Blue-Eyed Son

The Story of an Adoption

NICKY CAMPBELL

Blue-Eyed Son

The Story of an Adoption

MACMILLAN

First published 2004 by Macmillan
an imprint of Pan Macmillan Ltd
Pan Macmillan, 20 New Wharf Road, London N1 9RR
Basingstoke and Oxford
Associated companies throughout the world
www.panmacmillan.com

ISBN 1 4050 4718 6

'And Death Shall Have No Dominion' (extract)
from *Collected Poems* by Dylan Thomas (Dent, 1988)

Every effort has been made to contact copyright holders of material
reproduced in this book. If any have been inadvertently overlooked, the publishers
will be pleased to make restitution at the earliest opportunity,

'Little Gidding' (extract) from Four Quartets by T. S. Eliot (Faber and Faber, 1942)
'Sixteen Dead Men' (extract) by W. B. Yeats by permission of A. P. Watt Ltd
on behalf of Michael B. Yeats
'If I Only Had a Brain', words by E. Y. Harburg, music by Harold Arlen, © 1939
EMI Catalogue Partnership. EMI Feist Catalogue Inc and EMI United Partnership Ltd, USA.
Worldwide print rights controlled by Warner Bros. Publications Inc/IMP Ltd. All rights reserved
'A Hard Rain's A-Gonna Fall', words and music by Bob Dylan, © 1962 Special Rider Music.
Sony/ATV Music Publishing Ltd. All rights reserved. International copyright secured

1 3 5 7 9 8 6 4 2

A CIP catalogue record for this book is available from
the British Library.

Typeset by SetSystems Ltd, Saffron Walden, Essex
Printed and bound in Great Britain by
Mackays of Chatham plc, Chatham, Kent

To Breagha, Lilla, Kirsty and Isla

Oh, where have you been, my blue-eyed son?
Oh, where have you been, my darling young one?

Bob Dylan, 'A Hard Rain's A-Gonna Fall'

Contents

Contents

Contents

Acknowledgements

Where on earth do I begin? The whole team at Macmillan have been brilliant. They knew I was coming and they baked a cake. My editor Georgina Morley was fiercesome but fantastic. In truth, she was just what I needed. Years ago I interviewed the literary agent Jonny Geller. He wrote to me afterwards saying to get in touch if ever I wanted to write a book. I found his letter and came back to haunt him. His wise words and canny instincts have been invaluable.

Thanks are also due to the outstanding writer and journalist Chris Ryder whose books on Northern Ireland rank among the very best. His encouragement and advice in seeking source material helped me enormously. He put me in touch with Sir John Gorman who was so generous with his time. Thanks also to my dear friend Doug Carnegie for reading the almost final manuscript on his holiday, Graeme Mitchell for reading a very early manuscript on his holiday, Christopher Farrington, Denis Murray, the staff of Belfast Library and also to Tim, May, Ann, Kate, Rupert, Heather, Victor, Iain Glen, Robert Harley and Vincent B for keeping me on the right course and many more who received a perhaps unexpected mention herein.

I am hugely indebted to Julian Putkowski the historian sans pareil on First World War military executions and Piet Chielens the director of the In Flanders Fields Museum, Ieper / Ypres. They helped me identify Private Herbert H. Chase whose memory I honour.

There are some people in this book who I haven't identified: names have been changed to protect their privacy, especially if those identities are not in the public domain. Similarly, I have changed some geographical locations.

Francesca Harris is who she is in this book and my gratitude goes to Francesca and her team at the Scottish Adoption Association. They do wonderful work offering information, counselling and support to anyone who has adopted, has been adopted or is interested in adoption. They have a very helpful website at www.scottishadoption.org. For anyone who is thinking of embarking on this whole strange but wonderful process these other websites and addresses might also be useful: the British Library has an excellent website and offers help if you are interested in tracing children or parents, www.bl.uk; The Adopted Children Register contains a record of everyone who has been adopted through a court in England and Wales. The website gives information on applying for adoption certificates, receiving information on original birth details and making contact with adopted people and their relatives, www.gro.gov.uk; NORCAP offers searching assistance, counselling for adoptees and parents and also has a list of approved researchers, www.norcap.org.uk or write to: NORCAP, 112 Church Road, Wheatley, Oxfordshire OX33 1LU.

I would like to thank all my families – the families for whom I am the missing and somewhat tenuous link. Mum and my sister

Acknowledgements

Fiona have understood and supported me despite the emotional challenges we have all faced. I love them very much and always will. My wife Tina needed the patience of a busload of saints when all this was going on. 'You've already got a family you know – us!' Secreted away in my study for hours on end, flying off at weekends, or constantly on the phone to somebody or other or introducing her to my latest newly found relatives while life with a young family went on was a testing time. Esther Cameron's contribution to the story and the book will become clear as you read but it was so much more than that: she helped me delve and think and work a lot of this out. We not only share a mother but also the most incredible journey. I'd love to do it again sometime.

On the families' front thanks to my biological father for sharing his life with me and taking the trouble to read every word of the finished book, hard as that must have been for him. Likewise my cousin on the other side, Robert Lackey, whose letter commenting on the final text I will always treasure. I'm indebted to all the members of my new families for their astonishing understanding and tolerance of what I have done here. First of all I find them, they realize I exist and next – it's all in hardback. Thanks to all my father's children, his wife, his sister Evangeline whose love I cherish and also the amazing Doris Lackey. I wish I'd met her husband, my Uncle John. A word too for my new brother-in-law, known in the book as Patrick. He worked so hard to make a lot of this happen and has become a very good friend.

And of course to Stella my birth mother. I owe you so very much. Thank you for doing the right thing. Finally, to my late father, Frank Campbell. I hope you understand Dad. I had to do it. I hope you're proud of me. Love Nickelarse.

November 1990

I was committing adultery in Room 634 of the Holiday Inn in Birmingham when my wife rang to say they'd found my mother. It was ten thirty on Saturday morning.

I scrambled, receiver and all, to the other side of the large double bed. As far away as I could possibly get from Sarah. As discreet as I could be without appearing duplicitous.

'Hi. I've only just woken up.' I just wanted this intrusion to end.

Sarah looked angry. She was hating this. Why hadn't I remembered to unplug the thing last night?

Linda sounded urgent – excited.

'Your man has just phoned. He has found her and wants you to call him.' I'd been expecting his call but I still couldn't believe what I was hearing.

'OK. I'll ring him right now.'

'How was the programme?'

'Fine. Listen, I'll speak later.' At least I had an excuse for being perfunctory.

I started dialling the private detective's number immediately and then stopped, put down the phone and turned to Sarah.

'That was Linda.'

'I gathered,' she said, looking away, resigned. She knew I was searching for my birth mother and she understood it was important to me. Taking a deep breath she turned to me with a question that triggered a panic deep inside me. 'Did your natural mum have a long relationship with your natural dad?'

'No, it was just a casual thing as far as I know. He was most likely some fly by night – told her he loved her and cleared off. Probably married for all I know.' She looked right through me. She was thinking exactly what I was thinking: like father like son?

I attempted to placate her so I could get on with the call. She gave me some space, but withheld the benefit of the doubt. I grabbed a notebook, reached for the phone again and lay diagonally across the bed ready to call the gumshoe. Bolton's Bogart was a private detective called Steve.

I'd met him only eight days before. The show I co-presented every Friday night was called *Central Weekend Live* and was in its heyday, a must-watch debate show on Midlands ITV. From Monday to Thursday I presented a late-night programme on Radio One and every once in a lucrative while I went to Glasgow to record the glittery big-money game show *Wheel of Fortune*.

I adored presenting *Central Weekend*. Every Friday night was an exotic adventure in Birmingham. It was always lively, frequently raucous and almost invariably confrontational. The night before I'd hosted a debate on penis extensions. The previous week the subject had been rather more private dicks – the ethics of private investigators, starring, as ever, some compelling human exhibits. It wasn't what the producer called 'blood on the floor' but it was fascinating stuff.

Introduction

The hospitality room at Central's Broad Street Studios had a buzzing atmosphere during and after each show and when the closing credits had rolled we chatted and drank with the guests and rest of the team. It was a three-item programme so the green room was always milling with wonderfully diverse and picaresque characters. All human life was there: burglars and bishops, vampire hunters and balloon-breasted models; purple-faced fox hunters and po-faced psychics. It was like a magic mushroom mardi gras. They all had real opinions though. There was no masquerade about that.

Steve the gumshoe was classic casting. 'Central casting' you might say. He looked every millimetre the ex cop: broad shouldered, thick-skinned and no nonsense, apart from a bit of a seventies-style handlebar effort inching down the sides of his mouth. We got talking and I told him I was looking for my mother.

'I want to find out more about her and maybe get in touch.'

The 'maybe' was pure self-protection. The thought of actually going through with it still filled me with trepidation.

'Be delighted to help.'

I knew she used to be a nurse from Dublin who worked in some big hospitals there and I knew her name but that was it. He said it wouldn't be a problem but it might take a couple of days. A couple of days? I was staggered. He was blasé.

'We are all numbers. We are all on computer.'

'But isn't all that stuff confidential? Data protected or whatever?'

'There is no such thing as confidential, Nick. In my game it's all about favours.' His booze-fuelled braggadocio notwithstanding I felt I'd crossed a threshold. There was no turning back now. I took the step. I was exhilarated and terrified. Scared of rejection. Worried that the fantasy I had cradled for so long might be easier to deal with than the truth I would confront. Excited that I was on the verge of an extraordinary life-changing revelation. Anxious that I would break Mum and Dad's hearts. This was the undiscovered country.

A midweek call to Steve had produced no more than a vague reassurance that all was in hand. It sounded like a delay tactic. The Saturday-morning call from the woman I married produced a feeling I had never known before. Adolescent shivers of excitement, a deep spiritual yearning and the most intensely burning curiosity all bundled up together. Deal with it! Where would it lead? I rang Steve to find out what he'd discovered.

'Oh, hello, Nick. Yeah, listen, I've got a number. She has been away for some time, possibly travelling abroad or something, and hasn't been at the address in question for a while but is back there now. She appears to be single but was married. She went for a time by the name of Stella Newton rather than Lackey, her maiden name.'

I was frantically scribbling all this down. He gave me her address and I took the number down. With the international prefix and Dublin code it seemed to go on for ever.

'Thanks a million, Steve. Listen, send me the bill.'

'Let me know how you get on. Good luck, mate.'

Later, Sarah and I parted. When I got home I was shattered. *Central Weekend Live* beats the hell out of you. So do lies.

We phoned Stella that night. Linda felt my adoption was at the heart of all our problems. What she rightly saw as my own restless sense of incompleteness was tearing us apart. Things were bad between us in a hopeless tangle of cause and effect. For Linda, finding Stella was the great panacea. She probably had a point. I was certainly driven by a lurking and now consuming curiosity, which her promptings had drawn to the surface. Someday I had to know and now that day was tantalizingly close, the knowing became imperative.

But there was another reason. I was thirty. I was entering a new phase of life and it was clear that we would never have children. Linda had two teenage boys from her previous marriage and having a baby just wasn't an option. The realization I would never be a father led me to my mother.

It was another tired and fractious Saturday night but for once we had a common focus. 'Go on, phone her. Phone her tonight. Do it now. Phone her,' she kept insisting. 'I'll speak first if you want.'

'I am not sure I can speak at all.'

Ever a force of nature, Linda grabbed the initiative.

'Let's do it now.' She was on a mission, pumping with adrenalin. She's a strong and striking woman and right then she was so strong for me.

She stood in the hall and dialled the number. I was sitting on the stairs, rigid with fear, my head buried in my hands, my body folding into a foetal position. I really didn't think I could go through with it. I was petrified and exhausted. What the hell would I say? What the hell do you say? This woman gave birth to me. I needed an epidural.

I had held this fantasy in my head for years. I had a mental picture of a beautiful but driven career woman – a free spirit who found herself in this impossible situation and made an extraordinary sacrifice. She gave her baby away. Her baby was about to catch up with her. We were about to speak to her. I was about to clothe this idealized wraith in humanity. At twenty-nine I was about to make the first connection with my own flesh and blood, someone to whom I was genetically connected. That word – genetic – it had an almost sacred meaning for me. (It still does.) A genetic link; a magical bond. An inexpressible essence of belonging and being.

From my seat on the stairs I could hear the ring at the other end. It stopped. A woman's voice. Soft, Irish, hesitant and wary. 'Hello.'

ONE

A Proper Mummy and Daddy

My birth mother Stella made sure I was adopted into a good middle-class family and it was clearly stipulated in the adoption papers that I be raised in her own faith – Protestant. My parents, neither of whom gave a damnation about religion beyond the nominal, had heard about her predicament through their GP and close friend Ronnie Cameron who'd been ministering to Stella's needs while she stayed in Edinburgh, far from the prying eyes and wagging tongues of Dublin. Letters were exchanged, formalities completed, flowers sent and my parents' joy was complete. Fiona had a little brother. I was deposited in a smart nursing-home ready for collection. New-born babies available for adoption are rare these days but back then they were relatively plentiful and it was in general an easier business. Private adoptions were commonplace.

Before that first phone contact with Stella we'd told Mum, or rather my wife Linda had told Mum, that we were considering the whole tracing thing. As a result Mum furnished me with a full account of the story one weekend, when were staying at my parents' house – my childhood home in Edinburgh. Mum left it beautifully typed in an envelope beside our bed. It was addressed to 'Our darling son Nicholas'. When I opened it and read it, I felt raw. It was almost as if this was the day they'd long dreaded. As if they knew that one day they would lose their precious son and that now the day had come. As if my being there was only ever transient. But if the bonds were loosening and the ties were fraying where was I? They were my family. Mum and Dad and Fiona were my anchor. Why did I do this? Because I had to. How could I do this? Because now I couldn't stop. As I headed towards the unknown, there was no turning back.

Mum's letter made me want to retreat to a past of warm certainties and security, to be a little boy again playing on the stairs outside the bedroom with Mum and Dad there with me in the house. Dad smoking his pipe, Fiona with a friend in her room and Mum declaiming into the phone downstairs. I immediately wanted to go back to the land of toy soldiers and table football. Mum's moving account laid it all out for me. They went down the adoption road after she suffered her fourth miscarriage, this time at four and a half months. As prospective adopters everyone was rigorously checked out – even four-year-old Fiona, their natural child, was interviewed. 'Natural child' – that invidious comparative term – was I their unnatural child?

In late 1960 and early '61, Mum had been thoroughly depressed and increasingly pessimistic about the whole tortuous process. The Director of the Guild of Service – the adoption society to whom would-be adopters applied – had visited the house to assess their suitability. Mum rankles at the memory. It hurt for obvious reasons.

'She came to the house and she was *eight* months' pregnant,' recalls Mum. 'I thought how tactless to interview somebody who has just had a miscarriage at four months and lost a child and she comes along – bulging – I hated her.'

One morning Dad, claiming he had an upset stomach after a 'late night', went to see Dr Cameron. Dad told Ronnie that they didn't hold out much hope they would be accepted. They were desperate for another child to make their family complete. Ronnie perked up when he remembered an unmarried woman in his practice who was having a baby and had been released from her job to come to Edinburgh for the birth. She was very nice; an intelligent professional woman; a fine-looking woman with 'black hair and blue eyes' who was a couple of inches taller than Mum but the same age – thirty-seven. Her credentials were excellent. She wasn't some flighty teenager who didn't know what she was doing and might suddenly renege on the deal. There were still three months of her pregnancy to go but after she'd received a glowing impression of the Campbell family from the good and trusted doctor she agreed to let Mum and Dad have whatever arrived – boy, girl or twins.

My birth mother was the matron of a hospital in Dublin. The hierarchy in the hospital had thought a great deal of her abilities as it was the second time they had released her and kept her job open. Some time before she had come over to Scotland to have another child, a little girl who was also adopted – Stella had chosen Deirdre's name.

Mum explained that they never met my birth mother. They sent her flowers at the birth and Stella replied to Dr Cameron with a short note of thanks.

Dear Dr Cameron,

Please convey a sincere 'thank you' to Nicholas's parents from me for their very lovely gift of flowers.

I do appreciate this kind thought. It has given me much pleasure along with their good wishes and consideration for me which have been such a help.

My prayers and best wishes for the future.
Nicholas's Mother

That was the extent of their contact.

Mum recorded:

The Children's Officer had to be informed. She got more information that she did not share. With hindsight there was so much more one would like to have known but was reluctant to ask. Answers were vague, maybe to prevent identification or for other reasons.

Stella's daughter Deirdre had been born in the Eastern General Hospital in Edinburgh on 8 October 1959. After falling pregnant again and returning to Edinburgh only fifteen months later she couldn't face the shame of going back to the same hospital with the same nurses, but she did return to her old digs in Portobello – Edinburgh by the sea – and decided to have me there. She felt comfortable and welcome at those digs. Mrs Blackie ran a relaxed boarding-house, ably assisted by her daughters, and Stella was made to feel like one of the family. To this day the laughter is remembered as much as the tears.

After Deirdre, Stella's pregnancy with me was the second storm in two inclement years and this time she'd agreed to put my adoptive parents' choice of name on the birth certificate. She didn't particularly like 'Nicholas' but she concurred. It was actually a matter of some debate with my new mummy and daddy as well. 'Nicholas' narrowly beat 'Peregrine' in the play-off. I fear it went to penalties. Dad put his foot down. Thank goodness for that. 'Welcome to the programme. My name is Perry Campbell.' It would never have worked – and neither would I – much. Not in radio anyway – maybe something big in soft furnishings. Or 'a young man in Antiques' – to use Noel Coward's mischievous euphemism. I am convinced that somewhere within the nature–nurture debate we do have to factor in the key variable of a crap name. Character is formed by such things, isn't it? Whether by compliance or defiance. The great Johnny Cash told us that: 'My name is Sue. How do you do?'

Mum says I was smiling when she and Dad first came to see me in the Willowbrae nursing-home. The nurses said it was wind. After I had spent four weeks in Willowbrae, my new mummy was allowed to take me to my new home. There was such excitement in the family on that day. My adoptive sister Fiona recalls how she was prepared for my coming. She was five but it's a memory as strong as yesterday. 'I remember coming down the stairs and being told I wasn't going to school today. We were going to pick up my baby brother. I was ecstatic.' For some time she had been pretending she had a baby brother and telling anyone who would listen all about him. Now it was true. It got better. Later that day she went to her regular ballet class and excitement upon excitement: Mum took her new baby brother along in his pram.

I have known I'm adopted for as long as I can remember.

Mum told me how I was specially chosen. It's quite a conceit. Of course I wasn't the chosen one; I was just a very naughty boy. Fiona subscribes to the theory that it's the secret of my success and the reason for my failings. In fact, I think she's the originator of that theory.

Dad was a map publisher; Mum a psychiatric social worker. This is what Mum told me from my earliest years – in her own words. God bless her, she wrote it down for posterity. Posterity has come around.

Once upon a time there was a mummy and a daddy who had a little girl called Fiona and all of them wanted a brother or sister for the little girl but Mummy couldn't grow any more babies and that made them sad.

One day they talked to the doctor about it and he said he knew someone who had a baby and wanted it adopted. The lady was very nice, he said, and would like to have kept the baby herself but was very wise and very courageous and wanted the baby to have a proper mummy and daddy and a good settled home which she was unable to provide so she put the baby into a special baby home and that is where your mummy and daddy first saw you at a few days old.

'Come along,' said the nurse as we walked past a row of cots. Mummy kept stopping and looking and in one cot a dear little baby actually seemed to smile at her. 'Look, nurse,' said Mummy. 'Isn't that one cute? I wish I could have more than one baby so I could take that one home too.' 'But Mrs Campbell,' said the nurse, 'that is Nicholas, your very own adopted baby!!'

So of course Mummy and Daddy were delighted and wrapped you up and took you home and an excited Fiona helped to look after you when you were a little baby. Now you will soon be big enough to look after her! And Mummy and Daddy love you both very, very, much.

For three years following my birth Stella had sent Dr Cameron a Christmas card enquiring after my progress and then, nothing.

TWO

Edinburgh Boy

Thank you, Stella. Thank you for giving birth to me in Edinburgh, for ensuring the most beautiful city in my known universe was to be my home town. Thank you, Stella, for making sure I had a new mummy and daddy to give me the life that you couldn't.

And Mummy and Daddy love you both very, very, much.

They did. They couldn't have loved me any more. I couldn't have loved them more – my mummy, my daddy and Fiona my big sister. For my first three to four years I was a clingy child. I needed to be picked up and cuddled and hated leaving Mummy's side. This was probably because I was always being picked up and cuddled by my mummy. After her miscarriages and heartbreak she had this perfect little gift, the child that was meant to be. I had consistency at last – the same person to hold me and to bond with. Did those five days with Stella leave their mark? Did my sudden separation from my birth mother register in any way on my subconscious? What of the four weeks in the nursing home? I always had a fear of rejection. It strikes deep. I suspect it's just the flipside of chutzpah.

Every morning Mum had to bite her lip and walk away from

the little nursery school round the corner as she left me wailing myself hoarse for her. When I went to sit the test for the big school – the Edinburgh Academy – at four years old, Dad took me along so that I wouldn't be tempted to stick to Mum like a limpet. It worked, I passed and they were allowed to part with their money.

I had a wonderful childhood. I played Cowboys and Indians with my replica star-studded Colts and pheasant-feather head-dress. We played Japs and Commandos with sound-effect machine guns. I had a huge collection of toy soldiers. They waged wars of attrition with Pyrrhic victories. My talking Action Man was always ready for action, or so he told me. You see – a selection of toys and games to make the social worker of contemporary urban myth shudder to the depths of her Doc Martens. While you shudder at my lazy stereotyping, let me tell you about my castle.

Dad built it for me. It was a fantastic wooden castle for my little plastic men. He took ages, lovingly sawing, hammering, crafting and painting it. It was beautiful. Being the perfectionist he was he paid meticulous attention to detail – a moat, a drawbridge, turrets – everything my castle needed, my castle had. Dad was so wonderful with his hands. I can barely make a paper dart. I wish I could thank him right now and tell him what it meant to me. I know how much it meant to him.

One childhood passion kicked off on a bright May evening in 1967. I was six years old. This was the first significant toggle on my anorak. The sun was streaming through the windows and Dad half closed the curtains so he could see the telly properly. I was playing on the stairs in the hall with my toy soldiers but was gradually drawn to the room by the excitement beginning to bubble. He was a rugby man but he liked the really big football matches and was hooked on this one. Glasgow Celtic has an overwhelmingly Catholic support and strong links with Ireland. In 1967 they were playing Inter Milan in the European Cup final and were on their swaggeringly beauteous way towards lifting the trophy. From that night I became Celtic obsessed. They had a flair and style and passion I fell in love with. They exuded football glamour. Their Glasgow rivals Rangers were the antithesis – hewn from the bleak bedrock of Calvinism. The 'Gers' seemed stolid and prosaic by comparison, or as this wee boy thought – 'Boring'.

By the time I was thirteen my room was like a green and white emporium. Pennants and posters all but obscured the marching soldier wallpaper. Then it came, the icy gust of reality. The little green apple fell from the tree and turned blue. Friends started to say, 'What the fuck do you support them for?' The naked support for the IRA from the terraces was much worse in those days and I remember seeing lairy lads of my own age at matches in balaclavas and paramilitary gear. This was the time of some appalling 'mainland' atrocities and I recoiled at the sight of these ignorant and provocative little idiots. Supporting Celtic became untenable. I couldn't explain why I liked them. I couldn't justify it. I didn't know. 'Because they are the best' wasn't enough. Of course I didn't regularly encounter the raw bigotry of Scottish sectarianism. It was a received version if it. A genteel derision for cleaving to the wrong tribe. It mattered though. I switched to Heart of Midlothian. Rangers-lite.

Mum and Dad were not well off. All the family income went on school fees. Of course by the standards of society in general we were comfortable but at my school, with my faded and ill-fitting second-hand uniform, I felt like a pauper. Going to friends' houses – huge detached stone mansions on Edinburgh's Southside or on the boulevards of Murrayfield – was great. When they first came to my place it wasn't. I felt ashamed. What would they think of the peeling wallpaper, the shabby carpets and the bijou dimensions of the place? We only had one 'smallest room', never mind a utility room.

Every summer we holidayed in the Scottish Highlands. My affluent school pals came back from their holidays and changed for gym to reveal spectacular white bits untouched by the golden rays of exotic climes. I had no incidental suntan. I was *peely-wally* and covered in midge bites and nettle stings. I loved the Highlands though. I can smell the heather and bracken as I write. My parents had a cottage bought for a pittance in a Glen not far from Loch Ness. I told my friends we had acres of land and a dozen bedrooms. We didn't but we had the best view in the world.

I became obsessed with the Loch Ness Monster. I was zealous about it and read everything on the subject I could lay my hands on. I'd two twin aunts called Ethel and Beatrice who claimed to have seen the beast when they were schoolgirls in the nineteen thirties. That was proof enough for me. If they stuck their necks out the monster must have as well. Their story never changed either. My Nessie obsession spilled over into other mysteries. The Yeti, UFOs, Chariots of the Gods, ghosts, the *Marie Celeste* – you name it, as long as you couldn't solve it. This mystery mania went in tandem with a ravenous hunger for biographies. From a very early age I had to find out and know about other people's lives.

The stories had to be true. Mysteries and other people's lives. The amateur psychologist is working overtime here, of course, but the big unsolved mystery was in my own life.

I was passionately Scottish. I still am but within limits – normally about ninety minutes. With age and perspective, reason has calmed the beast. The history we were taught at school was raw meat for that beast though. We were fed tales full of tragic reversals and cruel misfortune all at the hands of and benefit to the perfidious English – our oldest and only enemy. The loathsome light at the end of our tunnel vision. Kenny Ferguson was my friend three doors up our terraced street in Edinburgh. The two of us joined the Scottish National Party just before the '74 election. We filled in the forms and sent them off to HQ. 'It's Scotland's Oil' was the slick slogan of the day. It seemed so glaringly logical to thirteen-year-old me. We could be like Saudi Arabia without the amputations.

Having received my application form, two activists turned up on the doorstep just a few days later. They were keen. When the bald and insignificant man at the front door and his frankly nondescript comrade saw an impish thirteen year old before their beady eyes they were, shall we say, disappointed. Mind you, neither of them was exactly Rob Roy. 'We have – er never had – er one this – er – *young* before.' I love the Aldington aphorism: 'Nationalism is a silly cock crowing from its own dunghill.' It leaps to mind thirty years later – except he wasn't a cock. He was birdlike though. He was a puffed-up little pigeon. Still, Kenny and I traipsed up and down tenement and pavement delivering leaflets and posters to the people of the would-be tartan Emirate. In return for our efforts we got badges, stickers and the dour gratitude of the bald man and his baleful buddy. In that 1974 election 'we' came a poor third or fourth and Edinburgh South, a safe Tory seat, stayed safely Tory. This was a long time ago remember. I felt vanquished. We had worked so hard and walked so far. Such ignominy. What was wrong with people? The message had seemed so simple and irresistible. It's Scotland's oil!

After one football match a year later it felt like Scotland's dunghill. We lost 5–1 to England. My friend Robert and I were grief stricken. After all our hopes had been crushed by some cataclysmic goalkeeping, we fled his house. Having pinched some of his dad's cigars we stole up Blackford Hill and attempted to blow away the blues. Unfortunately, we both ended up vomiting away the blues. But really, we felt bereaved. To beat the English at anything meant everything. To lose, hurt horribly.

The Edinburgh Academy was founded in 1821 by, among other pillars of the Scottish establishment, Sir Walter Scott, to provide an education for the young gentlemen of that most elegant corner of North Britain. Nicholas Andrew Argyll Campbell was sent there in 1966 and Robert Louis Stevenson had been there some time before. He'd lived near by and set one of his most famous stories in the cobbled back streets near the school. The Academy did have certain Jekyll and Hyde-like qualities about it. The school had some wonderful and inspiring teachers. Jack Bevan and Bill Stirling, both now dead, were English teachers of exceptional ability and men of true quality. They were great men. I'd love to have sent Bill Stirling this mistake-ridden manuscript for his perusal and would have read avidly and taken on board every one of his considered comments in beautifully written red biro. A lot of *explain this better* and *what do you mean by this* and *nearly there*,

I would imagine. I had a great education and made some life-long friends in my time at the Academy. The Hyde qualities of the school have been aired elsewhere many times and were, I believe, symptomatic of a darker age. Kids are far more savvy now. Back then we knew it was wrong but we didn't know it was right to tell.

There were, to my certain knowledge, two teachers in my time there who took an unhealthy sexual interest in small boys and another who took an unhealthy interest in hurting them. I suffered at the hands of the sadist and was touched by one of the perverts but not in the appalling way one of my close friends was. Of course, any way is appalling but there are degrees. Abuse is not an absolute term. However, when I think about what I saw my friend subjected to I feel sick. When he thinks about it now he feels angry. Back then, as nine year olds we simpered in front of this man and mocked him behind his back. He was loathsome.

They were such different times. When I was there the school still had one foot in the Victorian grave. One of the relics of a bygone era was in the person and office of the Rector, in actual fact a rather pompous name for Headmaster. The Rector was a terrifying character who made the staff in *Tom Brown's Schooldays* look distinctly Secondary Modern. He was called H. H. Mills. A hero of Arnhem, his face was constantly contorted in a twitching mosaic of intellectual restlessness. It was putty in his hands. The distance and detachment were deceptive though. He'd strafe you like a Spitfire.

The school was predominantly for day boys, although there was a significant boarding element. It was expensive and my parents adjudged it the best in town. They couldn't really afford it but sacrifices were made and cloth was cut; only the best would do. When the money ran out my sister was moved from Mary Erskine's Girls school to a comprehensive and I was kept in the Academy at all costs. The Edinburgh Academy had a high opinion of itself, an opinion not without substance. It had provided mainstays and leading lights of the Edinburgh, Scottish, British and Empire Establishments for generations. The newly rich and the habitually rich clamoured to hand over their cash. They still do.

In those days rugby was king and if you were in the first fifteen you were accorded god-like status. One of the associated perks to rucking and mauling *sans pareil* was a lead part in the school play. This was a source of amusement to those of us in the rebel units who revelled in the manifest truth that there are limited common skills in handing off a prop forward and holding a mirror up to nature. My great school and university friend Iain Glen is one of the finest actors of his generation. The first time he ever trod the boards was up at Aberdeen University and he was horribly good. I am reliably informed a much more holistic approach is applied at the Academy these days.

I was a barely mediocre rugby player. In a school of umpteen fifteens I 'graced' the Fourths. My dad had excelled at rugby and cricket and anything where a ball was required to be thrown, caught, kicked or hit and I never once let him come and watch me on a Saturday morning. When he came to pick me up I insisted he arrive after the game was over. He would have loved to stand on the touchline and would have been so proud despite my shortcomings. I deprived him of something every dad should experience if he can and I regret it to this day. He did as I wished because his own father had been a martinet and Dad naturally tended to over compensate. He was terrified of being despised the way he despised his own father. When he was dying I sent him a card saying how much I had always loved him and what a great dad he was. When I went up to Edinburgh and entered the hospice ward shortly after he'd received the card he just pointed to it with tears in his eyes and I kissed him. He went quickly. An unfinished *Telegraph* crossword. Hours before he died my sister Fiona left him late at night and said, 'We love you, Dad.' He already looked at peace and gently replied, 'And I love all of you.'

He was so incredibly proud when I got a history degree from Aberdeen University. Aberdeen – my exotic escape from Edinburgh and what a fascinating place it is. The city of schizophrenic stone. It's the granite you know. When it sparkles in the sunshine the place radiates beauty but on a dreich hungover Sunday, the greyness is unrelenting and the gloom unforgiving. Despite that I stayed on after graduating and went into radio.

After I'd left university in 1982 I secured one show a week on Northsound Radio, the local commercial station. Then I got a daily show. Dad and Mum drove up to Aberdeen to listen to every live second of one early-morning parade of eighties' pop peppered with 'personality'. Dad loved it. When I joined Radio One in 1987, after a two-year stint on Capital Radio, they listened religiously. They both came at every opportunity to sit with the gaggle of Glasgow Grannies in the audience at Scottish Television's studios to see *Wheel of Fortune* being recorded. This glitzy trashy game show was about as far away from Dad's life and times as it was possible to get. He loved it. He made a point of telling me just how proud they both were at what I'd 'achieved'. As far as he was concerned, I might as well have been representing Scotland at rugby – or his other great love, England at cricket.

On reflection Dad and I loved each other for the qualities we saw in each other that we didn't feel we possessed ourselves. Our differences bonded us. I loved his prowess at sport, his natural charm, his courtesy, his gentlemanly qualities, his artistic talent, his skill with his hands, his ability to talk to anyone. Qualities which I was wanting. He in turn loved the fact that I was quick and clever and a right little show off. It tickled him. He called me Nicko or Nickle-Arse and I miss him so much.

My mum and dad were married for forty-two years. Shelia, my mum, is indefatigable and always has been. A force of nature – she can be brash, and domineering; brittle and needy. She headed a psychiatric social work department in a large mental hospital but, as my sister Fiona asserts, could be astonishingly insensitive at home. Wise and obtuse. Giving and selfish. Self-centred and caring. As I write this, it occurs to me that if I have taken after anyone it is probably her.

My friends all think she is wonderful as she holds her own at any table and is so open minded and accepting. At eighty, she is still hurtling round the country in an absurd little Korean car and going on package holidays to far-flung places with her pals. Mum is an intuitive and intelligent woman. At her best she is an absolute gem and all that age withers are the things that used to infuriate us all so much about her. Dad's outbursts from the front of the car still ring in my ears. 'For Christ's sake, Sheila, will you bloody shut up!' Dad loved her with all his soul.

In about 1970, some vague acquaintances were chatting to Mum and Dad at a petrol station when they peered into the back of our dark red Cortina and, admiring the specimen siblings within, declared 'Don't they look like one another.' I felt as though I had passed some kind of a test. I was pleased as punch and so proud. What about my adoptive sister Fiona and me? Well, she's the one who hung me over the banister when I was small, giving me a life-long fear of heights. I am the one who crushed a banana in her hair when she was fifteen and about to go out to a party. She is the one who has a fantastic musical talent and wanted to crawl into a corner when Mum demanded she perform and play the piano for friends. I am the one who would bash out a cacophonous ditty for anyone who would listen. We are the ones who fought like cat and dog. She used to hate me pulling her hair. We are the two who laughed till we cried. I'm the one who borrowed and fell in undying love with her Beatles and Kinks cassettes. She is the one who is a social worker. I am the one who needs one. She is my sister. I am her brother.

She is worried about the banister business. We were laughing about it recently. 'I work in child protection – remember my reputation here!'

That Fiona was my parents' biological child was certainly always in my mind if no one else's. At times it *had* to be in hers. She vividly recounts our being at a house on the other side of Edinburgh – in the elegant New Town. We were playing in a garden with a group of children. There were older children there. There was a sense of threat. Fiona was maybe nine so I must have been four. They started picking on me with a singsong taunt. 'You're adopted, you're adopted, you're adopted.' Fiona was frightened. She didn't know how to handle it. She felt vulnerable and exposed. She also felt protective. She still does.

Dad and Fiona had a special bond – but fathers do with daughters. Mum and Fiona had a troubled and complex relationship but – well, the same again – that's mothers and daughters for you. Or more particularly it's Fiona and Mum. The fact that she was genetic and I was acquired merely nourished my sense of being different and, importantly, it gave me a reason and excuse to feel different. It inevitably influenced how I came to see myself and what I came to be. It was what I was.

Fiona thinks I was the blue-eyed boy from whose backside the sun was thought to brightly blaze, the brother who was treated far more generously and leniently than his big sister. Mum dismissively says that's often the way it is with younger siblings and boys in general. Different standards apply. That doesn't wash with Fi. She says there is a huge body of evidence on her side.

How is this for an accusation? Fiona came straight out with it recently and I coughed at last. I sang like a bird. 'You broke a whole set of Rachmaninov *Piano Concerto Number Two* 78s actually performed by him.' An act of cultural revolution on behalf of the glorious people's vanguard, I had dutifully destroyed the works of Rachmaninov, the bourgeois individualist and imperialist lapdog. Yes it was the late sixties but I just fancied breaking them. Fiona was in full flow. She'd been storing this one up for thirty-five years. 'You broke them and Mum made out it didn't matter. I was always the one at fault. I was meant to have had the foresight to avoid the problem. "I am not interested," Mum said.'

I remember that one well. I am not surprised at her lingering sense of injustice all these years later. I just saw these old discs on the bedroom floor and wanted to walk on them to watch them crack beneath my feet like a thin layer of ice on a pond. So I did and they did. Realizing the potential for trouble I mounted a pre-emptive defence. I ran downstairs crying, full of confusion and remorse, and it worked a treat. I walked away an innocent man, without a stain on my character. Was there malice aforethought? Who knows the mind of the sub-teen suburban guerrilla?

Fiona and I aren't in constant contact – not like my wife Tina and her sister, who are, well, like sisters, but we will never be estranged. When we talk – and she can talk at international level – and when we see each other in the midst of our hectic and chaotic lives, there is an ease you can only achieve with family.

THREE

Blue-Eyed Son

I always knew I was adopted but of course I became more self-conscious about it as I negotiated spots, puberty, serial masturbation and the claustrophobia of the teenage maze. I was terrified my school friends would find out I was adopted and my cover would be blown, exposed as bogus. I felt, in a way, invalid, ungrounded, ill-founded. It wasn't an all-consuming feeling but it was always there. Lurking, lingering, skulking in the shadows and striking in the dark. I'm given to arbitrary sadness or to put it better – sometime I get pissed off for no reason. That's when I felt something missing or that's when I chose to. It is so hard trying to articulate for the first time what I have felt all my life but never outwardly expressed. There's many a person wishes they were adopted. I just wanted Mum and Dad to be my real mum and dad. Grandpa fought on the Somme and I wanted to be his grandson in every sense. Dad was a major in the Indian Army, waging jungle warfare against the Japanese. When I was a little boy that made me so proud, but how could I legitimately claim to be a part of that heritage? My heritage was a great unknown. I was a kind of an interloper. Not even a real one.

I was about fourteen or fifteen and my great pal Robert and I were shopping in Edinburgh's Princess Street with Mum. Why on earth we were doing that I can't imagine but Robert asked me out of the blue why my eyes were blue. I stuttered and stammered and felt sick inside. Clearly neither Mum nor Dad had blue eyes. Robert is a very clever chap and I thought he was on to me. I was immediately on the defensive.

'It skipped a generation. Eyes are funny things.'

I asked Robert about this recently. He can't remember but thinks he can explain.

'I didn't know you were adopted till we were about sixteen so it was nothing to do with that. I'd probably just learned the reasons for eye colour in biology – we weren't in the same class for that, were we?'

'Thanks for reminding me.'

'I probably said, "Do you know why your eyes are blue?" and I was about to tell you.' It says a lot about my sensitivities at the time.

The first person I was actually able to tell was Morag, the girl to whom I lost my virginity. We were sixteen. Lying on my parents' bed, speaking to her in one of those endless teenage phone marathons – which were clamped down on when the bill came in – I confessed. It really felt like a confession. I was in tears as I told her and it took me ages to get the words out. I even remember quoting a Rod Stewart lyric to her: 'What do you see in me?' I was worried it would change everything. She was lovely about it and until she chucked me for Sam three weeks later, I felt we'd reached a new level of understanding. I survived. Three weeks is a long time in teenage politics.

By my late teens it ceased to be a problem and became a badge of rebellion. 'I am not your real child any way' was a regular strop mantra. I am cringing as I write this. All fifteen and sixteen year olds say vile things to their parents but that wasn't just hurtful – it was emotionally sadistic. My friend Iain Glen reminded me of one particular incident. I was at his house and Mum phoned to get me home. I dug my heels in. As Iain told me this recently he bellowed the words like the superb stage actor he is. I was shocked.

'No, I am not fucking coming home now. I am fucking coming home when I want to fucking come home. If you don't like it you should have adopted another fucking baby.' Harry Enfield's 'Kevin the teenager' has a way to go.

I meekly asked Mum about this.

'I don't remember that at all, darling. Are you sure? We probably didn't take any notice and I just dismissed it as teenage angst.' What wonderful parents.

On the other hand, Fiona remembers howling at Mum and Dad, 'God I wish I was adopted too.' She used to think that I was the lucky one because I was chosen. She used to yearn to be adopted and pray at night that in actual fact she had been. To her mind I was bespoke and she was off the peg. I saw it the other way around.

Mum recently said I never showed any desire to trace my mother when I was growing up. That's certainly what I told her when she asked me, but the very asking sent shards of insecurity through me. I always said words to the effect that if my natural mother didn't want me why would I want her. It was a diversionary tactic. I didn't want to think about it. 'Don't go there' as people all too often say now. Too embarrassing. Couldn't face having my boat rocked. When I was sixteen or seventeen she often broached the subject and even left leaflets in my bedroom offering confidential advice but no way was I emotionally ready for any of it then. She meant well but it didn't exactly drive out my teenage demons. She now acknowledges it was a mistake. I felt felt there was something treacherous about tracing too, something ungrateful. But I did know from somewhere inside me that one day I would find out the whole truth. One day I would find those missing pieces and fit them all together.

Thirty years later I was hearing *her* voice for the first time. Now I was pressing my ear as close to the phone as I could, while Linda talked. We stood huddled in the hallway, close again. It was that hallway that had made us put in a bid for the house. When we'd first seen the property we looked at each other and knew what we were thinking. What a brilliant place for a Christmas tree. A symbol of togetherness, childhood happiness and reconciliation. For the rest of the year that hall looked empty. Linda eventually fell out of love with the house and had it dowsed for negative energies by a fascinating little old man with two lively little sticks. He found it replete with negativity and we consequently had to move all the beds into the most unorthodox and impractical positions. If Dr Dowser had been with us that night my head would have sent his two wee sticks haywire. This was a strange energy I was feeling. Linda and I stood together by the phone. Linda was leading me to the conversation of a lifetime.

FOUR

Talking to Stella

'Is that you, Stella? Stella Lackey.'

'Who is this?' She sounded vulnerable and suspicious.

Reality was dawning fast for me. This was a human being, not the mythical figure of my imagination. Maybe she wasn't the perfect, strong, self-possessed creature of my own legend. I detected something fragile about her. She seemed crushed, dispirited.

Linda continued: 'It's to do with events in Edinburgh thirty years ago.'

'Are you sure you have the right number?' Then reality slowly dawned for her. 'Oh.' There was an unbearable pause. 'Is that you, Deirdre?'

Deirdre? I remembered. My adoptive mum had told me about Deirdre. She was the other child Stella had given up for adoption eighteen months before I came and went. She had only registered faintly on my radar at that time. She wasn't a sister – she was an abstract concept. Back to the womb and find my mother – that was my only focus.

Linda established the fact that she wasn't Stella's daughter. 'No, I am Nicky's wife. Your son Nicky.'

'Sorry, I thought you were – someone – else – Nicky? Nicholas? Heavens! Oh my goodness!'

Joy flowed through her voice. I started to cry. Linda hurriedly explained how I had traced her and that I was standing right there. 'Here he is.'

I was holding the phone. I'd shaken the tree of knowledge and the apple was right there in my hand. I don't know how I got the words out but I did. I felt so defenceless at that second. My voice felt weak. My hand was trembling. I said something like, 'How are you?' It could have just been 'Hello.' We were both on cloud nine. At that time I was the presenter of *Wheel of Fortune* on ITV. She watched it and enjoyed it. She'd no idea that the preening posing idiot was her son. Mind you, if she had said 'So you're that preening posing idiot, are you?' it would have been a blow. *Wheel of Fortune* paid loads of bills, but at the time I was unnecessarily touchy about the cheesy image of the show. Now I can see it for what it was – a bizarre and brilliant experience. Stella loved it anyway. 'Like finding out your long-lost son is Dale Winton,' quipped Tina years later.

Initial contact – the first phone call – it gives you a mighty euphoric rush. These really are the emotional rapids. The flow of information, however trivial, is utterly absorbing and totally absorbed. You're a sponge soaking up a lost river of time. From the subjects she enjoyed in school to her family details; from her failed marriage to her hair colour. Her brother had recently dropped dead suddenly and she'd been in hospital to help her 'cope with the shock'. I later fond out that her time in hospital actually pre-dated his death, but she had been deep in the doldrums and was obviously overjoyed to hear from me. She seemed to have great warmth. Granted, all my powers of objectivity were dulled by the sheer relief that she was actually taking the call. I didn't appear to be her worst nightmare come back to haunt her. A friend of mine told me what I thought was a shocking story about a friend of his. This girl had traced her birth mother and found to her astonishment that the woman was actually married to her biological father and they were living in a large house in an upmarket village in the north of England. Full of excitement she wrote an emotional letter asking to meet her mother at last and received a reply by return of post. It was painfully short and to the point: 'I don't want you in my life. Never contact me again.'

The fact that Stella had said 'hello' and did seem to want me at least on her phone came as an enormous relief. In this context the call was an unequivocal success. I was in no mind to absorb nuance. She seemed receptive. She seemed open. She was certainly shocked but she had a mischievous almost girly giggle.

The only thing I remember her being in any way evasive about was the issue of my father. I put this down to the natural reticence of a first conversation but she did confirm something that I already knew. Mum must have mentioned to me that he was a Dublin policeman. It has certainly lodged somewhere in my brain and become a part of my internal folklore. 'Father was a policeman; Mother was a nurse.' With prompting Stella added slightly to my sum of knowledge, telling me he was originally from the North and was a Catholic, but beyond that she steered the conversation away. She told me she was the only person who knew his identity. I remember wondering if he knew his identity. I didn't ask further. Even so, I was entering the age of enlightenment.

Enlightenment is enervating though. There's only so much

you can take and only so much you can take in, so after about an hour we agreed to write, exchange family photos and we both said goodbye for the first time. We had a bit of catching up to do. As soon as we could Linda and I were going to get over to Dublin and meet her. Life is full of surprises. Lying in bed I realized there was so much still to ask, so much I'd missed. Did my father know about me and was he still alive? What on earth happened? I did ask her about Deirdre. Stella confirmed what Mum had told me. Deirdre was her other daughter from another relationship – another policeman. A man from two summers before. Two kids? Two different men? Two adoptions? In two years. Too much to take in one phone call.

To give two babies away in eighteen months must have been heartbreaking. She must have been strong to have managed it but weak to let it happen in the first place. She wasn't some flighty teenager, as my parents had properly established before adopting me. She was a mature professional person. What on earth was going on in her life for that to happen? What on earth did going through the situation twice do to her life?

To adapt a line from a great Irishman, Oscar Wilde, 'To give away one baby may be regarded as a misfortune; to give away both looks like carelessness.' Careless in conception perhaps – but careless was the last thing Stella was when it came it organizing her babies' adoptions. She was meticulous and professional to the last detail. I hoped it was because she cared so much.

The only judgement I made at that stage was that she was a modern woman – a pioneering proto-feminist. She was strong and empowered. I chose not to draw any other conclusions. Who was

I to make moral judgements anyway, fresh from the bed of my mistress?

Stella and I started writing to each other. Her letters were particularly long but only occasionally legible. There was something we had in common then. We both had a scrawl that others hadn't a spider's chance of following. Thank heavens for the device on which my stubby fingers are dancing right now. In the first epistle from Stella she told me the gospel according to Lackey lore. They were a 'branch of the MacGregor clan which came over from Scotland in the 1700s' – hence the fact that they were Protestants. I was relieved. In fact I was delighted. Caledonia no more? Away with you. I had a legitimate blood claim to be Scottish after my emerging tartan identity crisis. I had long known about the Irishness in me, or behind me, but confronting it had it made it real. Where did this leave my Scottishness? The seventeen hundreds were absolutely good enough for me. I checked the clan map of Scotland Dad had published to see where 'my people' came from. I looked up the MacGregor history in another of his old books and thought of all the people I had ever known or heard of called MacGregor. All my kith and kin. I even had a close squint at the accompanying illustration of a manly MacGregor in Highland dress to see if he looked anything like me. He didn't, funnily enough. This was the behaviour of some ancestor-hungry Yank desperate for a bit of heritage to appease his dotage. It was the behaviour of a little adopted boy desperate for some sense of belonging. I was nearly thirty.

Stella sent me some photos but not many. I saw pictures of cousins with dark hair and dark eyes. Little girls with fetching smiles who were long since grown up and working all over the world. Maybe they were always children in her mind. The most perplexing photograph of all was of herself. In TV it is what they call a mid-shot. I had to look really closely to make out her features. I examined microscopically this elderly lady in coat and glasses beside another slightly shorter elderly lady in coat and glasses. They were both standing by a red-brick wall and a blue door and were almost but not quite smiling. They were just looking really; waiting for the person with the camera to finish so they could all go inside for a cup of tea. I needed to see her face animated to see it at all. I need to see her heart and mind in action. I could tell nothing from that snap. I needed to meet her. She was my birth mother.

Linda and I were lying in bed on Christmas morning 1990 and the telly was on in the room. The film showing was *Meet Me in St. Louis* and Judy Garland was singing 'Have Yourself a Merry Little Christmas' to Margaret O'Brian, her screen kid sister. It is one of the schmaltziest scenes in the MGM cannon. I love it. My Vincent Minelli genes were doing a Busby Berkley routine. At that moment I decided to phone Stella.

'Oh hello,' she answered in her gentle way.

'It's Nicky. Merry Christmas!' I actually rang her before I phoned Mum and Dad. I still can't forgive myself for that but back then it seemed as right as a new romance. It was a perfect dream come true and I was going to meet my birth mother at Easter. Despite the mess of my life all seemed set fair for happiness and resolution. What an Easter parade. I really couldn't wait.

FIVE

The Trip to Dublin

In March 1991, five months, a pile of Christmas presents and several phone calls after our first contact, Linda and I flew to Dublin to meet her. It was Easter weekend and all Eire was marking the 75th anniversary of the Easter Rising.

We had an alcohol-free dinner the evening we got there – some archaic Good Friday licensing law; what a bloody country. You could probably get condoms easily enough but they still wouldn't serve you a drink on Good Friday. We'd arranged to meet Stella in the lobby of the hotel at eleven o'clock the following morning. I was a nervous wreck.

To take my mind off it and also to get rid of some money for no good reason we spent the early part of the morning shopping. I felt physically sick with nerves. I couldn't concentrate on anything at all and it was all just building up inside me, crushing my stomach like a vice. What on earth was I going to face? The fantasy figure – the ideal – the abstraction – the vague notion – was going to look me in the eye. Maybe life would have been so much easier if I had never looked. Maybe I should have stayed at home, forgotten the whole thing and got on with getting my own life in order instead of trespassing on somebody else's. I didn't wear a watch. If I had, I would have worn it out with my eyes. Eventually we got back to the hotel and the clock was creeping towards the moment. We took a table in the lobby.

Eleven came around and eleven went. I'd already had two pints of Guinness by this time. In fact, this mother-and-child reunion was still an hour and a half away. Stella was horrendously late. Punctuality has always been a big thing for me and this minor transgression seemed almighty at the time. It disconnected me from her. I felt let down. Maybe I was being rejected again. It was the most awful feeling. It made my heart cold. I had another pint. The waiting was unbearable. Every woman over sixty who entered the lobby got the full treatment – the once over and expectant stare. I must have come across like some louche gigolo preying on unsuspecting widows. Linda kept me calm. She had been in the driving seat through all of this.

I'd just about given up all hope when a dishevelled and chaotic-looking woman shambled through the door and walked gingerly towards us. She apologized profusely. She hadn't been able to sleep for nervousness and had taken a sleeping pill which had knocked her for six, hence her lateness. It was her epidural I guess.

The Hollywood soundtrack stayed determinedly silent. There was no outpouring of emotion. Just awkwardness. My first impression of my mother was that she looked like . . . she looked like an old woman in her late sixties or early seventies. Think of your parents – they are timeless. You remember them as younger, as middle aged and as older – as they are and as they were. The millions of mental snapshots of their lives as you have known them merge together as one in your mind. Now imagine meeting your mother for the first time as she looks, or might look at seventy. Just an elderly woman.

I kissed her as I would a distant aunt. She kissed me for the first time since the social worker had taken me away thirty years before. As we sat down gingerly, I saw her looking at me and looking away. Looking at me and looking away so as not to stare. I looked at her and looked away. She told us about the accommodation she was living in. Her sister was there too and it was very comfortable. They had their own little flats within the building and were well looked after. I looked at her. She looked at me. I looked away. As I spoke it sounded like someone else's voice saying strange things like 'It's a really nice hotel this' and 'Well, it is really good to meet you at last.' I wasn't myself. I didn't know who I was. I needed a leak. Three pints and thirty years came cascading out. It was a huge relief and it was wonderful to be alone. The moment seemed endless. Going to the gents was like walking into a cathedral from the searing intensity of the Mediterranean sun. When I turned to wash my hands I caught sight of myself in the mirror. TV presenters and mirrors are on pretty good terms but this was an altogether different experience. I had a Stephen King moment. I saw my own reflection in the mirror but I didn't look anything like me. I saw new and different things about my face. I saw some of the features of the stranger who was my mother, sitting with Linda in the foyer. There was something frightening about it. It wasn't me. It was him. Who was he?

I sat back down in the lobby. What other extraordinary meetings were taking place at the other glass-topped tables dotted about the psychotically patterned carpet. If they only knew what was afoot at our table. I noticed Stella's fingers. They were long, slender and elegant. Mine are like chipolatas. If my fingers are a genetic mean between the length of my mother's and my father's respective digits and my fingers were already pretty stubby, it occurred to me that my biological father might be all but fingerless. I was escaping into a surreal internal world. We talked some more. I can't remember what about.

I kissed her goodbye with a cursory peck on the cheek and we arranged to go to her sheltered flat that evening for a meal. In the interim we repaired to our hotel room for the rest of the afternoon. She was going to cook us her speciality – Chicken Marengo. Why did I feel no bond? Why didn't I do what you are meant to do and embrace her and say, 'Mummy. My mummy'? I felt empty. I lay on the bed with Linda and watched TV like a zombie. I wanted to roll up into a ball and sleep for a thousand years. What had I got myself into?

A key to tracing your natural parents is to be prepared for everything. I'd rushed into it headlong without thinking about anything. I hadn't considered the consequences. Just like my birth mother on that night in 1960 really. People who do trace and take this momentous step in their lives, and in the lives of so many others, have to prepare themselves for all eventualities. They do their own research and have often thought about it for years before going through with it. I looked around the mess of my life, was persuaded it was necessary, got the bit between my teeth and just went for it.

As I lay on that hotel bed, whatever the precise ingredients of the complex cocktail of emotions, it was just too much at once. I wanted to go home. I wanted to be far away from this sweet, well-meaning but eccentric old woman. I hated myself. That evening, at her tiny flat in the retirement home, we were served Stella's Chicken Marengo. Cardboard Marengo? Whatever the precise ingredients of *that* complex cocktail of chicken and sauce and whatever else – I couldn't eat it. Chewing and swallowing the stuff were missions impossible. Clearly mouth, taste buds and stomach were acting in solidarity with heart and mind.

Drinking was easier. Drinking was a must. After a couple of glasses of her warm Black Tower wine, I relaxed a little and we talked. She showed me photo album after photo album, taking me through the family history. A world of strange sepia people by farm buildings opened up before me. They had stiff collars and severe expressions. There was a wedding or two and then an array of gaudy colour and ghastly clothes. Then a parade of grinning kids and smiling parents. It was overwhelming to look at grand-parents, uncles, aunts, cousins and all manner of . . . relations. Then she handed me the photograph of a baby on a bed – a tiny child, just a few days old. A helpless little bundle. A picture of me in another world, with another mother. It felt like someone else possessing my dreams.

She was clucking and fussing about, trying to be what she needed to be at last – a mum, or how she in her old maidish and unmaternal way thought a mum should behave. My God it must have been difficult for her. I say that now. At the time I was caught up in the intensity of my own experience. I thought, This is wrong. We can't just start of where we left off in 1961. Mum was my mum. Not this woman. It seemed false and presumptuous. It was ersatz, like a Diana doll or an Elvis puppet. I didn't know what this was meant to be about or what it would mean but it wasn't about her suddenly metamorphosing into Nicky's mother.

I shrunk back. I needed to keep a distance. By that stage in the weekend the whole exercise had boiled down in my head to curiosity and nothing more. That was my way of dealing with it. There is a broader point here. When you trace a birth parent and get beyond the ecstasy of discovery, what roles do you each then assume? It is all down to finding what we are to each other and what we need from each other. What we need from each other is governed by what we've never had.

This was such a great day for her though. No wonder she hadn't slept the night before. All the regrets of her life must have come at her in the night. The sadness at what she lost and what she missed. A mother who missed her child's life.

But there is an imbalance. Tracers tend not to be looking for replacement parents but the birth parents have been looking for and thinking of their children every single day of their lives since they were given away. Their offspring are 'adopted children' and they are forever children. It's only with hindsight that I understand this. At the time I just felt trapped.

The situation began to irritate me. I felt I was caving in on myself and was just desperate to get back to the hotel room for some mind-numbing late-night television. A younger but distant relative called Heather showed up at the tiny retirement flat to meet us and drive Linda and me back to our hotel. She jokily but firmly rebuked Stella after I had again been offered the tea I had already turned down three times. 'Leave the poor fella alone!' My discomfort must have been obvious. But poor heartbroken Stella was only trying her best.

*

Heather later told me her impressions of Stella back in the early sixties. 'When I was young Stella was an enigma. She was either busy or away. She was ill a lot. But she really never struck me as being at all maternal. Her sister Patti had a great affinity and imagination with kids. Stella had a much more formal approach.' It's entirely possible that Stella suppressed her maternal side so she wouldn't be exposed to feelings she longed for but feared. Her sister-in-law Doris, who is an immensely likeable person, put an interesting perspective on it. When Stella was helping to bathe her young nieces and nephews, Doris remembers how much joy it gave Stella, how good she was with them, and she realizes now how her heart must have been breaking. We all know some of the most unlikely candidates become earth mothers, domestic goddesses and paediatric experts rolled into one when they have children. It changes your world. How vulnerable to those feelings could Stella allow herself to be? She knew too well what lay over the precipice. The Slough of Despond.

At our first meeting Stella did divulge a bit more about my father. I thought, Enough already! *Enough already?* A bit of Protestant, a bit of Catholic – and now what's this? A bit of Jewish! According to Stella my father still resided in Dublin and was in the telephone directory. His name was Joseph Leahy. Joseph? Joseph? Joseph Leahy. His name. It went over and over in my head. That is my *father's* name. She mentioned that Joseph still had a book of hers – a book of quotations. She sounded like the matron she had once been when she declared, 'It was a lovely book. I bought it in a sale. The poetry and literature were lovely. If you ever see him you might ask for it back.'

Ever since then, whenever we've spoken on the phone about

her relationship with my biological father, Stella mentions this book to me – whenever the subject of Joseph comes up, in fact. This lovely book of quotations and beautiful poetry and literature. I wonder what it meant? What did this token symbolize? Words of beauty and hope and intimacy. Her despair explained. Her passion forgiven. Her secrets shared. Her guilt absolved?

SIX

Evening is Falling

The story has become clearer over the years, as Stella told me about Joseph and others told me about Stella. She was first introduced to my biological father, Joseph Leahy, in early 1960 when she saw a handsome young man in uniform talking to another policeman – a friend of hers – on the steps of the station where both men were based. She went up to her friend and said hello. I can hear her saying it now – her crisp and confident hello not her hesitant one. She was introduced to Joseph. A few days later she saw him on the beat and they arranged to meet for a coffee. Life is too short to waste time, isn't it? It seems that the attraction was instant and powerful. We have all experienced that. Joe-the-lad probably couldn't believe his luck. Stella, trying needlessly to justify events back then, once breathlessly said, 'Some people are just more passionate than others.' She was a free spirit, wasn't she? A free spirit in a suffocatingly hypocritical society. An old family friend not renowned for telling you what you want to hear said this to me recently: 'Stella – a real individual all right. A woman before her time. You know she had ideas and concepts not in tune with the mores of society. She was well educated. She was knowledgeable – a view about anything. A fascinating woman.' No wonder young Joe was impressed.

The very last time Stella saw Joseph was in late 1962 when she passed him in the centre of Dublin. He was standing a few yards away, resplendent, so he reckoned, in his police uniform, chatting and smiling with a couple of colleagues. He saw her. Their eyes met. Were they thinking of their child? He walked towards her and tried to be friendly. When Stella mentioned this her voice always took on the frosty tone she must have adopted on that bustling Dublin street. 'I just said could I have my book back and walked on.'

Cutting. But I wonder what it was she really wanted back.

'He was taken aback and the two with him were as well.'

Triumphant. And still so passionate.

In 1948 when Stella was twenty-five she'd contracted TB. Many of her colleagues died and while she was on the long and tortuous road to recovery her emotional equilibrium was struck a terminal blow. She had been engaged to a doctor at the large Dublin hospital where she worked. During her long months of confinement to bed, he turned his attention to another young nurse – one of her juniors – and fell in love. Her brother John, who so often in her life was Stella's knight in shining armour, had seen the man out on the town with a pretty young nurse. He made the morale-sapping journey by bike to the nursing-home to break the news. Ernie the doctor clearly didn't have the guts. What must have been going through John's head as he cycled furiously to be by his beloved sister's side. He knew her heart was going to be broken. It was shattered. Ernie was the great love of her life and this was the end of her world. Stella never recovered from the blow. Years later she told a friend that it made her feel 'wicked' towards him. Given Stella's love of literature and English language she would never use that word lightly. She meant it. She kept tabs on him. She phoned him and hung up. She despised him with all that Stella passion. She never forgave him. She never forgot him.

Everything I hear about Stella's brother John makes me so proud of my uncle. His widow Doris thinks he knew Stella's secrets, all about her daughter Deirdre and me. I have a photograph of him when he was a boy which I find touchingly familiar. When I look at him I don't see a stranger. It's a deep, thoughtful, caring face. There's a sadness there too. John cycled for Ireland and would have gone to the ends of the earth for Stella. I am sorry he died just before I contacted her in 1990 as I'd like to have known him. Just before Stella and I met, she'd suffered yet another terrible breakdown and had been taken to St Patrick's Hospital for treatment. John couldn't bear to see her like that again and he died with a broken heart. How many times did he think of that day when he cycled for miles to tell her the awful truth about the man she loved? He remembered what it did to her.

After fully recuperating from TB, Stella climbed the professional ranks achieving the status of matron. By 1958 she had become briefly involved with a man in the dark green uniform of the Gardai – the Irish police force. Her affair with Frank, the man with whom she conceived Deirdre, was short lived. 'He was a drinker.' A drinker he may well have been; an enigma he remained. For years and years I found out nothing about Frank. There was a limit to how much Stella would say about her policemen as they weren't her favourite topic of conversation. Frank, as far as we were aware, might have become somebody else's father or late father and grandfather, much loved and greatly missed, forever in their thoughts, unaware of his daughter, and all but unacknowledged by his former lover. He had disappeared into the void.

Two years later, in 1960, Stella, who was never far from the slough of despond, met our friend, my father – a younger policeman not long in town. Joseph came from the North and, like Frank, was a Catholic. Her parents would have been absolutely horrified if they'd found out. Her mother would have spontaneously combusted. When Stella's brother John married a Catholic girl in 1963, long after the young copper had sown his seed and scarpered, the family took a while coming to terms with it and it's only because his bride Doris is such a lovely person that they did so. Such was the tenor of the times, the wedding was a rushed and tense affair. It was quickly over, with everybody out the back door of the church with as much haste and as little bother as possible. Whatever reservations Stella might have had about her brother's choice on purely religious grounds, surely they must have been tempered by her own ecumenical sexual experiences. You would hope so.

There is another thing to mention here about the dashing young Garda officer she met and took an immediate fancy to. It's something I only discovered very recently. When she met Joseph, he was twenty-three and Stella was thirty-six. Theirs was an 'inconstant' relationship. You might say casual but Stella didn't: 'I don't like the word casual.' She found him attractive, intelligent and very easy to get on with. She was under the shining impression that he was doing extra-mural university study. A 'degree thing'. That's what he told her.

They were both working very hard but when free time did

permit they would sit in her rooms listening to the Italian opera records they loved, particularly Verdi and Puccini. Stella mentioned *Madame Butterfly*. It has become a staple of Hollywood soundtracks and a predictable fallback for the opera houses but there are sublime moments. The first act love duet, 'Viene la Sera' – Evening is falling – is a beautiful evocation of sexual intensity, an extraordinarily sensual piece. There are shimmering highs of passion as the two voices soar together, then serene passages of serenity where the world is safe and all that exists and matters is the moment. Perhaps there were such moments between my parents.

They discussed literature and poetry and they both adored dancing. She told me he was a very good dancer – 'light on his feet'. As matron of the hospital, it fell to Stella to organize the social evenings for the nurses and 'Stella's dances' were legendary. She loved her bright-coloured dresses and flamboyant hats. Shaking off the shackles of matronly formality was evidently not just a sweet pleasure but a necessary act. She also revelled in the formality though. She had a responsible, straight-laced image and comfortably inhabited this world of strict decorum, the blue uniform, the Irish lace collar, the matron's cap and the little silver bell behind the red velvet curtain that she'd ring to order tea. She could bark at the maid all right. One visitor asked one poor girl, who was from Donegal, why she let Stella speak to her like that.

'It's my job.'

Away from this of world of stuffy etiquette – when evening was falling – Stella was a different animal, a person her mother would never have recognized. A person her mother would never have believed. Both sides of Stella came out sometimes when she'd go to dances and comment on the different women there with a mixture of rebuke and admiration. 'Look at her,' she'd say. 'What a Jezebel.'

Occasionally she and Joseph would go to the pictures. Stella remembered going together once to the Bergman classic *Wild Strawberries*. It's a morality tale about a man's reconciliation with his family and his eventual redemption. More often they would stay in. I once asked her when 'it' happened. When I happened. I was amazed that she didn't change the subject as is her way. Instead she responded immediately.

'Before I went on holiday cycling down the east coast with my sister. We did fifty miles a day. It was in my private apartment. My matron's apartment. We'd been for a drink.' I asked her how she knew that was the one. 'You just know.' Do you? My wild and passionate mother. That must have been some dance.

When she gave Joseph the news that she was pregnant, she says he asked what she was going to do. She told him she'd leave Ireland for a while and go to Edinburgh. 'He didn't say much really. He didn't say "stay here". He was discomfited. Upset. I didn't see him for a while after that.' When she told me this, I found the alleged moral cowardice on my 'father's' part depressing. There was a huge age gap, there was an unbridgeable religious divide and now there was to be a baby but surely there was a more supportive approach than just disappearing into thin air. I ask myself again and again, What would I have done in those circumstances – twenty-three years old? An occasional lover? Much older woman? I don't always give the same answer.

She only had to take twelve weeks off work. She was fortunate in that she didn't 'show' too much at six months and, of course, she took care to wear suitable clothes. Her explanation for her enforced absence from work was that she had contracted bronchitis. Family and friends were told that she had 'gone to Scotland for her chest'. In her previous pregnancy, with Deirdre, she told everyone that she was going to work as a locum in Northern Ireland which is what she did indeed do – but not for as long as people thought.

Getting blood out of the Blarney stone would have been easier than inducing Stella to talk about this period. That's a measure of the pain she still felt at events back then – one of which was set in train by the brief episode on the sofa in her apartment. Thank the Lord for that brief episode – that's what I say. But then if it hadn't happened I wouldn't be bothered, would I? The only people she ever told about her two pregnancies were her sister Patti and the man Stella was to marry some years later. No one but Stella knew the identity of our fathers. Deirdre and I were two little secrets conceived in clandestine relationships and born an ocean away. She found it difficult to address these memories, for they were hushed up and locked in her heart for so many years. The great taboo of her life nurtured an offspring that stayed – her invincible guilt. When we spoke on the phone I could so often hear the shame and agony and wretchedness of 1961 in her voice. She would far rather have talked to me about anything else, so mostly we did. She told me about her brothers and sisters and her mother and father and grandparents. She wanted to hear about Linda and her sons. Long after Linda and I had split up, she wanted to hear about my wife Tina and my children – Stella's granddaughters. There was only one thing she ever willingly mentioned from that painful period so long ago: that beautiful book of poetry.

SEVEN

The Slough of Despond

The first few hours and days of a newborn child's life are such a magical and precious time for parents. I could no sooner contemplate parting with one of my girls a few days after they popped into the world than rip out my own heart. I am not a woman – yet another piece of trenchant self-analysis there. I asked my wife Tina, who at the time of writing is pregnant with our fourth child, if, given Stella's circumstances, she could have done what was best for the baby's future? How's that for a loaded question?

'Knowing the pressures from society back then I just wouldn't have got myself into the situation in the first place. I would have been meticulously careful.'

'But if it did happen. If you had to? If you had no choice?'

Tina winced. 'It would kill me. It would destroy me. It would torment my every waking moment. To do it twice – that's beyond my comprehension. You must have to make yourself dead inside to deal with it.'

I guess Stella bottled so much of it up as a matter of emotional and professional survival because of those pressures and prejudices. In the Dublin of the early sixties the moral opprobrium pointing at single mothers was unforgiving. Not many years after my birth, Stella's manic depression had become a case study at a Dublin teaching hospital. The notes dryly stated that she'd had two illegitimate children. The information made its malicious way to her employer and she was dismissed. There was no recourse to any employment tribunal back then.

The battle between her heart and head – the love of her children and the reality of her predicament – cries out of these extracts from her correspondence with Mrs Graham Davidson from the Scottish Adoption Agency. She was pregnant with Deirdre at the time of the first letter. They are an eloquent mixture of the practical, the trivial and the desolate.

26 June 1959

Dear Mrs Graham Davidson

To introduce myself: my name is Stella Lackey (Miss). I am a trained nurse and midwife (English Registration) and am personally employed as a midwife at the above address. Miss Martin, Matron, has advised me to write to you.

My problem is that I am, unfortunately, going to have an illegitimate baby at the end of September or early in October.

I'd be so relieved if I could have my baby in Edinburgh and have it adopted in Scotland. I belong to the Protestant religion incidentally. I wonder if you could help me please.

I'd like to keep on duty here as long as possible but I would be grateful for accommodation in Scotland in September and possibly August if necessary. I am very fit at the moment. I'd be perfectly wiling to do some duties in a nursery, free of course during my waiting period. I'd rather be occupied. I have given this matter careful consideration but I have decided that adoption into a good home would give my baby a better chance in life.

23 November 1959

Dear Mrs Davidson

As the six-week period is up now do I write to you and tell you when my mind is settled regarding Deirdre or do I wait until her tests are satisfactory? I understand she'll be at Willowbrae for some time. It is very hard to let her go but it is the only course I can take under the circumstances and I know life would be easier for her. Have you seen her? I'd love to see her once more but perhaps I had better not. Matron has promised to send me a snapshot. I am happy that she is being well cared for.

Hope you are keeping well yourself although the weather has not been to pleasant lately. There is certainly no shortage of water here!

I am very well and getting ready for our annual dance on Thursday.

Hoping to hear from you soon.

1 Jan 1960

Dear Mrs Davidson

I do pray she'll have a happy life. Wasn't she a lovely baby? Hope you had a nice Christmas. I was terribly busy but patients and staff

*enjoyed themselves so that was good. I must say I enjoyed it too. We
had singing, concerts, Santa Claus and all.*

All my very best wishes for 1960 to you.

14 March 1960

*I shall never forget you and my other sincere friends in Edinburgh.
You were all so kind. Will you please let me know if Deirdre is
well. I am sure she is but I am more contented when I hear from
you . . .*

31 March 1960

*Thank you for your letter. I was glad to hear the good news of
Deirdre and I'd love to keep her photograph. I was delighted to get
it. Thank you very much for sending it to me. Miss Wilson also
sent me one taken when she was about six weeks old. She is almost
six months old now. How time flies. I may go to Edinburgh for a
few days in May. My brother is cycling for Ireland in the 'Tour of
Britain' and I might see part of the race.*

I was born at 8 a.m. on 10 April 1961, just over a year after the
date of that last letter, in an out-of-the-way downstairs room at
her Portobello digs. She was staying with her 'sincere friends in
Edinburgh', the Blackies. They knew all about her situation; they
knew all about her problems and she couldn't have asked for truer
friends. I arrived after only an hour's labour and was delivered by
the landlady Mrs Blackie herself with Stella, who was of course a

qualified midwife, yelling instructions through the pain. All the time, however, she quite properly accorded her much-loved land-lady the respectful status – 'Mrs Blackie'. 'Now, Mrs Blackie, if you could cut the cord please?' Quite right too. Labour is no excuse for informality. By the time Dr Cameron, in his accustomed bow-tie, had rushed across town, I was already a citizen of the world. He'd had no fears though. He well knew that Stella knew what she was doing. In the following five days, Mrs Blackie's daughters May and Ann would help mix up my bottle and Stella would tenderly feed me. The awful day was looming though. The mood still darkens when May and Ann recall it. It rapidly arrived and was 'traumatic'.

'It was awful,' says May, shaking her head. 'Poor Stella was inconsolable. Inconsolable.'

The struggle between her heart and head must have torn her apart. She told Mrs Blackie and the girls she didn't think she would be able to dress me to go. It would be too much. Eventually though, she gathered her strength and insisted on it. The social worker, remembered as a kindly woman, arrived slightly early but there was no mad rush. Stella had a few moments alone with me. She kissed me goodbye and I was taken.

The next few days were depressing for everyone in the Blackie household. Stella recovered her composure after three days or so but as May points out – 'only on the surface'.

What must have gone through her mind? She had been in the same situation once before of course. As then the efficient ultra-competent matron Stella stepped forward. She was renowned for being practical, assertive and taking control when she worked and following everything to the immaculate letter. This was the person seeing the job through and handing over a healthy baby as per the agreement. This was the mask. As Tina said, she must have died inside.

When she did talk about our time together she took refuge in a warm tale about a little dog, a scruffy mongrel called Toby that slept under the bed in the room. Toby was half collie and guarded my cot devotedly. He wouldn't let anyone but Stella go near me without a menacing growl and was constantly trying to lick me clean.

Her pregnancy and my birth were a shock to the system for the twenty-three-year-old policeman. I asked Stella if he ever came to see her after she'd returned from Scotland. Had he been any comfort during her post-natal hormonal maelstrom as the little boy she bore smiled his first smiles at his smitten new mummy and daddy? I was praying she would say 'yes'.

According to her, Joseph rang up out of the blue one day and told her he was coming round. Initially Stella told him to sling his hook but the young charmer called forth all his powers of persuasion, said he'd really love to see her and she weakened. He came by. I wanted to know if he gave a damn – if he cared for me at all – for his baby son. Stella told me about the meeting.

'I hadn't communicated with him until that time. It was in my private rooms again. He was asking me if it was a boy, saying he'd always wanted a boy. He said he would come back and see me again but he didn't. I was annoyed about that. He told me that he had somebody. A relationship. So I didn't pursue the friendship any further. I didn't want to be upsetting people. I was a bit upset but what can you do?'

What can you do? The desolate cry of my mother. Those

deceptively fatalistic words were a howl of despair, a *sotto voce* primal scream. She said she was 'a bit upset', as if she were referring to a coffee stain on a favourite blouse. It was a piece of understatement belying years of denial.

Whenever we discussed the events surrounding my birth Stella was as apologetic as she was unforthcoming. Every time I met her and we talked seriously, every telephone conversation of any substance, it was the same. 'Sorry.' Sorry for what? For not having the abortion, which, given her contacts, I am sure she could have arranged. Sorry for not being more careful? Sorry for making sure I was adopted into a wonderful loving family? Sorry about Edinburgh? I said to her outright, 'You've got nothing to be sorry for. If it hadn't happened I wouldn't be sitting here drinking a malt whisky talking to you from a home where I am surrounded by love. Don't be so silly.' Maybe what she meant was that she regretted not keeping me and looking after me herself. But that would have ruined both our lives.

At the tail end of one lengthy phone call I had to get something sorted in my own mind. Now whether it was something I needed to know or something I was merely curious about – nosy about – I can't say. We had been talking for over an hour, much of it of little consequence bar the fact that we were talking. I popped the question. 'Stella, was there passion with Joseph *after* I was born?'

'Not much. Some. Yes. How's Tina?'

'She's in bed now. She's fine though.' My pro forma answer sufficed.

We small-talked our way to a close and I took the bombshell to bed. She has just given a baby away, he has become the invisible man, and the next minute they are back in bed with each other!

Who were these people? She must have desperately needed to be held.

Stella loved her father deeply. He was a farmer. Farmer George. The family had a small holding in Longford, two hours north of Dublin. She told me he was a man of few words, strong as an ox but quiet as a mouse. This latter attribute was in stark contrast to his wife Sarah, who some say terrorized the lot of them long after she'd shuffled off her indomitable but mortal coil. A 'forceful woman'.

'Stella's mother fucked her up. She fucked them all up big time,' one younger male relative told me. He was raised in different times.

Sarah Lackey was an imperious matriarch if ever there was one. She was very much the boss. Her husband had to go outside the cottage to smoke his pipe. And your problem is? You might argue she was years ahead of her time on that score but it was a telling example of a greater pattern. As some have it, she considered herself to be 'a cut above the buttermilk'.

'A snobby person but with nothing to be snobby about.'

This small-town gossip echoing down through the years may well be true, but Stella's mother utterly adored her oldest daughter. She was her shining light and could do no wrong. Stella spent half her life trying to win her mother's approval and the other half secretly defying her. If Sarah Lackey had ever known Stella's secrets – two illegitimate children by two Catholic fathers – there would have been hell and damnation to pay.

Sarah Lackey demanded the very best from her children and she was so very proud when Stella Margaret won a scholarship to nursing college. When she became a matron Sarah was thrilled. It confirmed and conformed with her sense of status. It is strange to think this is my grandmother we are talking about here. 'A cut above the buttermilk'? Nose in the air? I should hope so.

Stella spoke to me about her father with unequivocal love and longing.

She said he was just like the ploughman in Gray's *Elegy*; a piece Stella adored. 'That was him all right.' It's a vignette in a longish poem and it doesn't say an awful lot. Mind you neither did he.

> The curfew tolls the knell of parting day,
> The lowing herd wind slowly o'er the lea,
> The ploughman homeward plods his weary way
> And leaves the world to darkness and to me.

I think I know what she means.

Soon after her final encounter with Joseph Stella left to work in England and it was there that she got married. 'I didn't leave any address. I went to England. It lasted four and a half years. I made a bad mistake. He was an Irishman with Portuguese roots. A terrible combination.' A friend remarked that everyone was expecting him to be tall, thin and elegant but then he turned up: 'We got the shock of our lives when this gnome appeared.' Furthermore, he was a vindictive little gnome.

What she tolerated was extraordinary. Doris, Stella's sister-in-law, remembers him less than fondly. 'Newton – he was absolutely dreadful. Like Satan himself. We went to their house in London. I got the eeriest feeling – get me out of this house! Over their bed there was a photo of his late mother when she died – laid out. I asked Stella if she objected – "Not really".'

As soon as Stella even looked at another man he beat her up. When she told him about her two children he beat her up. When she didn't – he beat her up. She came out with all the hackneyed excuses. Doris remembers her explaining away a broken nose.

'I was stupid. I walked right into the door – the door belted me as I walked in.'

After she eventually left him, rescued by her brother John, his nastiness continued. Newton wrote a series of poison pen letters to family members making scurrilous accusations about her. He claimed she had given birth to two children out of wedlock. The rumours that he spread persisted but nothing was ever said beyond a quiet word by a flickering fire. 'I remember my mother wondering one evening whether there would be any truth in it,' recalls one family friend. The scuttlebutt was in whispers. Once again, hushed up and locked away. Did anyone ask her outright if it was true? 'It wasn't discussed,' a relative squarely told me. As for her husband, the British Rail Guard John Newton – he is dead now. It's his turn to be judged.

What Stella needed was a partner to share and understand her pain, not one to inflame it. She was suffering mentally and physically. When it did get to the dreadful point that her brother John had to come to the rescue and bring her back to the familiar environment of County Wicklow, she was a broken person. She suffered a dreadful breakdown and was sent to hospital.

When she took ill, she got giddy, excitable and uninhibited. She had surges of wild energy and became maniacal and fanatical about whatever she was doing. After that would come the unstoppable descent into her own hell. All the hurt and all the pain closed in and engulfed her. On so many occasions when we talked, she used the expression the 'slough of despond'. For poor Stella that literary allusion had a deep and awful truth. Maybe the passage from *Pilgrims Progress* was in the beautiful book she loaned to Joseph.

> This miry slough is such a place as cannot be mended: it is the descent whither the scum and filth that attends conviction for sin doth continually run; and therefore it is called the Slough of Despond. For still, as the sinner is awakened about his lost condition, there arise in his soul many fears, and doubts, and discouraging apprehensions, which all of them get together, and settle in this place: and this is the reason of the badness of this ground.

I wonder why she married that man – the 'terrible combination'. Gnomish and Satanic. In every attempt to escape from the hell of loneliness, she got sucked further in. Was her marriage the rebound from the rebound from the rebound? It was a last desperate throw of the dice for love and passion, the passion she craved. This final jolt precipitated another dreadful descent into that world of *fears and doubts and discouraging apprehensions*.

She held a number of positions for the rest of her working life, when she was well enough to work, including that of matron in an old people's home. She continued to take great joy in her nephews and nieces and then, in 1990, her brother John died. He meant everything to Stella and it was shortly after this tragedy that

I came back into her life. When Stella told her nephews and nieces that she'd had children, there was total astonishment. Sister-in-law Doris chuckles at the memory. Apparently Stella 'blew the lid' telling them one by one.

'Stella has children!'

'Bloody hell, when did this happen?'

'Jesus, if I'd known that.'

'What? Stella?'

They couldn't reconcile this extraordinary revelation with the rather fussy, stuffy, uptight aunt – the one who wouldn't let any of them touch anything when they visited her as kids. The last person they'd have thought . . . They didn't know the other Stella.

I once asked her if she was in love with Joseph.

'I suppose we could have got on all right. I was quite attracted to him, I'll say that. I could have been in love but I would have had to know him longer. The amount of time wasn't long enough. It was too off and on.' There was a long pause at the other end of the phone line. She broke her own silence. 'If you ever see him maybe you could ask for my book of quotations back? It was a beautiful book.' This from her adored Gray's *Elegy*.

> Perhaps in this neglected spot is laid
> Some heart once pregnant with celestial fire;
> Hands that the rod of Empire might have swayed,
> Or waked to ecstacy the living lyre.

It was all such a long time ago.

EIGHT

Big Enders/Little Enders

Our first meeting on that Easter weekend in Dublin was draining and depressing. I felt I had let her down. I'd danced back into her life and was now singularly incapable of feeling anything for her, let alone loving her, as she so clearly wanted. Maybe I didn't have the capacity to love anyone but myself. Maybe Linda was right.

I also felt so disloyal. Was I being completely selfish? There were Mum and Dad at home in Edinburgh sitting in their front room, thinking about nothing else while gazing vacantly at the box. They'd been very understanding. Well, Mum had. She at least sounded strong about it. Dad never once mentioned Stella, or tracing or birth parents to me – never in his whole life. I don't think I could have looked him in the eye even if he had. I couldn't bear to think how hurt he might be and how it would be eating away at him. I'm a compulsive worrier and I got that trait from Dad. His glass was forever half empty. The baby they had adored had grown into the son he loved so much. Dad's own father, an austere Victorian figure, had taken a lot of his confidence away. He wasn't outwardly emotional but there was boundless love inside him. I was terrified of breaking his heart.

As for Stella, I couldn't reconcile who I had come from with who I had met. I wasn't able to accept a mother whose image was so dissonant with the fantasy figure of my imagination. This fantasy – the independent, forthright, empowered figure – was intrinsic to my sense of self and I had cherished it in a special place at the back of my mind for as long as I could remember. Here was a challenge to my identity.

Where *was* the magical bond? The mythical cord? Lots of people feel distant from a parent or parents because they choose to or because they have drifted apart over time. They have the option. I fully expected to feel close and bonded to my natural mother until I understood that real life is a lot more complicated. I couldn't bond. Or I wouldn't. I'd naively thought I'd already know her and have an instant, almost spiritual connection. When I realized that wasn't the case I sounded the psychological retreat, looked around and found myself in a strange town, in a strange situation, doing one of the strangest things a person can do. Someone I did love was at home. Sarah, the 'girl from the hotel room', was going through the motions of her lonely weekend. So were Mum and Dad. I loved them too. Now I knew just how much. With all of this going on, that mighty question hoved into sight and blocked the view: *What happens next?*

Even now I am coming to terms with what happened *then* never mind *next*. You can't make up for thirty years in a day. It is a brand-new relationship with a stranger. If I had realized that – if we both had – things might have been better. We had different expectations and different needs. I soon found out that I didn't want a mum – I already had one. I wanted a puzzle solved. Stella expected to move forward in a mother–son relationship. I can understand why. I am her son. But in effect I was just another man, wasn't I? Another man in the line, only interested in satisfying his own needs and using Stella for his own purposes. But I had to know. And now I did. No more fantasy. Just the reality. Linda and I went back to the hotel. I got pissed.

The next day we ambled round Dublin and did a bit of shopping. Bookshops are the greatest escape and I bought a sack load on Irish politics and history – a bit of light reading about the mother's land. Since a pretty big part of me is Irish I wanted to find out more. If I did have a need for identity and connection I answered it in my new notional sense of Irishness. I'd had quite enough of me for one weekend so I filled my travel bag with those books. Books about anything, anywhere and anyone Irish. I bought everything from the poetry of Bobby Sands to essays on Loyalist extremism. A culture clash crash course. I absorbed every word of the quality Sundays. They were full of articles marking the 75th anniversary of the Easter Rising. One had a poll saying that most people thought the IRA men of the 1916 rising would disapprove of the violence of the modern IRA. The poll said nothing about the men of 1916 and everything about the modern Southern Irish citizens' discomfiture with the vexing situation in the North. A prominent writer on matters Republican once put it in his own nutshell after appearing in a TV debate I'd presented. With a glass of red in one hand and a chicken drumstick in the other, he explained to me through a volley of projectile breadcrumbs, 'If you lived in the South you'd want them strung up. If you lived in the North you'd want to fucking join 'em.'

I remember smiling at his saloon-bar generalization and laughing at the thought of Stella in a balaclava.

What did happen next? After we went home from Dublin Stella rang frequently, often at a bad time. We did have some good conversations though, amidst the many when she just needed to speak as opposed to talk. She was at her best when she was being matronly and waspish. Just as she had been when she asked for her book back from Joseph in the street in 1962, leaving him and his colleagues dumbfounded. On one occasion she phoned me full of savoured scorn for a man she had passed in a Dublin Street. 'Hello. I'll tell you who I saw in Dublin today?'

It wasn't, alas, the young cop to whom she had lent the book of poetry in 1960 although the legendary 'Joseph Leahy' did swiftly cross my mind. She immediately answered her own question in a testily disapproving voice. 'Gerry Adams. What a weasel-faced man.' This was of course a good while before Adams was having his hand shaken by Bill Clinton and kissed by New York's glitterati. There was no ceasefire. The guns were far from silent. Unlike the voice of Gerry. In broadcast interviews all his lines were spoken by an actor. This fatuous and wholly counter-productive ruling gave the leader of Republicanism a politically advantageous aura. It pumped him full fat with the oxygen of publicity. One TV friend of mine produced a Channel 4 interview with Adams round about this time and as a major act of rebellion against this dictatorial and anti-democratic Thatcherite fiat, left in one of Gerry's coughs. Snigger at the back of the class. What larks, Pip.

Stella wasped on animatedly about the man she'd encountered that very afternoon. 'I wouldn't trust any of them.' I wondered if she meant Republicans or men. 'Rogues. All of them.' I still wasn't sure. Prose and poetry gave Stella and me something to talk about – it was our thread of connection, although with her knowledge she left me in the shade. I remembered a line of poetry learned at school. I thought it rather fitted her strange encounter.

I met murder on the way. He had a mask like Castlereagh
Very smooth he looked, yet grim; Seven bloodhounds followed him.

She loved it. 'Who wrote that?' Typically I couldn't remember that it was Shelley, lines from 'The Mask of Anarchy' – a condemnation of the Peterloo Massacre of 1819. Lord Castlereagh effectively sanctioned the killing of eleven parliamentary reformers and the wounding of hundreds more by local yeomanry and Government troops at a peaceful protest in St Peter's Fields, Manchester. Castlereagh was the Government's spokesman on civil matters. Thereafter he was reviled – jeered wherever he appeared in public. When eventually he slit his own throat, he died unmourned.

Robert Stewart Castlereagh was of Presbyterian Ulster Scots stock. Stella's family, the Lackeys, seemed to have been of a similar religious strain back in the sixteen and seventeen hundreds. There are 'Ulster Scotch' Lackey descendents all over Delaware, Philadelphia and Maryland – I've seen their websites – but some of those who remained in Ireland and settled in the South were lured by the Bishop's purple and upped candlesticks to the higher church of the Anglican communion. Maybe, as they lived in the Republic, Anglicanism – the Church of Ireland – was a more comfortable ecclesiastical home. Some would say it's closer to Rome than it is to the Presbytery.

Southern Protestants have made a significant contribution to Ireland's political, artistic and business life. Many did so from positions of privileged status and economic power but, never the less, they proudly embraced and fiercely asserted their Irish nationhood. If Stella had engaged Gerry Adams about Wolfe Tone, for example, I am sure he would have waxed lyrical. Tone is, arguably, the father figure of Irish Republicanism. He was also, as Irish nationalists rush to remind you, a well-born Protestant. For some in the North this is a potent paradox. He was indeed a Protestant, but Tone was no Paisley. He was an anti-sectarian radical inspired by the revolutionary ideas of 1789 – Liberty, Equality, Fraternity. Members of the 'Protestant ascendancy' in eighteenth-century Ireland were determinedly Irish in the same way the English gentlemen who led the American Revolution felt themselves to be anything but *English* gentlemen. Eventually captured by the Brits, Wolfe Tone was sent for execution. On 19 November 1798 he assured his place in the Republican pantheon by defying his persecutors. He cut his throat with a penknife and died a martyr.

Stella was proudly Irish, with, of course, that aforementioned Scottish caveat – the cherished Lackey link to the seventeenth-century MacGregors. She *would* claim to be descended from Rob Roy! She always sent me thoughtful birthday presents. They were in the main books inscribed with her love and that fateful date – 10 April. One such was a simply wonderful tome. She gave me *The Story of the Irish Race* by Seumas MacManus. It is not just green tinted. It's emerald to the core, with flights of folkloric fancy and torrents of romantic nationalism and even some history too. It is great stuff. I treasure it. I wish I'd told her. As far as Stella was concerned, Irishness – and she wanted me to have an acute sense of mine – was nothing whatsoever to do with religion. It was everything to do with a sense of identity and belonging. Wolfe

Tone and Stella Lackey were great minds thinking alike on that one.

I had not altogether happy memories of George Bernard Shaw from university. We, being the aptly named 'Dramatic Society', had mounted a production of *Major Barbara*. I played what I thought was a scene-stealing starring role but was blown off the stage by Iain Glen in a relatively minor part. People watching couldn't take their eyes off him. I couldn't help thinking he was a better actor than me and you know – with his dozens of films and theatre triumphs, including *The Blue Room* with Nicole Kidman – I think I may have had a point. It was a painful discovery. Unfortunately this twenty-year-old wannabe thesbian was incapable of avoiding the green-eyed monster of jealousy – for years. It was a good play though, *Major Barbara*. In a roundabout way, it was about the arms trade. When I told Stella a rose-tinted version of my theatrical history, she was delighted that I was acquainted with the works of the famous Fabian, GBS. Stella had a high opinion of George Bernard Shaw and George Bernard Shaw had a high opinion of himself and an opinion on seemingly everything. Nationhood and religion were no exception. In 1912 he made a notable speech in London which further illustrates the ease with which the Southern Protestant could identify with the Southern state and proudly wear his Irishness.

> I am an Irishman; my father was an Irishman, and my mother an Irishwoman; and my father and my mother were Protestant . . . Many of the duties of my mother were shared by an Irish nurse, who was a Catholic, and she never put me to bed without sprinkling me with Holy Water.

Holy Moses! Could you imagine one of the bowler-hatted burghers of Portadown expressing those sentiments? Protestants in the South, the vast majority of whom are Church of Ireland, do not dump their religious, ethnic and national identity in the same drum, the way their distant brethren in the North do. For one thing there was no serious numerical threat to the established religion of the Southern state so no sense of rivalry was allowed to fester and grow. As one hardworking Dublin Prod told me, 'We just put our heads down, got on with it and contributed to society from our affluent ghetto.'

The doctrinaire authoritarianism of the Catholic Church didn't help matters. It merely reminded those who needed reminding what a heresy their alien credo was. *Ne Temere*, instituted by the Vatican in 1908, ordained that in any mixed marriage all the children were to be brought up as Catholics and a written promise to that effect was to be secured from both partners. Any marriage not following this precept would fail to be recognized. All unions had to be solemnized in a Catholic Church in the presence of a Catholic priest and all of this was of course heavily underscored by the special status the Church enjoyed in the Irish constitution. Unsurprisingly this had a devastating effect on the Protestant population and it was eventually rescinded in 1970. Thereafter more of an emphasis was placed on negotiation and persuasion and less on coercion. All this must have been in Stella's mind. Apart from her parents' horror, if she did ever marry a Catholic, her children would be lost to Rome for ever. In the event, of course, her children were 'saved', but lost to her.

The number of Church of Ireland adherents was and still is a very small proportion of the population of the South, but the effects of *Ne Temere* were borne out by the numbers. In 1881 6 per cent of Southern Irish people were Church of Ireland, but this proportion dwindled steadily over the following 110 years to a tiny 2.5 per cent in 1991.

Since then, there has been an upturn. The actual number of all Protestants has risen over the last twelve years in line with population growth. Now there are over 100,000 Church of Ireland adherents in the Republic of Ireland, which is still only 2.5 per cent of the four-million-strong population, but represents a significant increase in head count. This upturn in numbers is largely down to immigration and the more generally liberal atmosphere. However, it's fascinating to note that a mere 20,000 or so people declared themselves Presbyterian in 2002, while there are nearly three and a half million Catholics. This is a barely visible 0.5 per cent of the population – just enough to fill Trafalgar Square.

If a superior intelligence from a far-off planet were to ponder any of this they'd be perplexed. They might well have a good old belly laugh too. It's all light years away from logic, isn't it? One vastly superior intelligence closer to home and reality did address it rather well. Jonathan Swift, another scion of the Irish Protestant ascendancy, put it all too beautifully in *Gulliver's Travels*. Stella adored Swift. This was partly down to his literary output and partly to the fact that 'Stella' was the name he gave Hesther Johnson, who many maintain was his secret wife. He wrote this for her.

> Stella this day is thirty-four
> We shan't dispute a year or more
> However Stella be not troubled

> Although thy size and years are doubled,
> Since first I saw thee at sixteen,
> The brightest virgin on the green;
> So little is thy form declin'd
> Made up so largely in thy mind.

In Swift's time, of course, the Anglican Church was, because of English rule, the established Church in Ireland, even though the vast majority of her population were Catholics. As one of the rich and powerful minority, he could afford an enlightened swipe at the religious divide. In that more substantial and enduring work, *Gulliver's Travels*, the great satirist describes the Big-Enders and the Little-Enders and their ceaseless bickering over which end of the boiled egg to lop off for eating.

There was an extraordinary display of egginess in July 1949. Douglas Hyde, the first President of the Republic of Ireland, was a Protestant. That fact in itself was something that would never have been mirrored in the Northern Irish state – at the time so much a Protestant state for a Protestant people as to render the possibility of a politically prominent Catholic inconceivable. However, at Hyde's funeral in Dublin, the Taoiseach and his entire cabinet remained outside St Patrick's Church of Ireland Cathedral. They stood on the steps. They sat in their big black chauffeur-driven cars. They did anything but go through the Godless portals of the Protestant cathedral where Jonathan Swift himself had once been dean. They avoided this lest they got egg (from the wrong end) all over their faces.

This was Stella's world. 'Scratch-the-surface sectarianism', is how a friend of hers described it to me. The marriage options for a young Protestant girl were narrowly focused in Southern Ireland. When a good 'un came along, my God – whoever's bloody God – you were lucky. If he kicked with the same foot, as they say in Glasgow, he was worth his weight in bread and wine. The doctor who ditched her when she was twenty-five had a status that appealed and a religion that matched. He was a Belfast Protestant. She was also head over heels in love with him. It was all too perfect.

Her brother John met and fell in love with Doris, a Catholic girl. They really were made for each other so nothing and no one was going to stop them, but in those days it was an unholy struggle. Doris told me how their forbidden love grew and grew in spite of the reservations of friends, family and society.

'We'd first got together in the social season – cycling dances. It was never anything serious, being aware of the rules of the Church. I went to Australia in fifty-nine. I came back in sixty-two. Stella's mother then realized it was serious between us and she relaxed a lot. She wasn't well by then. She *was* good to me. We became good friends but she was very old fashioned in her ways.' The old lady mellowed with illness and age. It was one thing her son marrying outside the Protestant faith. It would have been quite another if her golden child Stella had done it.

What a palaver it was for Doris, John and the two families. First of all the happy couple had to get permission from the Archbishop. A sympathetic Jesuit Priest helped Doris word the letter to the big man. They applied to have their wedding on 8 August 1963 and didn't actually have that date confirmed by the authorities until the evening before. Two conditions were imposed on the ceremony: it had to be in another parish and it was to take place at eight thirty in the morning. When they got the great news it was all hands to the pump. John, an Irish champion cyclist, had to hurtle round town and get in touch with the relatives one by one, telling them that the wedding was on, *and* they had be up with the lark. Meanwhile Doris frantically got on with her own last-minute preparations.

Only members of the two families were in attendance the next morning. Doris told me about the greatest day of her life: 'I was allowed to walk up the centre aisle but not back down it and then we had to get married in the sacristy – you know, the room where the priest gets his robes on. It was upsetting for me but we so much wanted to be together. They did everything they could possibly do to stop us getting married but we defied them.' She told me *that* with such gladness in her heart.

Old Mrs Lackey was poorly at the time and didn't make the ceremony but the young couple dutifully made their way up to the house straight after the service to pay their respects and the old lady was there for them in her finest suit.

Doris does remember Stella's mother with understanding and affection.

'Sarah Lackey was very straight laced. Very Victorian. With our babies we Catholics might put a little religious picture in the pram. Sarah said one day, "I'd prefer you not to put that in the pram please. It might get the baby's eye."'

No more pictures appeared, for the sake of the old lady's feelings.

Stella's absolute insistence that both Deirdre and I were brought up as Protestants was hardly aberrant. The backdrop was a society tolerant of non-Catholics on one level but acutely aware of religious differences on every level. At that time, in that society, anyone would have done the same. Her faith was important to her and more than once she expressed to me a deep scepticism for the authority priests exercised over their flock and the Catholic Church over society. She didn't want her children to grow up in that atmosphere.

Religion was never important in my family beyond *Songs of Praise* with the smell of Sunday supper. I was aware of it but largely immune from it, save the merest whiff of snobbery on the wind. I detected a sniffy Edinburgh conceit that Catholicism was the lowest common denomination. This wasn't from my parents. Its provenance was less precise. It was just in the air. Anyway, Mum was staunchly secular. A humanist fundamentalist. She had no doubts about her certainty on that score. When I was about thirteen or fourteen, I went to Scripture Union camp for a week to play football and other games all day long in beautiful surround- ings with some of my best friends. They were fantastic times. The quid pro quo was a gentle religious indoctrination, which was, God forgive me, ever so slightly insidious. It was hard not to attribute to Jesus himself all the credit for the brilliant fun and amazing camaraderie – ergo we wanted more of it – ergo I found myself asking him into my life. We all did actually. Robert Harley, Iain Glen and myself. As long as our faith lasted, which was for two or three weeks, we'd admonish each other with the self- righteous rebuke, 'That wasn't a very Christian thing to do.' Very quickly it turned into the Spanish Inquisition. Such is the way of religion and human society.

I returned home from camp laden with tracts, prayer guides and page after page of *Good News For Modern Man*. When I got back I sneakily hid them all under my bed, safe from the search-light eyes of the Commissar Mum. It was like smuggling Bibles into Cold War Albania.

However, at one level the whole religious thing mattered even to Mum – not because of any theological issues. Even in its most bitter form sectarianism seldom hinges on canonical debate. Particularly in its most bitter form! It's something else entirely. When I first took Tina to Edinburgh when Dad was still alive, I could tell they both really liked her and they couldn't believe my luck. Mum sidled up to me when we were alone in the kitchen and told me how lovely she thought Tina was. 'What religion is she?' She didn't bark it. She just gently asked it as a mother might if hopeful of wedding bells. She was desperate for this one to work and was checking out any possible impediments to her dream scenario. She was also instinctively adhering to her class, culture, tribe and, above all perhaps, her generation. She was OK. Tina and I both open the same end of our boiled eggs. I like soldiers though.

NINE

Something Good

Whatever I had been looking for when I traced Stella, I did find something: a strong feeling of connection with Ireland. Maybe *she* – Ireland – was my long-lost mother. Her political and historical furnace became my burning interest. I looked back on the horrors of the Troubles through my parents' eyes. Guildford, Warrenpoint, Birmingham. I remembered vividly Dad's anger at the murder of Mountbatten of Burma. My adoptive father had served as a major in the Indian army during the war and had fought in the jungles of Burma. He was sickened by all the slaughter in Northern Ireland but his reaction to the murder of the former Viceroy of India sticks in my mind. He thought it senseless and vindictive. After the members of an IRA cell were killed in Gibralter by the SAS, I recall people thinking it was a fair cop. They got their just deserts. My parents had scant sympathy for the 'terrorists' starving themselves to death in the Maze and expressed abject disgust at their dirty protests. They were madmen. 'Bloody fanatics' as far as Dad was concerned.

In our house my sister and I had to observe ritual silence during the BBC News. The contents of this programme were to be revered. Pray silence please for Mr Kenneth Kendal. I remember news reports when the Troubles were at their height; people blown to smithereens for ends surely unattainable by those means. Dad just sucked on his pipe, shook his head in disgust and muttered the c word in plural. He was never prudish with the language. God knows what the memories of those outrages bequeath to children still grieving, people still suffering; mothers and fathers numbed to everything else by their loss.

Then, in the early nineties, armed with my books and my burgeoning curiosity about this labyrinth, I was determined to find out more and go in search of that illusive and illusory substance – truth. The Aberdeen University history graduate merged with the adolescent anorak and found voice in the broadcaster with pretensions to be a serious journalist. As well as the talk show on Central Television I was presenting a late-night programme on Radio One at the time and had enormous latitude as to what I could play and say. Music radio was very different then. I indulged myself on all fronts. Much of the late-night chat took on a distinctly Northern Irish flavour with guests galore to slake my thirst and bewilder many a listener looking for some late-night relaxation. From Paul Hill of the Guildford Four – 'Gerry Adams is an elected representative' – to the Reverend Iain Paisley – 'Let me tell *you* about history' – they came and declaimed between Bowie and the Beatles. I was in radio heaven. I interviewed Dr Paisley a few years later when he was on the election trail, and he was a different being from that avuncular late-night incarnation in my dimly lit studio. At times almost wise and at times almost vile, he personifies the complexities and paradoxes of Northern Ireland. The more I read about it, the more complex and paradoxical it all seemed.

Throughout all this, of course, peering from the darkness was the mysterious Northern Catholic who was my father. Maybe I was looking for him.

The fragile Southern Protestant who was my birth mother came over to London within a year of our first meeting. It was difficult. It just didn't feel right. It was as unsettling as our first meeting but without the sense of excited anticipation. She came, we had lunch, we talked, we went for a walk and she went. I slumped into the sofa and felt free again. Making myself analyse how I felt – and really thinking hard about *why* I felt that way – I get angry. Angry with myself for not coping socially, never mind emotionally, and for behaving like a dodgy computer – freezing and malfunctioning. But also angry with her for abandoning me. I should have been grateful. I should have loved her for that alone. She gave me away to a better life and God knows what she saved me from. It's illogical but feelings so often are.

I have blocked my mind to so much of my life back then but I remember the kiss when she arrived and it felt even less comfortable than before. I was cold and cursory. I said how good it was to see her but there was no embrace. No warmth. Where were my twelve pieces of silver? It was like going up to a strange old lady at a bus stop and kissing her cheek. The sensory wariness is difficult to explain. I love and adore the smell and touch of those whom I love and adore. They are heady aromas. A familiar smell or scent caught in the air can be utterly transporting. There is no sweeter fragrance in the world to me than the smell of my children's hair. Is there a sublime tactile experience that matches that of touching the warm skin of your lover's body as you both awaken to the world? As my lips brushed Stella's cheek I was as far away from her as it was possible to be. What made me afraid? Why did I recoil? I knew I would smell a stranger so I made sure I smelt nothing. Those five days we spent together after I was born were light years away.

The feeling of recoiling is the opposite of bonding. It's all in the mind but it's real enough. What forces are at work here?

This may all sound crass and perhaps brutal but I can't help thinking there is something psychologically if not anthropologically significant about our reactions. A solid relationship with another adult isn't about nurturing or being nurtured. It is about establishing things in common – ideas, interests, beliefs, values, goals – and sharing them with one another. We had, on the surface, nothing in common save a bumper bundle of DNA. This was a painful lesson. It was a struggle in the midst of our meetings for my mind to grasp this, and the disparity between what she was to me and what she meant to me began to suffocate and frighten. What she meant to me and what society would expect her to mean – my long-lost mother – was another unconscious pressure. All the time I had to maintain a veneer. I've always fancied myself as an actor but here I was struggling. I was wooden and I fluffed all my lines. I was scared and I felt enclosed. My brain funnelled the complex emotions into a basic sense. One I understood. Tens of thousands of years of human culture and civilization were rendered irrelevant. I was afraid of her smell.

I was afraid of eye contact too. It made me uncomfortable. Of course I didn't analyse any of my feelings at the time nor have I really done so until now. Back then my emotional landscape was just too cluttered. The birth mother stuff became just another reason for confusion and self-doubt. In a bid to make sense of everything else going on at that time I was persuaded to try therapy. I tried three therapists in all – if at first you don't succeed – but I didn't talk about Stella to any of them. 'There ain't no magic – end of story.' That's all I thought back then.

The magical bond can be there, I am sure. But only if you want it and more to the point if you need it, but you need to work at it and it takes time. Angels aren't just going to hand it down from on high, polished and golden. You create it yourself. Thankfully, from Stella's perspective (and for my conscience) our meeting was a wonderful turn of events. She was delighted when I found her. Heather, her younger friend, distant relative and occasional confidante, told me it was great for her. It changed her life. I am just sorry that it was a time in my life when I was dealing with my own emotional quagmire. I was in my own slough of marital despond. Beyond that, the manic and superficial world of being a radio and TV presenter can suck the empathy out of you – if you let it. I'm sorry I couldn't meet or understand her emotional needs. She deserved better.

It can be so different. I met a man recently who traced his birth mother when he was in his mid forties. I'm good friends with his half siblings – her other children – and his arrival created quite a stir in the family as these things tend to do. We got chatting and exchanged experiences. I asked him if he bonded with his birth mother. 'Instantly,' he replied. 'There was an immediate connection – like we had been waiting for each other all our lives and our moment had come.' His eyes filled with tears as he told me. I thought how lucky he was and I envied him. I asked him how he got on with his mum and dad – the parents who had brought him up. 'They were cold people. They sent me to boarding-school when I was seven.' That's the difference. One day out of the blue his mother turned to him in the car. 'Oh, by the way, darling, you are adopted.' He was ten. Thinking about my mum and dad and their unconditional love for me I thought how lucky *I* was.

What happened to Sarah, the girl in the Birmingham hotel room? She finally walked away when she realized I wasn't brave enough or cowardly enough to leave Linda. We talk every so often, often on the anniversary of Margaret Thatcher's resignation. Why? We were on the concourse at Euston Station once when a big Caribbean woman selling orange juice started yelling, 'She's gone. She's gone,' in a glorious calypso lilt. Two hours later, the lunch-time liaison in that same Birmingham hotel had a historic but not very erotic soundtrack, as BBC television news blared out the momentous events. The 'end of an ear ache' as a friend put it. As for Sarah, now happily married and far away – *where there was discord – she brought harmony. Where there was despair she brought hope.* When there was no longer hope she walked away. The lady wasn't for turning. Another kiss goodbye. 'Nicky, I deserve better than this. I am worth more than this.'

Linda and I finally got divorced in 1996 and it was a new beginning for both of us. We weren't divorcing each other so much as divorcing ourselves from the hell we had both created. We have our moments in time though – our *Madame Butterfly* moments when evening fell and the world stood still. She rang Stella a couple of times after it was all over. I found out years later what she'd said. 'There is some good in Nicky.' When I heard this I repeated the phrase over in my mind with a different emphasis each time and it seemed to mean something slightly different each time. Am I self-obsessed? Is it just me me me? Maybe I should disappear for a while, lead the life of a hermit and use it as a kind of self-fulfilling mantra. Stella latched on to it. She swaddled those words, nurtured them and wouldn't let them go. Neither would I.

After my divorce, and I don't know how, the story of my finding Stella crept into a couple of the tabloids. This following scoop appeared in the *Sunday Mirror* in October 1996.

TV and radio star Nicky Campbell has been reunited with his long-lost mother who gave him up for adoption when he was a baby. Radio One DJ Nicky, who also hosts the hit TV show *Wheel of Fortune*, had a tearful reunion with real mum Stella Lackey-Newton, 72, after a year-long search. Stella, a retired nurse who lives near Dublin, said: 'The meeting was difficult for both of us, but it was definitely worth it. There were some tears ... but they were tears of joy. Nicky first contacted me some months ago and has since come to Ireland to see me. Of course we are still in contact but it's a private matter and we are only just really getting to know each other. I told him he has his life and I have mine, although I hope we can become good friends.' Stella refused to go into details about why she gave the radio star up for adoption.

My adoptive mum had a call in Edinburgh from someone purporting to be from the National Register Office needing to 'just check a few routine facts on my birth certificate' and Mum, being recently bereaved and ever helpful, was in no mind to doubt his bona fides.

Stella had an unscheduled visitor to her sheltered housing

project in Dublin. She phoned me to tell me about the strange appearance by a quite charming gentleman and their subsequent conversation. I went up the wall. I felt fiercely protective of my mum, Sheila. Dad had just died of cancer and I was furious with Stella for saying anything. I was very uptight – petty and petulant perhaps – why on earth would poor Stella have any media savvy, for God's sake? I've got precious little myself and I am a denizen of that murky world – but I still felt terribly uncomfortable with the whole situation. I was glad I knew about her but facing up to it, dealing with it and rationalizing it in my own mind were still a universe away. Why should everybody else know this stuff when I could barely come to terms with it myself? As I scolded her it felt bizarre and unnatural. She had never scolded me in all my life. That is part of a mother's role, isn't it? This was role reversal without the reversal. She often spoke about my Red Top rage incident but never to me. She reminded others – and helped convince herself 'There is some good in Nicky'.

Even more upsetting for her was the time she phoned me when Mum was staying. I had told her about Mum's visit but it hadn't sunk in or seemed important. She couldn't understand why it would never be all right for her to meet or talk with my mum. I was livid. This struck an arrow right at the heart of my guilt and stirred up the nest of emotions I wasn't willing to acknowledge existed let alone deal with. I know my outburst made her sad and confused and she cried about it often but never to me. She was defiant and angry with me though: 'Am I not good enough? Is there something wrong with me?' She just didn't understand. And neither did I.

It's funny – when my ex-wife Linda phoned my birth mother

back in 1990 on that nerve-fraying Saturday night, Stella had assumed it to be her daughter Deirdre. Deirdre's new mummy and daddy had rejected Stella's choice and named the child Esther. When Esther made contact with Stella in 1996, our 'mother' thought her long-lost daughter was but another duplicitous journalist with a devious ploy. She was ultra-cautious. Once bitten, twice shy. Granted, it wasn't a maxim she had applied in certain other areas of her life, and neither has her son, but she pulled it out of the flames here. The woman formerly known as Deirdre and forever more as Esther recorded what happened.

> Our first contact was by letter. She took my letter to her solicitor because she thought I was a journalist trying to wheedle information from her about her other child. I discovered that I had a half-brother called Nicky, also given away for adoption in Edinburgh. He was a pretty well-known national radio personality in the UK. Stella was obviously incredibly proud of this, but she had paid the price, in the form of a few scurrilous articles about it all in the papers.

Esther's journey had started. She was heading straight for my life.

TEN

When Nicky Met Esther

I was living in a small flat on Hampstead heath with big bright windows looking over one of the scenic little Heath lakes with ducks, geese, a pair of swans and the odd soul in a nylon football shirt fishing for carp. The flat was interestingly appointed. The fabrics, furnishings, kitchen surfaces and flooring had all been painstakingly chosen by Linda, by now my ex-wife. When we'd split up I'd moved in. It had all seemed fine to me but Tina had expressed violent objections to the whole style of the place. This was partly though clearly not entirely down to differing taste. I spent much of my time there staring out the windows at the Arcadia of NW3, scribbling material for my radio programme – thoughts, jokes, one-liners and miscellaneous ad-libs – and writing music for the album I'd been dreaming of making since I was fourteen. The one on the Never Never Land label. One evening Stella phoned. Down went the six-string.

Rather than my usual terse and snippy, 'How are you? Listen, you have caught me at a bad time – I'll phone back at the weekend. Bye,' I settled down for a reconciliatory chat. After the ear bashing I had given her over speaking to the creepy hack it was the very least I could do. She was probably thinking that there was some good in Nicky. On the firm instructions of my guilty conscience I sat on the low leather stool by the main phone and braced myself for some deadening small talk. I couldn't have been more surprised. It was gigantic talk. She was bright, excited and animated. She had purpose. She was engaged and coherent.

'I have spoken to Esther. She wrote to me and we have made contact.'

Of course at that stage I didn't know Esther from Adam – all a bit Old Testament for me. The only Esther I could think of was the legendary and powerful TV presenter who lived in a mansion over the lake, through the trees and on the other side of East Heath Road. It did cross my mind that Stella had really gone too bloody far this time.

'You have spoken to Esther?'

'Your sister. I knew her as Deirdre. Her given name is Esther.'

'And she's doing very well?' A line from Ian Dury. Even at a time like this I couldn't resist an adolescent wisecrack. It's like comfort food, though, isn't it?

'She is that. She lives near Bath. She is married and has two children. She is something to do with computers.' She said that like someone who wanted nothing to do with them.

'Would you mind if I passed your number to her so she could get in touch?' Graciously I consented. Inwardly I was thrilled. I was pleased that she had expressed a desire to see me and now it was happening it re-ignited all the feelings of belonging and connection that had originally made me embark on this journey. I'd suppressed them and ignored them over the last few years as I floundered in an emotional swamp that had sucked in everybody's energies. Life was so much better now though. I had a wonderful new relationship, a daytime slot on Radio One and the fact that Esther had found me seemed to be a part of this new beginning. The mythical Deirdre has appeared in the corporeal form of Esther.

Stella sounded genuinely enthused by this latest lurch in her life. It really meant so much to her. Her children had now come back and if they could get together it would be a remedial and even redemptive event. The circle would be complete. We were always meant to be together. Fate had cruelly dictated otherwise but now – now we would fulfil her dearest wish and all the agonies of the past would be erased. I saw this part of the process as entirely divorced from her. This was about my sister and me.

It was only a day or two later that Esther rang. I hadn't been expecting it to be that soon. Jesus! She said, 'Hello, is that Nicky? It's Esther here,' in the way that she still does. We talked for an hour. Tina was amazed.

'The most you can normally manage on the phone to anyone is two minutes.' We felt an immediate affinity. Apart from DNA we had loads of common ground. There was the whole Edinburgh private school thing, which always entailed finding friends and friends of friends we both knew or knew of. Esther and I were mutually recognizable creatures. She may well have been from Venus and me from Mars but we were both from Edinburgh and that counts for a lot. We encountered familiar attitudes in one another. My wryness and dryness was returned with interest. She saw her middle-class Edinburgh reserve and inner core of curtain-twitching snobbery coming right on back at her. Obviously we both had the experience of tracing and meeting Stella. For both of us finding Stella had been more interesting than enlightening. It hadn't been transformative – it had merely satisfied our natural curiosities. It solved nothing. It answered no questions. Clearly in her time our mother was a formidable, capable and highly respected woman but a woman with two devastating secrets. However, she had had such difficult times over the years. The mother, the fount of our lives, who was maybe at one time more like us, had been changed by the vicissitudes of her own life. What caused the manic depression that came upon her in those difficult times and what was caused by it is a moot point. Maybe both Esther and I were afraid to look too closely.

Acknowledging the shared sense of anticlimax was liberating. In fact it came as a massive relief. An exculpation even. It wasn't just me then. Maybe I wasn't such a selfish bastard.

Esther had similar experiences to me in failing to bond. When Stella hugged her she sometimes held on just too long and too tightly and in resisting the intensity Esther found herself hardening and missing her adoptive mother. Esther *had* been looking for a mother in a sense, as her own mum had passed on. In her grief, I think she half expected to find if not a replacement then certainly an alternative. Stella had far too much to live up to.

Stella's kids arranged a rendezvous. Esther was coming up to London for a business meeting and would pop over in the evening to meet me and my then girlfriend and future wife Tina. I was excited although I had learned from the previous experience to take things as they came, rather than build them up before they had happened. This was surely different though. This wasn't a reunion for a start. This was a beginning. I was going to meet my sister for the very first time.

I remember the buzzer going. I panicked because I was on my own. Tina wasn't yet home to hold my hand. It was a jolt to the system. I had done live television with millions watching – I had spoken to large crowds – including 80,000 at Wembley once before a Rolling Stones concert. That was fine. This was really bloody frightening. I pushed the entry button and up one small flight of stairs she came, emerging from the darkness, literally and metaphorically, and walking into the bright flat, her chic boots clicking and clattering on my Canadian maple floor. I was a bit like Felix – the prissy guy in the *Odd Couple* – about my floor, just because of the incredible unnecessary expense of it really. She scuffed it. Get a cloth later, I told myself. To do so now wouldn't look good. Never mind the boots, she was tall. Lanky. She was a different shape from me. Her features were someone else's. At first glance they seemed somewhat lugubrious but, for all that, striking. There was certainly a touch of melancholy about them. This could have been nerves. Mine probably.

We looked at each other, not as the sociable Great Apes that we are tend to look at each other, but more in the way some people might peer at an intriguing painting in a gallery. A painting they can't quite work out. I appraised her appearance as I stared a little too intently. A little too intensely. As with my first meeting with Stella, we looked and looked away, looked again and looked away. There is a lot to look at. Eye contact stirs up a range of feelings. I know you from somewhere? Am I in there somewhere? What have we missed? Do I want to go there? Do I stay away? Who are you?

Who the hell was this? She was dark. She looked absolutely nothing like me. What is going on here? I thought. Is she related to me? I was under the impression relatives – brothers and sisters especially – were meant to look like each other. I didn't see this in the small print. There is an element of narcissism to all this, you know. Where was my face in hers? I wanted to look at her and see me. But looking alike is superficial. Being alike is more profound.

She looked every stitch of her smart outfit, the businesswoman. She looked like someone who would be very in control in a professional situation. This wasn't quite one of those though. Later Esther told me she'd written books on management techniques and in one of those there's a whole section on body language and what it means. I am so glad I didn't read that before we met. I'd have feared she was going to suss me out. I wondered if she had thought hard about appropriate apparel. She was wearing what my mum would call a trouser suit. I was in jeans and a scruffy old shirt.

The minute we got down to talking properly she was as sharp and perceptive as she had been on the phone. I was immediately put on my mettle. Now I was worried she would suss me out. An inferiority-cum-superiority complex is a really irritating neurosis – for everyone around. For once spare a thought for the sufferer. I started to perform. Deflective position. Defensive position. Default position. 'There's a picture of me and John Major. Me and Denis Law. There's me and Keith Richard. He is the best interviewee I have ever had. Barely alive but a walking quote machine. Bla bla bla bla.'

She seemed interested and of course this only encouraged the cabaret. I felt exposed and I needed Tina. I had never been alone with Stella, you know – it's only just occurred to me as I write this. Talking on the phone is not the same thing, is it? Here I was expected to shed the trusty carapace for only the first blood relative I had been alone with since I was five days old. Esther is a brilliant observer and analyser. She must have had a field day with me.

We spoke about places and people we knew in Edinburgh and the whole middle-class world into which we'd both been adopted. The Edinburgh private school cabal had done rather well out of the irksome shift patterns of nurses and policemen. We began to realize we knew a lot of the same families and then we discovered something extraordinary.

It was summer 1978. I was in my final year at school going through the humdrum traumas of exams. Scotland's catastrophic World Cup campaign was in full plunge. That was far more serious. We had to beat Holland by three clear goals to avoid expulsion from the tournament being piled on the already massive slag heap of embarrassment. We had already drawn with Iran and lost to Peru. Iain and I dashed away after school to my friend Matthew's large detached stone house in Edinburgh Southside's genteel Lauder Road. We couldn't wait for the match. Hope springs eternal with Scotland.

We were sitting in Matthew's den, smoking fag after fag of John Player Blue with our shirts out and school ties raggedly de-knotted. We just didn't care, I tell you. It was a cracking match and then it happened. Archie Gemmel shimmied and jigged his way past the Dutch defence like an elf through a phalanx of trolls. He scored the most wondrous, beautiful, spectacular goal I have ever seen. We went mad. We were hugging and kissing and jumping and punching. Come on Scotland! It was three–one. We needed one more goal.

The commentator on Scottish television declaimed, 'And the

Mendoza miracle – is – on!' It was, but not for long. The Dutch scored immediately. What Esther and I discovered as we chatted in Hampstead eighteen years later was the other miracle going on that afternoon. Matthew's sister Julia was having an old school friend stay with her over the summer. Julia and this friend were mooching about in the kitchen next to the den and generally being completely unengaged by the momentous events in Argentina. I always cast an eye towards Julia Kreitman as I reckoned she was borderline fanciable. The friend made no impression other than as an indistinct presence. The friend was Esther, Stella's other child by the other policeman. As we talked all those years later she remembered Matthew and his scruffy friends lounging about after school watching the football. Little did she know one of them was her brother.

Out life stories tumbled out. Esther lives in Bath and is married to Duncan. She consults and writes her books on management techniques and organizational change, applying her big-brained first in maths from St Andrews to the task. I am useless at maths – really useless – so that must have been from the other father. The other policeman. Another calculating copper.

She and Duncan have two gorgeous children. She lost a third child eight and a half months into pregnancy and, as I later found out, this anguished event gave her the emotional imperative finally to trace her birth mother. The search for that genetic essence of belonging and being. The need to assuage her loss by following back her own umbilical cord. She traced Stella in 1996. Two months before the baby died Esther lost her beloved adoptive mum to motor neurone disease. It was a terrible time for her and Duncan. They were in deep shock and went to register her stillbirth in Bath. As Esther remembers, 'We sat in a cold council office and through the bleakness I noticed a poster on the wall. "Trying to trace your birth mother? Call this number . . ." I didn't write down the telephone number but something clicked deep in my psyche. That was the moment it all started.' Like me she had always known she was adopted. Like me she didn't really know what she was searching for.

Eighteen years on from Scotland's World Cup debacle, we were sitting in my flat searching for similarities – something of ourselves in each other. As there was no obvious facial resemblance, I suggested we look elsewhere. By the time our shoes were off and feet and toes were being compared, I felt we were on to something. Our second toes are both longer than our big toes. With hindsight I realize she considered this as mildly irritating as I'd found her scuffy boots. But I really felt we'd struck genetic gold down there. I must check our elbows sometime.

For those who have always taken such things for granted this must seem odd. For me at that meeting on that evening it was the most natural and normal thing to do. Where *was* the missing link?

She has a great sense of humour and showed it then. Laughing at my nervy, gabbled monologue was probably just good manners but she made some razor sharp comments herself. She was in fact extremely funny and when she laughed her face lit up magnificently. The melancholia melted. As first meetings with a like-minded person of a similar age and something sort of familiar round the eyes go, it was pretty good. That vaguely familiar look around the eyes was a fleeting glimpse. Here now and then gone. A tantalizing wisp of partially shared parentage. Now you see it, now you don't.

I was mightily relieved when I heard the key in the door though and saw Tina walking in. I was enjoying Esther's company enormously but it was high-octane stuff. She was my sister, for goodness sake. Not long-lost – more at long last and now *at* last I could have a breather. Like going out for a fag or having a pee at half-time in a massively important and consequently nerve-racking televized football match. There had been rather a lot of reality for my liking really. My world was full of escapism. You can't beat the preparation for and delivery of a daily live radio show and a once-a-week TV debate show for pretty failsafe avoidance of life's complications.

Esther and Tina quickly hit it off and I began to worry that Esther felt she was having her first encounter of the evening with a normal human being. To regain the initiative (in other words to get some attention) I kicked off my shoes and socks again like a Vegas showgirl, implored my new sister to do likewise and gleefully pointed out to Tina the uncanny similarity in our semi-sibling second toes. These things matter a lot when you are in the position Esther and I were in. All things are relative and we were relatives. Tina pretended to be utterly thrilled by this podiatric demon-stration but curiously and hurriedly changed the subject, announcing with a fixed grin, 'I'm starving. Let's go for an Indian.' I put on my socks. We all trotted up the hill, over the road and round the corner and the fresh air was lovely if not very fresh.

We went round to the Shag Bag as we called it – our favourite Indian restaurant in the area. By this time I wasn't so much hungry as dying for a drink. A lovely icy draught pint of Indian Cobra Beer was waiting for me like a pot of cold gold. We sat and ate and talked and I was much more comfortable. We both were I think. Back in the flat I had certainly been acutely aware of what she might be thinking of every nuance of everything I said and it had made me far too self-conscious to be myself. And the more I realized that, the worse it got. Now we had a different setting, low lights, Tina, nice food, soft Sub Continental music and of course those delicious restorative pints of draught Indian Beer.

Here is Esther's account of the meeting on that enlightening November evening in North London.

Stella excitedly gave me Nicky's phone number. 'Give your brother a call. He'd love to hear from you.' I knew exactly who he was. I'd heard his afternoon programme on Radio One before, but wasn't a huge fan. I was also aware of the *Wheel of Fortune* history because Stella had sent me some clippings from various newspaper articles. I had certainly never met a shiny-suited, blue-eyed quiz show host before and had absolutely no idea what to expect. One of my friends, a lifelong Radio Four listener, raised a critical eyebrow and dryly commented, 'Well, that's interesting. A compere for a brother.' I could tell he was unimpressed. However, I was open-minded and quite excited.

I made a list of questions before I called the number, the systematic approach favoured by the management consultant in me. How often have you seen Stella? Do you get on well? Do you call her 'Mum'? Has she met your own mother? When I finally got the courage to dial the number, he answered immediately. His first question came shooting at me at 100 mph: 'What made you look for Stella?' 'Overwhelming curiosity,' I answered quickly. I couldn't tell him all about how my third child had been stillborn, and how it had made me think about Stella's painful loss. He would think me weak and needy. No, that was not the way to go at this stage. I drank some more wine, and lit another cigarette. This was turning out to be a bit stressful.

We talked for quite a while on the phone, and arranged to meet at his flat in London. There was a complication about timing. He was keen that I met Tina, his girlfriend, and was pretty insistent that she would be there when we met. In fact there was no question of any other arrangement reaching the table. I got the impression that I should arrive after Tina was home – around 7.15 p.m.

It was around November time. London is always too hot and it's difficult to know what to wear. I went to an excellent conference during the day. What a line-up: Chris Argyris, the renowned thinker on management learning and double-loop change in the afternoon, and Nicky Campbell the renowned radio personality in the evening. It felt a bit like I was walking on air.

Naturally I had been completely preoccupied with my choice of outfit. What do you wear for such an encounter? I remember choosing a green suit, which I thought gave the right mix of soft and interesting with a thoroughly in-control professional appearance. I could tell he was impressed by my first in maths, but naturally wanted to avoid any trace of accompanying geekiness. When you have a nerdy qualification like this, you don't generally tell people, because they regard it as a certificate in madness. However, I told Stella to make her proud I suppose, and she told Nicky. Perhaps Nicky was expecting me to be socially hopeless and rather serious. Oh God, perhaps I was!

The taxi drew up in Hampstead around 7.10 p.m. I rang

the buzzer. 'You're early. Tina's not home.' I remember thinking that there was no way I was going to wait. This guy talks to millions of people every day. He can't be shy. It was cold outside. He said something about not having time to get changed. I walked up the stairs and we met in the doorway.

I noticed his height first. I was hoping for more of a reflection of myself. Although I had seen him on the TV before, seeing someone right in front of you is quite different. 'I was expecting someone a little taller.' I meant someone lanky like me. He hitched up his jeans. 'I am tall. I'm 6 foot 1.' This was hard to believe. He commented that people who've seen him on TV always expect him to be bigger when they first meet him. I wondered whether he thought I was coming to meet him because he's a broadcasting personality, rather than because we have DNA in common. This notion irritated me slightly because there was some truth in it.

He was looking quite scruffy in a pair of jeans and a pretty nondescript T-shirt. Where was the shiny suit? He poured me a large glass of wine and we sat down on a turquoise leather sofa at right angles to each other. It looked like the set of a late-night talk show. I felt out of place in this rather glamorous-looking apartment. He talked about his ex-wife and her influence on him. 'She encouraged me to find my birth mother. She thought it would sort me out. We split acrimoniously and she went to the papers.' He seemed to think I had read about all this in the news but I had studiously avoided doing that. I thought it might make our relationship rather one-sided if I knew all about him and he knew nothing about me.

I learned that Nicky already knew I existed, but chose not

to seek me out. There were some limp-sounding excuses. I immediately labelled them as apathy. Why didn't he search me out? Did he run out of energy, or just not want another sister? I began to feel like a bull in a china shop – like I feel when I'm presenting a proposal to a client and I can tell they don't have much of a budget, or much appetite for any real change.

We were surviving without Tina. He made some black jokes about my natural parentage. Stella was manic depressive; Frank (father) was an alcoholic. 'Impressive pedigree!' We laughed. It began to feel like we were getting on.

He is sure that we have different fathers. So is Stella. 'Now I should know!' she had chuckled. When I looked at Nicky that November evening, I saw quite a lot in him that is certainly not in me. And vice versa. But the similarities began to emerge. It's about an energy and a sense of humour. He is much bolder than me, but we share a thread of arrogance and an ability to be chameleons with our voices and styles of communicating. Of course he's much better at this than me (he'd be upset if I didn't put that). We both think we're intelligent. He is orally quicker than me – it's his job. I am more considered. That's my job.

I was interested in how he works, how he thinks. I have a natural fascination in this area, which was heightened by the nature of this situation. It was obvious he had a huge amount of drive – with a natural dominance and a physical presence that made him difficult to ignore. I wondered what he was like when he wasn't happy. Worth avoiding I reckoned. He had a hard time listening to my side of the story. He cut over the end of my sentences. I started to speed up my speech. He cut over the beginnings of my sentences instead.

Tina burst in. She was lively, expressive and enquiring. I wondered then whether people said he was lucky to have her. She was warm and funny, and intensely interested in me. She asked me a stream of scattergun questions end to end. 'So have you met Stella?', 'How long have you known you were adopted?' I was breathless. 'Wow. You can tell she's a journalist.' We laughed.

Tina suggested that we should go out to eat. They took me to an ordinary-looking Indian restaurant near by. Afterwards I wondered whether they had talked about taking me somewhere modest. Were they trying to play their enormous wealth down? I fantasized. The glum waiter moved us from one table to another, even though the restaurant was totally empty. I thought, Doesn't he know who this is? Maybe I even said it. Tina urged Nicky to sit next to me. Nicky avoided the issue, and instead nestled himself comfortably beside Tina on the other side of the table from me. I felt awkward but grateful to Tina for her warmth. I noticed her stepping in to protect him once or twice during the evening, and thought I spotted a pattern. That's what we management consultants do – we spot patterns.

Nicky says he's relieved I don't live in a council house in Mid Calder and have five screaming children. I find this cruelly funny and feel myself warming to him. 'Well, you don't want tinkers coming up the path.' Perhaps I was a tinker of sorts. I certainly didn't have a massive brand-new flat-screen TV and a 100 per cent black chrome kitchen. And no sign of a turquoise leather sofa in my house.

We talked a little about his job and my job (mostly about his job, to be honest). We moved on to tabloid topics. I was hoping he wouldn't talk *too* deeply or too fast about politics, as I might have got lost rather quickly. He commented that the Spice Girls were having such an extraordinary career they should be keeping diaries. I made a joke. 'Do you think there is a Literate Spice?' We enjoyed a little shared snobbery. Why not? We were both from Edinburgh.

Time was ticking by. We went back to the flat and listened to Nicky's tape of his own songs. He played me a song he wrote for his dad who had died earlier that year. I was touched by his openness. They were good songs. He talked about the emotion behind the songs in a way that surprised me. He operated using this peculiar mix of candour and distance, which was disarming. I began to find it hard to concentrate because I was feeling a lot of different things.

It was time to go. I needed a break from all this. It was quite intensive. But I liked him right from the start. It's a winning combination, all that strength and vulnerability in one small package. I liked him a lot, but with my over-cautious style, and fear of rejection, I would never say so!

I reached out my hand to give a brusque business-like shake. Work habit. He kissed my cheek. He was stiff, but genuine. I was relieved.

I travelled back home on the last train wondering what it had all been about. What happened now? Family holidays? Birthday cards? They were getting married soon. Perhaps I would get a invitation.

The next day I was working – doing some coaching out on a client site. I drove back to the office mid afternoon and flipped to the Nicky Campbell show on Radio One. He told my Spice Girls joke within five minutes. I felt pretty good.

Meeting Stella and now Esther had certainly induced 'double-loop change' into my life. I don't know what it is but I'm sure I had it. Maybe I was really on the road of making sense of everything. Perhaps this was the beginning. We didn't see each other for another seven months but our relationship was under way. Getting to know each other properly has been a gradual and wonderfully worthwhile process. It's a process without end. Like life itself – a work in progress. Why hadn't I traced Esther before? I knew it would happen one day – I was convinced of it – and when it did the time would be right. I don't really mean anything gnomic here. Day-to-day realities rather than the universal mysteries brought me to this conclusion. I had just been through a period of mayhem and divorce and was slowly settling into a new relationship. Life wasn't yelling at me to do it. Life was saying, 'Get yourself together and calm down.' On the other hand, maybe this is just a trite explanation and lazy conclusion – but it is easy to think it's meant to be. There speaks an agnostic teetering on the brink of belief.

I kept the meeting with Esther quiet from Mum and my sister Fiona though. I would have loved to have invited her to our wedding but it couldn't be. Everybody would be wondering who on earth she was. It was going to be a huge day for Mum without Dad. Can you imagine? 'Ladies and Gentleman – I have another very special announcement for you today!'

I didn't want Mum or Fiona to feel undermined and I found

it all far too entangled a subject to verbalize. How could I put this into a string of words and make sentences out of my confused thoughts? How could I explain this to my family – and they were my family? It would be the ultimate in rejection. Mum and Dad gave me everything. I concluded it would only hurt them and even though Dad was gone, I still saw it as active disloyalty. The best way to skirt the issue was to keep it hidden. I kept it secret from them, deep down in a vault they didn't even know existed.

ELEVEN

A Long Time Coming

From the time I traced Stella it was to be another twelve years until I was ready to look for my biological father, the 'other half of the sky'. Why so long? The nineteenth-century Irish nationalist, parliamentarian and Protestant Charles Stuart Parnell said, 'No man has the right to say (to his country), "thus far shalt thou go and no further".'

This was about my self-determination. Once on that path I couldn't turn back. All I had to do was get off my backside again and follow the yellow brick road. Move along. Simple as that. I knew I would one day but this time I had to be better prepared. I had to have my own impetus, my own reasons, and also the strength and security to face the challenge and deal with the possible rejection. I needed that strength or I might again immure myself from feelings. Block myself off from the experience. Attempt to do it but not feel it. That, I fear is what happened when I met Stella.

But it's not that simple. If it were I would have done it years ago really and the older I got the more I understood the implications. Tom, a friend who works in music radio, thought long and hard about tracing his birth mother and father. The breakthrough came when he discovered his father's name and address. He wrote and received a lovely letter back. They arranged to meet. When the Saturday came Tom could hardly believe it. Like me in Dublin he was beside himself with nerves. He got the train in from Hertfordshire to the centre of the city, got off and walked up Euston Road towards the pub where his father was waiting. He slowed down as he approached the door and stopped. He stood there for a minute. He thought about everything. He thought about his whole life. Then he turned round, walked back to the Tube station and went home. Somewhere, the old man's still waiting.

I always remembered that story and it made me incredibly sad. I thought of the chances gone. Why now? After twelve years? Did I wake up one morning and say to myself, Today is the day? It was gradual, but gradually it grew. So much happened in those years. I got divorced, Esther appeared, Dad died – my only 'Dad' – I gave up *Wheel of Fortune* and moved away from music and speech on Radio One to concentrate on journalism and news on Radio Five Live. Best of all, I met and married Tina. After my divorce and Dad's death from cancer I'd gone off the rails and had walked out of far too many nightclubs at three in the morning looking for a party. Tina stuck by me and rescued me from myself. We fell in love and we've been falling ever since.

I met her at Radio One when my marriage was on its final legs. Richard Evans, the regular news reader on the show I presented, had broken his leg sliding down a Swiss mountain on a couple of fibre-glass planks. She came in to the studio to stand in for him on a couple of the greatest legs I had ever seen. When we met and talked the legs ceased to matter. I'd been caught by evolution's sweetest trick. Legs alone weren't going to give the relationship legs or underpin a lifetime's bonding, but they sure gave it a kick start. Tina is a fine journalist. She is smart and warm and funny and forgiving. She loves me, which amazes me, and frequently astonishes her.

Personally and professionally I was more able to inhabit my own skin. That is a great feeling. In the following four years three little girls transformed my life, put it in the starship's transporter and beamed it to an entirely new dimension. It all started to have some kind of a logic and having my own children – little people genetically related to me – changed everything. We are so lucky to have our three beautiful little girls and I don't know how we lived without them. What on earth did we worry about for a start? Being a father made me wonder all the more about my father. The day Breagha, our eldest, was born, I was, as dads are, overwhelmed. I was a weepy mess. Where did this beautiful thing come from? I remember holding her as Tina was being sown up after the emergency Caesarian section and ruminating on life, the universe and everything.

I had found my mother – I had met a sister and here was my daughter. I was actually a father! Me – I was a dad. I thought of Dad. How proud he would have been now, and I thought of my genetic father. I wondered what he would think? Whoever he was, wherever he was, he came to mind. If there was 'some good in him' he would care deeply about this moment. He was there – somewhere – I was here and so now too are my children all on a line through time. As I held Breagha on that November morning back in 1998 just seconds after her birth, my mind was darting all over the cosmos. What ghosts have left the best and worst of their selves behind in her? Been given another lease of life in this beautiful baby?

There was Breagha in my arms, squinting at the light and nonplussed by this abrupt removal from her warm home. She would be open to a myriad influences but all along attended by countless previous generations. Whether she's blessed or blighted by their legacy may well be her own choice. Whatever the legacy of these strangers, they were men and women from different worlds. There are some genes from Stella's imperious mother in there. 'A cut above the buttermilk' she reckoned she was. Will my little girl be formidable like her great grandmother? Will she brook no nonsense? Will she be the boss? Is her Great Grandfather George in her? Compliant, biddable, and anything for a quiet life? Will she be like Stella? Strong, weak, spirited, fragile, passionate and emotionless. Like her mother? Like her father? Or, setting all this genetic determinism aside, will she be just what life allows her to be? Catherine, a woman we love dearly – a lady in her seventies who lives in a little Highland village – when asked if any of the children resemble Tina or me always sagely replies, 'Neither of you. She looks like herself.'

Breagha's birth and the overwhelming love I felt for this little girl and the responsibility I had to care for her drew me to thinking about death for the first time in my life. My death. This hopefully wasn't a Woody Allen-like morbid fixation, it was a cold passing taste. From Wilfred Owen:

> Bitter as the cud
> Of vile, incurable sores on innocent tongues –

Here now, and then gone – with the laughter of children in a down-stairs room.

It is not unlike catching a fleeting glimpse of that hooded figure with the scythe. He comes around, doesn't he? But it wasn't just my death. What if my biological father was dead like Dad? I couldn't have contemplated finding my natural father with Dad still alive. When I traced Stella I am sure it was bad enough, but for him to feel he was being directly replaced and usurped by starting to look for Joseph would have been intolerable. I couldn't have coped with that guilt. Dad loathed his own father, who was a remote and tyrannical figure, and given Dad's gentle nature, it must have been a loathing deserved. I wanted to protect him. Needless to say, we never spoke about it. Our communication was in the subtext of impassioned, triumphant, frustrated and despairing phone calls after Scotland's rugby matches. Mum was stronger in a way. I felt she could handle it. I made far too many assumptions.

When I did think seriously about taking the next step, rather than just vaguely maybe possibly – you never know – contemplating it at some stage, I did have that terrible thought that it might be too late. My genetic father, even if I had even figured in his thoughts, might be gone. But here is the thing, I didn't want to regret never having at least tried. As far as I then understood from Stella, Joseph was slightly younger than her so there was hope he was still around. She had demurred on the full thirteen-year age gap. It was evidently another sensitive issue. 'Toy boy' was an eighties expression. Stella once again – a pioneering spirit. She had said he was in the Dublin Telephone Directory and I'd looked at his name there once, back in 1990 in Dublin, but since then I'd never had the guts to look again. Seeing the number in front of me would have been too tempting, too terrifying. I panicked just thinking about it.

When I had gone looking for Stella, I had a profound belief that this was more than just piecing together a jigsaw puzzle. There were important truths and meanings I could uncover. I thought there was something telling about the genetic link, that you would instinctively appreciate, only if you had never had it, never taken it for granted. Finding Stella, though, hadn't unlocked any chest of knowledge. The secrets remained illusive. Perhaps the key lay elsewhere. I wouldn't know until I looked, would I?

There was a wholly practical side too. Tina was heartily sick of going to the doctor and partially blanking her when being asked the standard stuff about family medical history. Is there this in the family? Is there that in the family? 'Don't know.' She never pressed me to search though – she just said that she would support me and it would actually be useful apart from being absolutely fascinating to know. I think that was a big factor with her – wanting a bit of background on the man in her bed.

Lilla was born in May 2000 and Kirsty in December 2001. As the black-cloaked Presbyterian minister said at her baptism in the old stone village of Kirk: 'God knew Lilla was coming. Oh yes he did.' I thought the Rev was right. God must have. The births of Breagha and Lilla and Kirsty, all such different personalities, edged me step by step – psychologically, emotionally and spiritually – towards the day I would resume the journey. My courage was growing. Life really did have a logic at last and now it wasn't just about me.

Now family was all that mattered. What was more important than making sense of my origins and Kirsty's origins? And Lilla's?

And Breagha's? Piecing together the final parts of my family puzzle was important.

I'd made the first difficult step and traced my birth mother. Maybe this next step was another cry for help from a little boy lost. I knew now that love and family are all that really matter. New priorities, new responsibilities, and a new decade of my life all played their part too. I felt well prepared and truly ready for another – please pardon an expression Grandpa never used – mind fuck.

I decided to get on the phone to my trusty private detective and give him another case.

This time I harboured no great expectations, no soft-focus idealization waiting to be splattered on by reality. My father was likely to be a flawed and complex human being just as Stella turned out to be. Just as we all are. I consoled myself that only a man not worth meeting would turn down the chance of meeting me – his own son. But what about his other children if there were any? What about his wife if she existed? What about his life, if he still had one? This was a leap in the dark but I think I knew enough about him to be ready for absolutely anything. Whatever the situation, I had to know. I also had a *right* to know. And so did *he*. A son and three gorgeous little grandchildren were there for him. But you just don't know what's on the other side of the door. Inside the vault.

TWELVE

Two of Us

In October 2003, Esther and I were flying up to our home town of Edinburgh for a day and a half – travelling together in more ways than one. We were going up to see Francesca Harris from the Scottish Adoption Association, who'd kindly put aside a couple of hours to meet us late on a Friday afternoon. I'd been up since three-thirty that morning to prepare for the breakfast programme on Five Live but I was fired up at the chance to meet Francesca. We both had a million questions for her and I had a story to tell her. As Esther and I sat there I felt very close to my travelling companion. Since our initial meeting in my Hampstead flat in 1996 the fuse had burned slowly. We'd all go down to Bath to see her and the family or they would visit us in London and we'd get together every six months or so. We spoke fairly regularly and always with uncanny familiarity but since the imperative to trace my father got hold of me, our relationship moved to a different level. She has helped me, we have helped each other, we've talked each other through it and we've shared the ups and downs of the whole mad mystery tour. We've been Stella's kids – in it together. We really have become like brother and sister.

Esther had given me a form to fill out a few weeks prior to our Edinburgh adventure and having ducked its trickiest questions till the very last moment, I completed it and returned it to her as we readied for take-off. It's one of the things she does for her living. It gives people a structure with which they can look at themselves and helps them to discern their habits and preferences so they can see their strengths and work on their weaknesses. In the ever-changing corporate world it's a valuable part of the survival kit. On a personal level, when you are trying to think about your feelings, anything that gets you to, well, think about your feelings, is pretty useful. While Esther was interpreting the answers and assessing my score, I asked if she was a Scientologist and she half laughed. That is what I like about her – she knows when to humour me. When she said it would be worthwhile, I half believed her. We share a sense of humour if not a father. She didn't share lunch though and rejected a British Airways sandwich as she was on a wheat-free diet. As I excavated my notebook from the mayhem in my briefcase and jotted down some questions to ask at the Scottish Adoption Association later, Esther was doing her calculations. She asked me a few pertinent questions to put the dryness of the questionnaire into a better context and then the proverbial puff of smoke appeared and she pontificated in the nicest possible manner. 'Are you ready?'

'Yep.'

She told me we shared a personality type.

Poor you, I thought.

'ENFP,' she explained. 'Extrovert, Intuitive, Feeling, Perceiving.' These were the opposite of Introvert, Sensing, Thinking and Judging and my four-letter type was just one ramification from the sixteen available options. I am not great at thinking and judging sometimes, that much is true.

I wolfed my chickenesque sandwich down and as I spat crumbs of wheat over poor Esther in an unthinking, ill-judged kind of a way, I told her about my meeting with a friend earlier that week. Jack also works at the BBC and we'd sat in one of TV Centre's smartest coffee bars and talked about why he had never felt the urge to trace his birth parents. He was a journalist, for goodness sake. Hadn't curiosity got the better of him?

'Yes, I am a journalist but this is about me not something else and I just can't be arsed,' he said decisively.

'But, Jack, this could be a fascinating story. The fact that it's about you is a bonus.'

He looked at me with puzzlement. The way an introvert might gauge an extrovert. Maybe there is something in this personality type malarkey.

He thought for a minute. He was *sensing, thinking and judging*. 'I just can't be doing with the bother. I've got all the people in life I need right now with my wife and my little girl.'

I shot back, 'But having all the people I need in *my* life has had the opposite effect on me and given me the strength to go and seek. It's given me the impetus.'

Jack looked thoughtfully at the selection of panini and disgusting croissants full of chocolate goo up at the counter. Another colleague scoring her morning caffeine fix brushed by and then stopped to chat. When all the gossiping and 'she said what and he did this and well I never' was over she sashayed away to sort out the nation's news agenda (just more gossiping really), and Jack got on with his explanation.

He is softly spoken anyway but this conversation was at the softer end of his range. He said his reluctance to trace was nothing to do with any strong bond he had with his adoptive parents, as he's not close to them. He swigged his café latte and leaned forward.

'There is the possibility of what I might find. The unpleasantness. I am a person who likes to avoid complexity. I'm not that fussed about relatives. Not interested. Being an only child made me very self-sufficient so it doesn't emerge on an emotional level for me, any of this. It's practical. I don't go through the story in my head all the time and wonder what happened. I am not a great one for what ifs.' He took a pause as we both took it all in. I was aware it wasn't something he had really spoken about before and it was as if it was new to both of us.

'Finding out for my little girl is the only thing that might sway me and maybe – maybe – there would be nobody to meet. That would be easier.'

I tried again. 'Jack, if I walked off and left the name and telephone number of your birth mother in an envelope on the table would you open it?'

'Yes.'

'There you go.'

'No I don't. I would look at it but I'd probably do nothing about it. The thing is, Nicky, I don't want the bother.'

Esther listened intently as she sat beside me in row 17. For 'adoption junkies' like the two of us, such testimony is compulsive. Jack didn't want the bother. Neither did I for many years after meeting Stella so I did know what he meant. Why do we want the bother? Esther suggested part of it was to do with his introverted personality, in that introverts find it hard to meet new people. The thought of what you are letting yourself in for when you trace is daunting whatever your personality type. The difference is that some of us revel in the risks of this extreme psychological sport. I certainly didn't 'think' about the prospect of dealing with other people's baggage. Neither Esther nor I even considered for a moment the implications of our own baggage. As far as we were concerned we were travelling light. Little did we know we had a blooming aircraft full.

Francesca Harris, a gentle and committed woman, deals with people who put themselves through this 'bother' all the time. She shares their joy and relief, their disappointment and, on occasion, their heartbreak when a long-lost son or daughter or mother or father just doesn't want to know. After parking the little hire car, all too aware of the attentions of the legendary Leith police traffic dept, we trekked to the top floor of an Edinburgh regency building occupied by solicitors and design consultants. It had high ceilings and big doors and was full of small people with low voices. We arrived on the top floor and entered the frugal but comfortable offices of the Scottish Adoption Association.

Ahead of our visit I'd wondered if the chairs we'd be sat in would be soft or hard. In the event they were somewhere in between. A strategically placed box of tissues lay on the low table between ourselves and our mother confessor.

Francesca had sent me my adoption documents two years previously when this phase in my search was just beginning, the quest for my biological father.

Esther too had come here as a first stop when she traced Stella back in 1995. She later wrote:

It was surprisingly easy to find my birth mother. I contacted the Scottish Adoption Association and managed to work my way towards Stella. Luckily she was in the phonebook under her maiden name, even though she had since married, separated and become a widow. Naturally I took it that she wanted to be found. The Scottish Adoption Agency told me something totally unexpected. Stella had given birth to another child, a boy who had been adopted eighteen months after me. 'It looks like the two of you have the same father,' said the advisor. I put this on the back burner for later investigation.

I took advice from someone in the local county council's Adoption Services unit and wrote a rather obscure letter to Stella. This was intended to be meaningful to her, but opaque to any family member who might pick up the letter. She didn't reply.

I eventually found the right phone number and spoke to her late one evening in 1997.

It was a stilted conversation. She explained why she hadn't replied to my letter, and before long she was excitedly telling me about her 'son', Nicky, who was 'very well known'. She had been bothered by the local press who wanted her views on this unusual relationship with a well-known figure. After our first telephone conversation, I wrote Stella a long letter telling her all about myself, highlighting all the good things of course. She sent me a huge batch of photos of herself and her brothers and their wives and families. No one looked anything like me, which was really disappointing.

Francesca looked at the two of us and agreed that we didn't look very much like each another. We all then cheerfully concurred that real similarities often lay deeper. Francesca is in an unusual position. She is a social worker and people come to her for help. They actively want her assistance. No two cases are the same and she has seen so many different outcomes. There was the woman who traced her son and found he was serving a life sentence for murder. She still loved him as her long-lost baby boy. There was a birth mother in her eighties who was found by her fifty-year-old son, causing one of her other sons to reject her. 'She found one son and lost another.'

There can also be problems when people who make contact find they are from different social and economic backgrounds.

'It can be difficult if there are big differences.'

'That shows how important environment is – nurture,' I suggested. Esther pondered. Francesca told us more. We were drinking this up like cold beer after a desert march.

She has seen new relationships burn with the intensity of a love affair, with people wanting to be together all the time and their lives becoming dominated by it, and then she has seen the same people suddenly and dramatically fall out with each other. In time, with a bit of luck, the relationship can settle down into something calmer and more comfortable.

I mentioned that Mum told me I was chosen and expected Francesca to confirm what an astute and sensitive approach that was to telling a child he is adopted. I was proud of my psychiatric social worker mum as I said it and wanted to fly the kite of her professional expertise in full view of the impressive professional sitting opposite. I was rapidly disabused.

'You were chosen – no! People don't say that now – what a

burden!' said Francesca. Esther laughed at the brotherly beast of burden beside her. When it was the orthodox approach, some parents thought it need be said only once and thereafter the deed was done. That was precisely the experience of my friend Jack from the BBC. He has a vague half memory of his parents saying 'something about being chosen'. He was five or six years old at the time and it was only when he was sixteen that a family friend tipped him off that he was actually adopted. He went and checked his birth certificate. They were right. No wonder he is an island. Thank goodness for my mum and dad. I am glad I chose them.

It is painful for some parents who adopt to ever address the issue though. To so much as think about it reminds them of the original reason for it – very often infertility – and adoption doesn't take away the pain of infertility. Adoption is just a solution to not being able to have children.

Another recurrent pattern Francesca recognized was the fear adoptive parents have that they might be usurped by birth parents not so much in the eyes of their children but in the eyes of their grandchildren. They are happy about their son or daughter finding their origins but the thought of being replaced by another grand-parent is harrowing.

I leant forward for a tissue. Moved as I was by what Francesca was saying, and she hadn't even started on us, my lunging for the paper hanky was more to do with the cold I couldn't shake. Doing early shifts means they hang on in there however many vitamins you blast into your body. Francesca took her cue though.

'People come in here confident, articulate and successful and when they start talking about the whole subject of adoption, they feel like small children again. It arouses childlike emotions – a feeling of not being in control. Someone else has the facts on you and at the meeting with the birth mother there is very often a partial regression to being a child again.' I thought about my first meeting with Stella and how disorientated I had felt. Esther being Esther articulated it beautifully. 'When I met her I remember not knowing quite how to *be* – whether to take over or go and play in the garden while she was cooking.'

Francesca had our files on her knee and slowly flicked through them, passing each of us the occasional document we might not have seen before. Then she pulled out an MI83 form – my second questionnaire of the day.

'I sent you this, didn't I, Nicky? A couple of years ago. I'm pretty sure.'

'Can I have a look?' I recognized it at once. 'Yes, that was right at the start of my search for him.' She handed me the full photocopy and I got a shiver down my spine all over again. It was seeing his name there and all those other sketchy particulars as dictated by Stella to a social worker with terrible handwriting. His name and Stella's name together – on the same bit of paper. This MI83 form was a vital strand in the tangle of red tape. The Adoption Act 1958 insisted upon it.

Name: Joseph Leahy
Address: Paternity not admitted. Not established by decree.
Occupation: Policeman (BA)
Description: 5ft 10 ins. Well Built. Fair. Blue Eyes.
Why is child offered for adoption? For future good of child.

My eyes were drawn to the letters of qualification again – BA.
There were some other observations jotted on to the top and
bottom of the form, crawling over all the available space, in that
barely legible script.

I saw this mother by request of Dr Cameron and the
Campbells on 8/1/61. Infant (expected in March–April), superior
type of person. Matron of a hospital. Very nice appearance. She
feels ILLEGIBLE this is the only solution. I will see her again
soon. She has a TB history but now all clear.

Father of the child is Policeman also BA of Dublin University. Sister of mother of child knows but not the grandmother.
G Father deceased.

2/3/61 Saw mother again. Father quite keen on sports, art,
music, graduate of Dublin University, ILLEGIBLE good music,
art, English + History. Good concerts. (Father's mother very
musical.)

24/4/61 Saw mother again in bed. Infant at Willowbrae and
doing very well . . . She had been engaged to be married to a
doctor before she went down with TB ILLEGIBLE she wanted
to break it off but fiancé said no, so after getting all clear she
was set on getting married when fiancé broke it off. She feels
she became ILLEGIBLE. This is her second infant; in 1959 she
had a girl . . . she did not tell me this when I saw her first as she
explained she could not in front of Mrs McIntyre. However I've
enquired and the doctor informs me that the Campbells already
know this. I saw Mrs Campbell this afternoon. She has been
very good and written to the mother and sent her flowers and I

had a long talk with the mother which I hoped has helped her, as she was feeling very down and very ashamed and she really is quite a nice person.

I still couldn't decide whether that last phrase – 'she really is quite a nice person' – was tender and touching or judgemental and patronizing. There were hints about her manic depression in there. I asked Francesca whether Stella would have been asked about her mental health. 'Yes, the agency would have written to her GP and she may well have been less than forthcoming but of course back in those days it wasn't recognized as it is now.' It was all too often put down to problems with the 'nerves'.

Francesca pointed out that our mother was what was described in those days as a woman of 'privilege', although all things are relative. This explains the rather arcane description of her on the form as a 'superior' person. Her mother would have loved that description, as long as she hadn't seen the rest of the form. Being a matron, Stella was a woman of means and could afford to fly over, have a private room and pay for her children's time in the nursing-home. She needed no financial help and this was uncommon for someone in her predicament.

Francesca sat there with all the details of Stella's careful planning and the beginning of our little lives in two buff folders resting on her lap. Francesca is a fascinating person. She does a brilliant job and seems by experience and instinct to understand the fears and needs and feelings of the people who come to her office looking for that essence of being and belonging. She is extremely easy to talk to. I wish I had a quarter of her ability to listen. Over the course of our two-hour meeting, which seemed much more like twenty minutes, both Esther and I asked our questions, pursued our shared and separate lines of enquiry and told our stories. I was full of the experience of meeting my genetic father. 'He was a Catholic – both our fathers were,' I told Francesca. 'He was a fair bit younger than Stella was.'

'How's the whole experience been?' she gently enquired.

'Amazing.'

It was fifteen months since I'd first heard his voice.

THIRTEEN

There's a Message on the Answerphone

In October 2001, two years prior to the meeting with Francesca Harris in Edinburgh, Esther and her family were coming up from Bath for the weekend. Well aware of my born-again tracing zeal, she came bearing documents relating to our birth mother and to our different fathers. Our adoption papers. I had already sent off for mine and agreed for another copy to be forwarded to Esther. Francesca sent me a copy of that questionnaire – the MI83 form, in effect, Stella's statement. Just before Esther was due to arrive, she sent me this e-mail.

> Nicky, I have contacted Scottish Adoption Centre for information on our fathers – don't expect too much. I will bring whatever they send. Stella said you called and had a good chat. I suspect father-centric motivation on your side, but then I'm a suspicious type. Do you think she needs to be involved in the reunion? Maybe disturbing for her (and maybe for you too?).
>
> Looking forward to seeing you all. Ailsa is particularly keen to see Breagha.

Father-centric motivation? Her suspicions weren't entirely misplaced, but talking to Stella about him and gradually drawing the
information out was also a way of getting through to her and she
to me. I think we both knew that. It was a game of cat and mouse.
I would ask, she would give a teasingly vague or incomplete
answer, I would probe further, she would change the subject and I
would ask again in a different way. The original trauma and the
march of time had conditioned Stella's mind. She had programmed
herself never to talk about it and, as far as possible, never to think
about it. I was pushing her against all her well-practised survival
instincts. I hadn't yet told her I was going to trace my father. It
felt too delicate. I was worried she would feel used and rejected –
again. I didn't want her to feel like that. I held this guilt that it
would seem as if I'd made only a token effort with her and was
now going to make a momentous one with him.

When the adoption papers arrived I sat down and read them.
What they told me was rare and priceless. I wondered whether the
details had been wheedled out of Stella as I had to wheedle
information out of her or whether she'd offered what she could
out of a sense of responsibility to her child, to his new parents and
to posterity. Sitting alone on the hallway floor, I felt a spell
working on me. Like Hamlet beholding the spectre of his father
through the mists of Elsinore, I began to discern the vaguest
outline of a human being. But whether he was a *ghost rendered up
to sulphurous and tormenting flame* or a retired copper propping up
a bar in Donegal I had no idea. Was Joseph dead? Stella seemed
sure his mortal coil was still firmly attached. I hoped she was right.
But maybe she was living in some kind of dream, frozen in time.

I knew the name already but seeing it written down there on

that grey photocopy, right beside that of my birth mother was quite a different matter. It was as if I could now see flesh and bones or clothes on the mannequin. Here were the tantalizing snippets of information Stella told the adoption agency so that suitable and, ideally, physically similar adoptive parents might be found. I read it again and again – and then again, trying to absorb every last detail.

Occupation: Policeman (BA)
Description: 5ft 10 ins. Well Built. Fair. Blue Eyes.
Father quite keen on sports, art, music, graduate of Dublin University . . . music, art, English + History. (Father's mother very musical)

I am just over five feet eleven inches, I have fairish hair and blue eyes, I love sport, I'm fairly musical and I have a degree in history. At that instant I felt like my father's son, give or take an inch. It stopped me in my tracks. I'd heard some of these fragments from Stella before but reading them on this official document, their names in concert, made me shiver. The cold facts of my parents' relationship were right there in bureaucratic monochrome and it *was* like seeing a ghost. As I read, the words wriggled in my stomach. Strange as it was, the feeling wasn't bad. I was excited, full of anticipation. I was going to find him. Whoever he was.

Address: Paternity not admitted. Not established by decree.

Esther and her family arrived for the weekend. She and I were really looking forward to comparing notes but we were on very different missions. I was on a search for my genetic father. Esther plainly wasn't but she had her own question to answer. Were our fathers different men? There were fewer details on Esther's form than were on mine. Her father was unnamed in the paperwork. We knew from Stella that his name was Frank but she'd chosen to withhold that from the adoption people. Stella had given them a description though. He was tall, dark haired and in very good health. This last fact was at odds with her previous indications that he was a heavy and possibly terminal drinker. The form told us he originally came from Limerick. 'Limerick? There was a young fellow called Frank,' I ventured. 'Stop right there,' said Esther. When she'd first contacted Francesca Harris at the adoption agency before meeting Stella, she'd been told something that she had never fully dismissed. Francesca, noticing our fathers' shared occupation, had told her, 'It looks like you and your brother have the same father.' It was only after reading both our forms and seeing the discrepancies, that Ether had finally and definitively banished the theory from her mind. Now she had proof. Tall and dark is not fair haired and five foot ten. Any policeman will tell you that.

After dinner, Esther and I sat with a bottle of wine in the kitchen mulling over our respective cops, poring over our newly obtained documentary evidence and boring our respective spouses rigid. I liked the idea of the tough sharp cop who loved music and art. I was getting an Irish Inspector Morse or a Columbo with culture. I thought Esther would be swept along with my enthusiasm but she seemed bewildered by it and kept asking me why, wondering what I was looking for. She seemed churlish about it. I tried to explain it to her. I told her it was about the kids and about knowing the family health history. She said something like, 'Oh really.' But later told me she thought, 'Bollocks'. It wasn't total bollocks. All that was somewhere in the mix but she was right to inwardly scoff at the fact I'd made it the headline.

It's worth saying that our relationship has developed immeasurably since that night in the kitchen. The tracing process and the journey we have both been on since then has taught us about ourselves and about each other. It's galvanized our friendship and cemented our kinship. When we talk now about how we felt back then we have to qualify it to each other with all kinds of corollaries and caveats which huddle under the umbrella explanation – 'I know you so much better now.' Back then our minds met only sporadically. Now they are in league. She is kind and wise, astute and sympathetic. She can be elegantly cynical. Who knows what drove him to drink but Frank must have been an exceptional man.

Esther remembers, 'I thought you were mad to embark on more risky searching. These people could be anyone. They could take advantage.' She remembers feeling slightly panicky even thinking of it. She thought I was mad. Maybe it was madness. Maybe it was my antic disposition. I was clearly intoxicated and it wasn't the Saturday-night booze that had done it. I was off on one, a man with a purpose. I rebuffed or ignored her further probing as to why I was doing it and her concerns as to the consequences. I can see now that I was insensitive when it came to Frank and too caught in the rush of my own trip. I was determined to follow the process right through, not only finding out about Joseph but also making contact and even getting to know him. If you'd asked me if I was prepared for the implications of bringing this man into my life full time, I suppose I would have said that I'd deal with them if it happened. One step at a time, sweet *bejesus*.

Of course I hadn't thought it through, but I never really do. I wasn't being driven by reason but I reasoned that this time I'd be indestructible if I spun off the road. Recently Esther and I discussed my drive to go for it 'full throttle' and her instinct to 'put the brakes on'. She felt, our different fathers notwithstanding, as if my search was her search and she just wasn't ready. 'I thought I would be dragged into it,' she explained.

Knowing what Stella had told her about her genetic father Frank – 'he was a drinker' – she pictured, if he were still alive, a rather pathetic figure who might need looking after and one who would inevitably give her yet more to deal with. She already took much of the responsibility with Stella and during my frequent periods of non-communication, Esther was the one making excuses and telling our birth mother that I was asking after her. Tina would usually take Stella's untimely calls for me and as Esther says, 'I don't have a Tina.' Her husband Duncan would not quite see 'communication surrogate' as his given role. So, what on earth was I doing, Esther wondered, taking on another genetic parent when I had scarcely coped with the first? Taking on more people when she and I were still on the starting blocks with each other? We still had a long way to go to know and understand each other properly.

When Esther came clean about all this long after that night in the kitchen, I looked at her squarely and said, 'You were right there then.' After a knowing glance she told me that near her house there is a hall of mirrors. It's a bizarre and disorientating experience. You are surrounded by the strange and surreal. You glimpse yourself and other people coming from all directions in all shapes, all forms and all sizes and you're really not sure who is real and who isn't. When you find the exit and return to daylight, it's a good feeling. Esther explained more: 'I felt I had just come out of it with Stella, you and the whole regressionary experience.' She explained she didn't want to go into another hall of mirrors. 'I didn't want to put myself through any more distortions of reality. You think you are looking at other people but, in fact, you're looking at yourself.'

Esther called it the 'hall of mirrors'. For my friend Jack at the BBC it is 'bother'. They mean the same thing. As to why I wanted to go into the hall of mirrors, take a trip on this emotional helter-skelter or leap on the Elsinore ghost train, Esther says she doesn't think *I* really understood why.

'You're perfectly good at understanding the motivations of others, just hopeless when it comes to your own.'

'Yes, you're probably right but I'm not alone, am I?' I replied, only to be rewarded with another one of her knowing looks. I've tried to explain why I waited twelve years after meeting Stella before finding Joseph and cited a variety of reasons. Losing Dad, meeting Tina, sorting my life out, having children, finding happiness, reaching forty with all the existential baggage that went with that, the need to determine who I was and the need to see myself in the context of some cosmological continuum. All the factors cleared the road ahead but what drove me on?

Maybe it's primal. Not something our twenty-first-century sensibilities can easily come to terms with. The basic need to get near. There's the external mystery of who your mother and father really are and the internal mystery of why you really need to know. Maybe we don't really know until we've got there. Isn't there a song? *Well I still haven't found what I didn't realize I was looking for*. As a boy I loved mysteries and biographies. Other people's. In these journeys to the centre of the self, I'm the main player.

As far as anyone could, Esther understood; well, she would do – she was uniquely placed – but it was that understanding that made her pause. She recognized the thrill and the folly. I only saw the former. She considers things slightly more than I do, weighs up the consequences a bit more deeply. Just a bit mind. I am a toddler with a box of matches. She is eighteen months older – about four years old maybe – but she is still playing with fire. My devil-may-care approach to this psychological extreme sport was reckless.

Whatever cavils Esther had with me over my periods of non-communication with our birth mother, Stella and I were actually talking more than ever before. My ever so slightly 'father-centric' chats with her continued and centred ever more on my father. I told her I had seen the dreaded form (the paper one not the ghostly one) and she changed the subject. I asked her what he was like and she changed the subject but not before saying, 'He was quite good looking all right but not as good looking as you, I would say. Are you working hard at the moment?' Was she putting him down or flattering me? Was this a subtle compliment to her own bone structure? Then one evening I plucked up the courage and told her I was intending to trace him. 'Are you really?' she asked with interest. 'Would you like some help?' I was astonished and relieved. She must have guessed I was gearing myself up to it. And there was I thinking I was being wily and sly in my questioning. Now she had something to give me. Something I wanted. She said she would make enquiries through her solicitor about him and in the meantime she offered to get me his address. That was simple; he was in the phone book.

At least she was convinced it was him. She had seen his name in the papers a few years back in relation to solving some crime or other in County Wicklow and she was sure he had retired and was living in a particular part of Dublin. She went and got the directory. She had always told me his name was there. I'd never even had the courage to open the page and see it in print. I knew it would be too tempting. Seeing a number – I wouldn't be able to resist ringing it and – and what exactly?

Hello. I have reason to believe I am your son. Have you got a minute? You did in 1960? No but seriously . . .

Or maybe just the old jape – ring the number, let them answer and speak in a funny voice. Pretend to be someone else. The trouble is, I am someone else. I'm a boy called Nicky and I'm from Edinburgh.

After two or three minutes burrowing around her room she was back on the phone. A name in a book. Was it this easy? She gave me the number and address. I manically jotted it down. It was there in my hand – in my own bare scrawl. This was a potent bait all right. I couldn't have been more mesmerized by a sequence of numbers and letters than if it had been the secret ancient code to the sacred casket of infinite and eternal wisdom. The ordinariness of the address belied its deep personal meaning. What amazing human discovery trod on its swirly shagpile and stared at stunning Alpine scenes on its anagylpta walls? Here was the hallowed number. Here was the holy see. It was in the Shankhill area of Dublin. That was a new one on me. Shankhill? Dublin? All those associations of strife-torn Belfast and the barbarism of the Shank-hill butchers juxtaposed with the elegant urban heart of Southern Ireland. It sounded as strange as Hackney in Paris.

What to do now? Stella's solicitor never materialized, so that seemed a non-starter. I sat on the address and number for a week or so and then decided this definitely looked like a job for my original private detective from Bolton. I rang an old friend at Central Television to ask him to grab the number from the files.

'Liam, it's Nicky.'

'Nicky.'

'Do you remember that show we did on private detectives in 1990?'

'No.'

'Could you get me the list of guests please?'

'Is Tina playing away?'

'Yes.'

'Hang on,' he said, pleased with his quip. A few minutes later the conscientious hack came back and read me out a list of four guests, one of whom was called Steve. A bell rang.

Liam also gave me the agency's name and I looked it up on the Internet. Their proud website informed me they were the largest surveillance operation in their part of England and had introduced quality film evidence in employee liability and personal accident claims. All I wanted was confirmation that I had my father's number, not miles of secret film of people walking their dogs in the Shankhill area of Dublin. I rang the agency.

'Can I speak to Steve?'

'One moment please. Can I say whose calling?'

'Nicky Campbell.'

I spoke to him. He sounded like my man but evidently was someone else's.

'No, Nicky, that was the other Steve,' he explained. 'He left a few years back. He's gone freelance.' Freelance? What the hell did that mean? Maybe for security reasons they were all called Steve. I explained my situation. Could he ascertain whether the man at the number and address I had got from Stella could conceivably be this elderly ex copper. At this stage Stella had only told me Joseph was slightly younger than her. I didn't yet realize that slightly meant thirteen years. Indeed one of the reasons that the search took on such urgency once I had decided to go for it, was the fear I might just miss him. He might not be long for this world. Steve said finding him would provide few problems and he would get back to me in the next day or so.

Another day. Another threshold. I couldn't believe how easy it was. That number had been there in the book waiting for me all those years and all I needed to do was pluck up the courage, write it down and get somebody else to phone it for me. In the meantime I got on with some private investigations of my own. I had the number but I needed to find out more about the man, at least to confirm the scant information already there. Stella told me often he'd been doing a 'degree thing' at one of the universities. Indeed, as she had gone so far as to have the fact unambiguously recorded on the adoption papers, I was convinced this was the key lead.

I phoned University College Dublin: no record of a Joseph Leahy. I phoned Trinity College Dublin: no one of that name, at that time. It was like trying to get hold of *Fly Fishing* by J. R.

Hartley. Maybe 'the degree thing' had been concocted to impress the bookish Stella? Could it have been used to cover his tracks and provide an alibi for another assignation? My mind was spinning. The mystery got a whole lot more mysterious. But this was a blow. Since I'd met Stella she had maintained that this man – my father – had academic ambitions. Could she have created a fantasy man, the kind of man she wished he'd been – or the kind she wanted the adoption agency to think he was? He may have been a Catholic but she wanted whoever had to know that he was an extremely intelligent individual who was going places.

A few days later, gumshoe II rang back.

'Nicky, it's Steve. We rang the number.' It was one of those slow-motion moments. It elongated as I waited for the amazing revelation.

'What did he say?'

'Not great news, I'm afraid. He is far too young. It isn't him and we were aware of young children in the background. He isn't your father.'

I sank like a stone. This was desperate. 'It must be. It'll be his son that answered and his grandchildren you heard.'

'No. According to our investigations, we can rule this one out.' I had to defer but I wasn't convinced. This had to be my father. Stella had said so. She'd kept tabs on him just as she had done with the doctor who had ended the relationship with her all those years before. I had a good mind to ring the number myself.

'I still think it might be his house.'

'Nick, we know it's not.'

'How do you know it's not?'

'We have established it.' He sounded unequivocal. He had

established it. I was so deflated I forgot to ask, out of curiosity, how on earth he had managed that.

'We'll try another route. He was in the police, you say?'

Heavens. Where was this going to lead? It was like a drug. The deeper I got into it the more obsessive I became. The option of doing anything else but following it through to its bitter, sweet, or bittersweet, conclusion was the only one I could make out in my gimlet-eyed focus.

The clock was ticking and the meter was whirring fast. Steve came back within forty-eight hours with the news that there were precisely 376 Joseph Leahys in Ireland. He had a contact in the police pensions department and he would see if there were any in receipt of a Garda pension. The phone stayed silent for a week or two. The trail must have gone quiet.

I wanted news instantly. I had no time for any nonsense. Any delay or period of due reflection in which to consider whether this was what I really wanted and how it might affect me emotionally was so much humbug. Sod that. The toddler had the matches in his grubby little hands. Strike a light.

Then, a while later (God, this seemed to be taking for ever) Steve the Detective got back to me and told me his cunning plan. He suggested I write to an intermediary he had identified, asking for the letter to be passed on to Mr Leahy for his consideration. He gave me his contact at the Garda pensions office. This go-between would be aware that Joseph needed to be contacted but didn't know exactly why. All I had to do was write the letter. What should I say? What do you say? How could I let him know who I was without alerting anyone else in his nuclear family to a nuclear situation? What about his wife, if he had one, and his children if there were any? More sisters? Brothers? Who knows, but I couldn't just burst out of the cake – it's the son nobody knew about. 'Hi there everybody!'

Dear Joseph,

I am a radio and television presenter/journalist of a certain renown working in the UK. I am forty years old, married with three children and looking for a different challenge.

To that end I have decided to investigate the possibility of writing a social history of the Garda. I was wondering if I could come and meet you sometime to tap you for some experiences. Maybe we could merely talk.

I of course guarantee complete confidentiality and I think that you could find it extremely rewarding. I got your name from Stella Lackey.

Perhaps you would like to further discuss the parameters of the project and want more details. I would willingly oblige. Please do not hesitate to get in touch.

I also enclose a return envelope.

All the very best

Nicky Campbell

'A certain renown.' Pompous arse that I am. But I needed to make an impression. I was desperate to tell him I'd been successful so he wouldn't reject me. Look at me, old fella. Esther says she thought my letter was 'totally nuts', but that on recent reflection she agrees she felt something similar when she contacted Stella. She just couldn't wait to tell her about her academic achievements.

I put on the stamp and took it round the corner to the post box with great ceremony. I needed to double check that it had been posted properly. I pushed it through the slot and then pushed my fingers in to ensure it had fallen down into the main pile of post and not become lodged by fate or freak for eternity on some shelf. Then after walking away back to the house I returned obsessively to check again. I was so churned up with excitement and thought a reply would be only days away. But there was nothing for days. Nothing for weeks. I thought I'd allowed for its necessarily circuitous route via the pensions official and then out into the rural wilds of Ireland. After my great expectations I was left feeling frustrated and confused. I began to ready myself for the disappointment not of rejection but of silence. No response. No nothing. To cope with this I buried it away and reconciled the situation in my mind as best I could. At least I'd tried. I'd done my bit. Nothing ventured. Et cetera, et cetera. It was hard though.

I'd posted the letter on 21 January 2002. As the days turned to weeks and the weeks slipped into months I resolved to channel my disappointment into a mission to find out more. It even crossed my mind to get the detective agency to do some real rooting about so that I could know about him and maybe begin to understand why he didn't want to know about me. I might have to be content with information but in my heart I needed communication. Speak to me.

Then, on 3 May 2002, he spoke. I came back from a run – running round the common from old father time – and as I puffed and sweated my way back into the house Tina headed me off in the hallway. 'There's a message for you on the answerphone. It's Joseph.'

FOURTEEN

All My Sons

A wave of fear, excitement, relief and God knows what else swept through my body. I started to climb the stairs towards our bedroom – away from the sitting room where the answerphone was. Tina couldn't believe it, 'Well, aren't you going to listen to it?'

'I have waited forty-one years so another ten minutes won't matter.' It was a pretty lame response but in truth I needed to get my breath back, have a shower and freshen myself up so as to be properly prepared to absorb and interpret whatever was to come. Halfway up the stairs I turned to Tina, 'Is it OK?'

She looked at me quizzically. 'Yes,' she replied as if she really didn't understand why it wouldn't be.

I showered, shampooed, shaved, changed and came down stairs scented, minted and ready to meet my maker – or at least a major contributor to the process. I was ready for him. Our answerphone has seen better days – and much worse ones, having had it for ten years – but I put my ear right next to it and pressed the playback, with my heart in my mouth. Here goes.

What a beautiful voice it was. Like a wise old rascal. Deep and warm and gravelly, sounding nervous as a deer. It was Irish. It sounded like it had taken quite a bit of courage to make the call. It sounded like a call he had been longing to make.

Hello, Nicky. It's ... er ... It's Joseph here. I ... I got your letter. I'll ... er ... I'll ring back sometime. God Bless. Bye now.

1471.

You were called today at one forty-one hours. The caller withheld their number. Please hang up.

Tina had been tending to one or other or all of the children and it was one of those calls she just decided to let ring and get back to later. If only she'd picked it up.

What if he doesn't phone back? I wondered. He has to now. I thought. I listened again. And again. And again. The 'God Bless' sounded from the heart – maybe from a heart that might have long had a place for the son that got away. He coughed twice on the way through. Had that been nerves? I called out for Tina and she came to listen with me. She reassured me: 'He's bound to ring back.' I thought he would too. The ice was broken now. But I wondered when it would be. It was three and a half months since I'd sent the letter to the contact at the pensions department. Why the hell had it taken so long? There had to be family complications. As with Stella, and her side of my genetic bequest, I was clearly top secret. The unmentioned and unmentionable. I concluded it might be a good while until he could again find opportunity and courage combined. Because our answerphone was from the Ark I couldn't remove the message and save it on some other format. I wouldn't have known where to start and there weren't any sockets to facilitate such an operation. The thought that this might be all I would ever have of him did occur. I even tried phoning my friend Mark Goodier who is Mr gizmo techno-freak and would have all the answers. He was engaged. I abandoned that plan and slapped a verbal preservation order on the short recording. It was of historic importance all right. All messages left by Emmas, Claires, Felicitys and Arabellas, were just telephone ephemera, to be summarily expunged. This crackly message was of a different order. It was my line to antiquity. The entrance to the time tunnel. I can't tell you how many times I listened to it. If I did you'd probably think I was a little bit weird.

Because he had phoned, I felt confident he would again. But because he clearly had to await his opportunity, I wasn't holding my breath. I was right not to. May turned to June. June burst out all over and blazed into July. By the time July wound down into August, we were winding down for our annual break in the Scottish Highlands, my childhood paradise. I love the solitude, the children revel in the freedom, and Tina adores a blazing fire as the warmth of the late summer day subsides. I was co-presenting *Late Night London*, the deftly named late-night current affairs debate pro-gramme on ITV in the London area. It was modelled on *Central Weekend Live*, the fiery argument show I'd been doing when the original Steve 'the Gumshoe' had got back to me with Stella's details. The last two editions of *Late Night London* overlapped with the first two Mondays of our holiday so I zipped down from the land of *Ring of Bright Water* to the city of recycled toilet water.

I would get off the Monday-morning plane from Inverness to

Gatwick, whizz back to my home in South London, grab a suit, pick a shirt and hopefully a matching tie, dash to the studio, prepare and present the programme and drive home after midnight for a bit of sleep and an early start back to Gatwick so that I could return to the clarity and sanity of the wilds.

On the first Monday in this whistle-stopping culture-shocking gallivanting from the sublime to the ridiculous, I dashed into the house with about forty-five minutes before I had to leave for the studio. I checked the answerphone. I couldn't believe my frantic ears. He was on it. His voice. He was here. He was in London. He was calling from a car by the sounds of things and there seemed to be someone with him. At the end of his message but before the call was over, he made a brief aside to the mystery companion. It sounded like he was asking which button to press now. What did the message say?

> Hello, Nicky. It's Joseph here. I am in London at the moment.
> I thought I would call and see how you are and maybe have a
> chat. I'll . . . I'll phone later.

1471.

> You were called today at fourteen forty-one hours. The caller
> withheld their number. Please hang up.

I hadn't long missed him. If he was in London, he must have family here. Bloody hell! 'I'll phone later,' he had said. What if he did phone later? Or tomorrow? I'd have finished my debate, be sitting on an aeroplane, roaring up to the land where the only debate was whether to go for a walk, do the garden or nip over to my friend Jimmy's for a whisky. I needed to give Joseph our number in the Highlands. I then composed myself as much as possible and recorded a pretty damn strange new out-going message, once I'd eventually managed to work out what to press.

> Hello. We are not here at the moment but we will get back to you when we can. If however you are Joseph – hello Joseph – please phone me on this mobile number and we could maybe meet later tonight 07767, etc., etc., or at this number in the north of Scotland 014555, etc., etc. – which is where we will be for the next three weeks. If you are not Joseph, ignore that.

I skipped into the shower, picked a suitable suit, leapt into the minicab, and headed for the studio in the knowledge that we were getting warmer and warmer but aware that this was not as straightforward as it might be. Clearly, there were complications. If he was married, and that seemed more than likely, I had been conceived and born prior to that. Maybe the shame of having a child born out of wedlock had led him to lock the secret away. Well, now the secret was having his day. The quest was irresistible and the puzzle was compelling. This was the beginning of an extraordinary sequence and accumulation of events, discoveries and revelations that would change my life and stir up a few others, and the pace from here on would be relentless.

It was a glorious summer in the Glen. The house, proud on its promontory, has breathtaking views of both the Isle of Skye and the majestic north-western seaboard. We went for walks, read books, sat on the deserted beaches, swam in the crystal-clear waters, basked in the heatwave, and at the going down of the sun lit the log fire and remembered how lucky we were. We saw otters and dolphins. We spotted eagles and pinemartins. I remembered the endless Highland summers of my boyhood. We were having one of those, plucked straight from the nostalgia tree. I'd spend those long-gone holidays reading Gavin Maxwell's books. He wrote about his life in the tiny lighthouse keeper's cottage overlooking the Isle of Skye and I'd dreamt that one day I'd see, smell and feel the fantastic place he'd brought to enchanted life in his prose. And, like walking into a cinema screen, there we were. From the house we could actually see the islands of the bay where he lived and wrote and all the magic of childhood was undimmed. As for those endless summers – it's funny how memory filters out the rain, the damp, the voracious winged insects, the sheep ticks and the clouds of midges taking succulent chunks out of our young bodies.

One afternoon, not long after returning from my rather hardcore London commute, I was in the house on my own. The rest of the family were away playing pooh sticks on the little bridge down the road. I was due to meet them and some friends in the pub for lunch. We'd have a nice boozy time and our children would run around in the garden and play by the shore. The phone rang. I escaped from everything up there and was, as a matter of course, mildly irascible when the outside world dared to intrude.

'Hello,' I answered, thinking, This had better be good. It was good. It was very good.

'Hello, is Nicky Campbell there please? It's Joseph Leahy here.'

My heart leapt like the salmon that used to teem in the local waters before the fish farms came.

'Joseph, it's me – Nicky. How are you?'

'Oh it's good to talk to you,' he said with such a smile in his voice.

'This is a bit strange, isn't it?' That really needed to be acknowledged. It is more than a bit strange. When you are speaking to a parent or sibling you have only just found, you have constantly to check yourself, remind yourself what is actually happening and share the amazement with your new partner in wonder. You need to because the thought is ever present.

'It is a strange thing, isn't it?' he agreed and he said how overjoyed he was that I'd written. We started to talk. We started to talk all right. We had two lives and a hundred and five combined years to catch up on. It is a nerve-racking business but the burning curiosity and amazement of the moment swept the nerves away. He had a soft Northern Irish accent. We talked with the joy of mutual discovery. He is a wonderful talker. He could talk for Ireland and, from what I gathered, he certainly wouldn't want to talk for anywhere else. The experience is and was a curious mixture of the intimate and the distant. We were strangers but we seemed to know each other. The thought that this was my father and that I was his son informed every word of the adrenalin-powered dialogue. Whether some ethereal bond already existed or whether we both just wanted one to be there is moot. Whatever the answer, we clicked.

'So tell me all about your life,' he said emotionally. Touchingly, he was eager to know about my mum and dad and the home I'd been given. I told him what fine people they were and how fantastic my upbringing had been. I felt a wee bit protective of Mum and Dad here. I needed to tell him that this was nothing to do with anything lacking in my relationship with my parents. This was bonus time. This was to find out what went before. I tried to explain: 'They were my mum and dad and always will be but I wanted to find you and maybe meet up before it was too late. I could go out and get run over by that tractor and you would never have had the pleasure.' He laughed. That felt good.

He was thrilled to hear about my three little girls. He asked their names and got me to describe them. He wanted to know all about Tina. He had three children too. That floored me. Three more siblings? I had a brother, and two more sisters. A whole world was opening up here. He was justly proud of them. Joseph Junior was in advertising in London and was extremely successful. He travelled and lectured all over the world and was a 'strapping tall handsome fella'. He wasn't married but another 'sister' Helen was. She ran an IT company in North London with her husband Patrick and they had three young children. His third child was an accomplished artist and had her own little girl. What parallel universe had I landed in? Don't beam me up yet, I want to stay here a while.

'I've got two sisters up in the North,' he said.

Bloody hell, I thought. Aunts.

'And will they be surprised by this if you tell them?'

'I'd say they would be.' He paused for a thought. It came. 'But not completely.'

Joseph had been married since 1963 and he and his wife Mary lived in a quiet corner of the Republic, extremely far from the madding crowd. She didn't know about this. He had never told her. 'I should have but it got too late.'

He was retired now and had been in business after his time in the police but had got his fingers burnt during the eighties downturn when interest rates soared like a sputnik. He gave me a hint or two of some of the heavy-duty front-line Irish police work he'd had been involved in during the seventies and early eighties. 'There were lots of dealings with the "boys",' he said. I don't think he was talking young offenders. We had already been on the phone for an hour. It was flowing and it was fascinating. It was very easy and completely, totally, utterly surreal.

The only person he had told about this contact and my existence was his son-in-law Patrick – the man with the IT business. Patrick must have been the background presence when Joseph had left the most recent message on the answerphone. I already sensed that this was a son-in-law who made things happen. The feeling of intimacy grew as the conversation progressed. Joseph told me how delighted it had made him after cheating death and beating cancer. It had struck him in the throat. He said he was fine now, fit and healthy. He was overjoyed and determined to get this secret out in the open so that I could meet what he described as 'your brother and sisters'. And so that I could meet him. Then he coughed. He did that a lot. Like a reminder of mortality. Then his voice dropped to a near whisper and he said, 'I spent nights awake thinking about you. Wondering.' I didn't know what to say. I wondered if he was just saying it but then the very fact that he was on the phone meant that he hadn't forgotten me. I must have crossed his mind. What a cross to bear. What a weight to carry in the dead of night. Could you forget?

Joseph then told me the story of how he'd received my ever-so-carefully worded letter. The intermediary at the pensions department had sat on it for a few weeks before passing on the missive – and, I suspect, a hint of its contents – to a local district police welfare officer who eventually took it upon himself to drop in on Joseph. 'He turned up. A little ol' busybody. Initially I thought it'd be something to do with my pension and they were checking to see if some retired old guy was doing OK. Mary my wife asked him about pension rates but he said fuck all. He just stood there assessing all the pictures on the wall. He couldn't look me in the eye. He was a gobshite. A gobdaw.'

'Gobdaw?' I enquired.

'An Irish word for eejit.' Apparently this gobdaw, the social welfare officer, had decided that tact and discretion were the better part of nosiness and beat a temporary retreat. Three weeks later Joseph got another call from him and they met at the end of the lane. Mr Gobdaw handed him the letter with a salacious glint in his beady little eyes. Joseph opened it. He read it and the little man asked if he knew anything about it. 'He was on to the fact that it was a paternity issue. I said, "This letter is a whole load of crap." I disavowed it. They are mouthy these amadans.'

'Amadan?' I asked.

'It's a bit like a gobdaw.'

Joseph rang me at the first available opportunity and had told the whole truth and nothing but the truth to his devoted son-in-law Patrick as soon as he was in London to see daughter Helen and family.

'I saw you on the telly when I was in London. And I thought, Jeez, put a green uniform on him and that's me thirty years ago.

I drank a half bottle and watched it with tears running down my face.' As he said this I didn't know what to think. It was all so intense but all so unreal. It must have been just like that for him seeing me prancing about a studio on his son-in-law's television screen. 'And might I, by the way, as an ole' cop congratulate you on your line of questioning.' I didn't want this extraordinary conversation to end and it was nothing to do with the flattery, I promise you. He told me more about his battle with throat cancer. I'd been right. Time had been of the essence. He had nearly died but pulled through. The chemotherapy had taken a lot of his hair and all of his teeth, and the surgery had robbed him of part of his neck and most of his sense of smell but he was still here. This explained the coughing and the gravelly voice. He had trouble with his saliva glands and liked to have a glass of water at hand. He said he loved horses and rode out every day. That kept him fit. He went on to describe my piano-playing grandmother and my gentle, idealistic grandfather. He started talking politics too and was extremely knowledgeable and insightful. He set forth his Irish nationalism and fished subtly for my position. I said I tried to understand both sides. I always said that. I said it so often I'd come to believe it. He was sympathetic to that. He was engaging, intelligent, passionate and had a winning turn of phrase. No gobdaw he.

Eighty minutes had passed in a flash. So had forty-one years. We both had to go. Tina was back downstairs screaming that she needed my help with the children 'for a change' and I sensed Joseph's window of opportunity about to close. I was in a daze and I am sure he was too. I told him how amazing it had been. 'Likewise,' he said. 'Likewise' with a sing-song voice. We had packed a lot in. He asked how Stella was and went off on a wistful and not entirely plausible tangent. 'It was just one of those things. She had these wonderful, what I would call Asiatic looks and we just fell in love as people do.' I didn't entirely swallow the *Madame Butterfly* scenario but let it pass. Maybe once evening had fallen it seemed like that. Poetic licence was understandable in the circumstances. He didn't know how important it might have been to me that they really loved each other and had a deep and meaningful relationship. He didn't know what he needed to explain and what he might need to apologize for. I told him he had absolutely nothing to worry about. I reassured him while trying not to let on that I was reassuring him. As the call came to a close, we agreed to talk as soon as we could. It was a thrilling phone call. I dashed downstairs and told Tina. I was on another planet but the children were hungry and screaming so I got on with being their father.

The pub in the Highland village we love contains the most wonderful mixture of locals, holidaymakers and a sizeable contigent of the Barbour brigade who do tend to gravitate towards the Western Highlands of Scotland. The inn was busy and there were a good few green wellies galumphing about. Loads of kids were running around laughing and making a wonderfully raucous racket. As I stood at the bar, still in my post-paternal conversational aftershock, I ordered the pub lunches from Mhairi the barmaid, trying to second guess what my wife would want, as she'd temporarily nipped away to a nearby cottage to look at a painting, some curtain material or something that required urgent pre-prandial attention. While I was at the bar, a charming member of the aforementioned officer class marched up beside me. I offered to buy him a drink.

'Love a pint,' he said. 'How are you?'

'I don't really know. My head is a bit crammed. I have just spoken to my biological father for the first time in my life.'

'Really!' he said. There was a short silence and he glanced out of the window at the Isle of Skye. He looked back at me and said, 'How long are you up for this summer then?' Family secrets aren't everybody's cup of tea and, to be fair, there was a lot going on. There were children running riot in the pub and there was the child running riot inside me, thinking about his father.

Mum came up from Edinburgh to spend some time with the family. She was oblivious to what was going on, as was my sister Fiona. As far as I was concerned, that was the way it had to be. They knew I had traced Stella years ago and was in contact but I left it there and never let the subject be broached. I'd told them nothing of Esther. As Joseph had said about the secret me: 'I should have but it got too late.' Neither did Mum or Fiona have any inkling of my recent discoveries. God forbid. It was easier that way. I selfishly thought I had enough to contend with so I compartmentalized it. How could I share my joy with them without hurting them? Of course the longer it all went on and the more extraordinary it all became the more and more difficult it was going to be to tell. And the more it became an excuse not to. The secrets just became locked away deeper and deeper in the vault. Unconsciously and unthinkingly I'd turned away from Esther too. I became wholly absorbed by the paternal journey and so rapidly did the chain of events unfold, I was sucked in by the addictive adrenalin of revelation after relentless revelation. I'd barely absorbed and processed one thing, when I got whacked by another. I was like one of Muhammed Ali's hapless victims. Nicky 'the amadan' Campbell, first the jab, then the left hook and before I had got my bearings I was caught by the sweetest upper cut. Fate was dancing round me and I was punch drunk.

Just a week after first talking to Joseph, we woke up to a scorching cloudless day and all piled into a pal's boat with towels, wine and kids galore and headed for an idyllic beach in the breathtaking heart of this country's last true mainland wilderness. It was a magical holiday outing, the sort of day you remember for ever. And because of what happened later, I would certainly never forget it. Mum, remarkable for seventy-nine, had a whale of a time, although she gave the windsurfing a miss, and by the time we'd all got back home in the early evening, with the sun still blazing, we were absolutely exhausted. I had a mild touch of sunstroke and lay on the bed for a while. Out of curiosity and boredom I turned on my mobile to see if there were any intrusions. There was one. It was a text from work:

Ring Joseph Leahy on 07836, etc, etc.

I immediately assumed Joseph must be back in London already and had felt emboldened enough to give me a number. I was so tired I didn't particularly question why he had phoned the BBC when he had the number in the Highlands. I rang it. A young man answered. Joseph Leahy?

'Speaking.'

'It's Nicky.' There was a pause for breath.

'Hi, Nicky. My name is Joseph Leahy. I think you've spoken to my father.'

It was my brother. I gasped.

'Oh my God – this is strange.'

'It is so strange,' he replied warmly.

'I can't tell you how weird this is.'

Naturally we kept conferring and concurring about the weirdness of the situation. It was an emotional conversation. Joseph Junior told me how happy he and his sister Helen were about this, although their father – our father – didn't know that they knew. Their mother had to be protected at all costs, even though my birth did pre-date their marriage. The whole business would just be such a shock. Joseph Junior told me he'd always wanted a brother and despite the understandably mixed emotions they were experiencing and the myriad issues it had brought to the surface, they were keen to meet me. He reassured me and perhaps himself: 'This is nothing to do with him as far as we are concerned. This is about our connection to you. We have found a brother and that is a good thing.'

He was intelligent, sensitive and direct. He said he had 'sort of heard of me', which was sort of comforting. Not a fan but he knew I existed. Perfect. I liked him. I also felt that strange closeness that has no real reason or right to be. Again, whether I created it or whether it just existed is irrelevant. He told me he didn't see eye to eye with his dad. Joseph Senior, our mutual father, was a complex man who in his time had been a pretty hard-drinking cop. He'd lived the life. Joseph Junior and his sister Helen, both of whom lived in London, had found out about me from Joseph's son-in-law and confidant Patrick. The man in the shadows. It was a shock but, in another way, no surprise. Nothing would really surprise them about their father. I remembered the aunts. They wouldn't be completely surprised either. The call was chastening and exhilarating. It was uplifting and depressing. Families are complicated things.

We exchanged numbers. We put the phones down. I shouted for Tina. She shouted back that she was busy. I shouted back that it was important. Mum yelled up asking if she could help. 'No I need to speak to Tina, Mum. Could you tell her I need HER? Now.' I had to keep all this from Mum. Talk about a tangled web. Reluctantly, Tina traipsed up to the bedroom. I told her what had transpired and she sat down to take it all in. I then phoned Joseph Junior back to see if he was OK. I felt protective towards my brother. I'd immediately assumed this mantle for the first time in my life. I am a man with a brother. It's a whole new psychological standpoint. I wanted to check he wasn't upset, and to say that if this was all going to be too difficult I would pull back now. He said that was ridiculous. He knew it was impossible.

I was deep in Esther's Hall of Mirrors. What was real here and what was an illusion, distortion, or rather a warped perception? Joe Junior and I exchanged numbers and agreed we would meet back in London sooner rather than later. I was completely exhausted. Perhaps psychosomatically, my sunstroke got worse, and I had to take a couple of Nurofen and lie down with the curtains closed. I have had only about three headaches in my life and this was the worst yet. My mind was darting around all over the place and my body was shivering. What a day. Did I want out? No, but even if I did, there was no exit. There were mirrors everywhere and the door was gone.

FIFTEEN

Something Wonderful

Back in London and back at work. I was rehearsing in the
Watchdog office for the first in a new series of the BBC1 consumer
programme. We were going live later and were working hard
getting the cameras and lighting sorted and our words in the right
order when my mobile burst into the overture from *Carmen*. I'd
recently changed from 'Scotland the Brave'.

'Yes?'

A rather timid voice was on the other end. 'Hello, could I
speak to Nicky Campbell please?'

'Who wants him?' I said like a pompous pratt and she told me
in a roundabout way that she was my sister. She didn't actually say
the S word. She just said that she was called Helen and had got
my number from her brother Joseph Junior who was the son of
Joseph Senior, my father. I metamorphosed from consumers'
champion to blabbering fool. I rushed into a quiet corridor,
stuttered an apology for my initial offhandedness and said how
good it was to speak and that I would ring her when I got home
but things were a bit busy right now. Mark, the studio floor
manager, was yelling for me: 'Nicky. Nicky love. We need to try

the Peugeot link again. Whenever you're ready.' But I was too shaken up. Another sister. What on earth was going on? 'We've got to press on, Nicky. Whenever you like.' I had the frenetic butterfly excitement of a new love affair and the driven unquench-able curiosity of the most compelling personal mystery. It was fast-tracked family. Fast-tracked and furious.

I'd discovered my father and now these siblings from the past or was it the future, and I was terrified of telling Mum or my sister Fiona. To share it with them would be to hurt them. To explain it would mean having to understand it. Understanding anything was the last thing on my mind. I was a man possessed. In 1990 I knew no one to whom I was related by blood. Then I found a birth mother and a sister and since 1998 I'd fathered three children. From August to September 2002 I had traced a father and three more siblings, and heard tell of aunts galore. I had no gears left. I was in genetic overdrive, seduced by the speed and thrill of it all. It's easy to ignore the feelings of others when your own are so churned up.

Later that night I phoned Helen and we had a long talk. She was eight months pregnant and she stressed that she and her brother wanted to meet me for themselves and it was nothing to do with the 'old fella'. I found that touching and I was grateful for it, though I did wonder whether this had more to do with the old fella than they were letting on. Their relationship with him was clearly complex. I ascertained Helen was a good pianist and I remembered my adoption papers and Stella's description of my father's mother as being very musical. That would be 'our' grand-mother. I swooped on these shared talents and characteristics like a gull on a fishbox. I'm a self-taught pianist and have long lived under the delusion that with a few lessons the Paris Conservatoire would have been gagging for me. Tellingly, it conveniently slipped my mind that Esther plays brilliantly by ear.

Helen, who graduated from UCD in Italian, lived not far from us in London and she sounded lovely. I thought about what Joseph Junior had said when he phoned me in Scotland. About how much he wanted to meet; how this was a good thing, a joyful thing. I listened as she said exactly the same thing but in her own sweet way and I thought again how fortunate I was. Unlike Esther and me, they weren't searching. They were just living their lives and then – like the words superimposed over the old *Batman* TV show fight scenes – bam biff kapow – holy foundling Robin! Here's a brand-new brother and by the way, he's forty-one. Not only had I made contact with all of them in the last couple of weeks, but Tina and I had an eight-month-old baby, Kirsty, who had just augmented the family and shaken up our world – not to mention our hormones. For me, emotionally, it was bam zap pow followed by crash sock splatt. No wonder it knocked me for six. As for Joseph Junior and Helen, they had been inadvertently found and they'd embraced it. Some would have reacted very differently I'm sure. Who the hell was I anyway? They'd every right to treat me as an unwelcome intruder disrupting their lives; they didn't.

Helen said she wanted to meet sooner rather than later. I recognized the behaviour of the pregnant female of the species wanting to get everything done, dusted and ready before the big day. No loose ends. We agreed on Saturday coming – my place –

2 p.m. She would check with Joseph Junior and get back to me. She rang straight back. 'See you on Saturday.'

'I can't wait.'

It was another nerve-jangling Saturday morning, but my state of mind and body had nothing whatsoever to do with the afternoon's vital Euro qualifier between Scotland and the Faeroe Isles. I was pacing up and down like a big cat in a small cage, aching for the time to pass before curiosity killed me. As two o'clock approached I was desperately trying to work out what I would say and how I would say it. I was worried about the way I would come across, as I felt too nervous to be sure of making any sense at all. I was certain to portray myself as a gobdaw full of gobshite. At least I had Tina and the kids there. Facing Esther alone had been tough but this time there were two of them.

The buzzer went. I looked at Tina. The children were blissfully unmoved. 'You answer it. You answer it,' I wittered pathetically to the wife.

'You answer it. They're your relatives. Answer it,' she snapped back. Tina employed the tone with the forty-one year old that she'd mastered with the two year old and the four year old. Then she was emollient. 'Just go to the door and open it.' She seemed as calm as Lauren Bacall in *To Have and Have Not*, showing Bogie how to whistle. 'You just put your lips together and blow.' Easy. I attempted to swallow my pride and go but found I couldn't swallow. 'Just go to the door and pull it open, then say hello.' I went to the door and pulled it open. They were standing on the doorstep. They looked at me. I looked at them. Then I looked down at the welcome mat and let out an amateur dramatic scream for imaginary help.

'Aghhhhhh', that basically said, Isn't this the fucking craziest thing? I just haven't got a clue what to do! Do you feel the same? Help. They laughed. Thank God.

Helen looked petite and pregnant with reddish hair and was chicly but casually dressed. It is a real gift to be able to look stylish at eight months' pregnant. Joseph Junior wore a pair of smart jeans and a short-sleeved designer shirt. He was tall, thin and chiselled with dark hair. Both had soft southern accents and piercing blue eyes. What peculiar things genes are. Tina reckoned he was gorgeous. As she put it later that evening when she phoned a friend, 'He was like a better looking, younger, thinner version of Nicky.' My, how we laughed.

I took the two of them into the hall and we walked across to the sitting room. That walk took an eternity. I should have been sponsored for it. We all sat down and talked the smallest of talk with the deepest of subtext while giving each other the most penetrating of looks. I knew this intense ritual from my previous close encounters of the genetic kind. It is the staring game. On one level you are forensically and minutely examining their every feature and looking into the depths of their eyes, unaware they're aware of it. It's as if they're on the other side of a trick mirror staring at the human subjects. The part of you not engaged in this subversive process is awkwardly conscious of it and of the fact that they're doing the same thing right back. This all happens in seconds. It is so brief. The feelings are fleeting and unexpressed.

Thoughts are barely formulated, it's as feelings they remain. Feelings of connection, loss and the disquieting notion of a brand-new past.

We sat down and I started chatting to these fascinating people. I was feeling painfully self-conscious. What did they think of me? Was I making a fool of myself? Was I making sense? They were intelligent and perceptive. They might rumble me? Remember, I'd had that feeling with Esther when I realized she was a force to be reckoned with. Nerves, insecurity and the surreal nature of the situation initially conspired to put me on the back foot, but pretty soon the fascination of the afternoon generated its own life and energy. Afterwards Tina told me, 'I couldn't believe you were in that room for so long talking to two people you didn't know.' That is what she'd said about me and Esther when we'd first met. Talking to complete strangers with such ease is not something I'm noted for outside professional circles. What do you say without descending into the ultra banal? But were they people I didn't know? That is the strange thing. You don't know them, but you feel you should and in a way you do. It's akin to that gnawing feeling when you're sure you've met someone somewhere before but can't for the life of you remember where or when. Of course, knowing that we were half siblings, we were disposed to open up to each other. We shared a history if not a past. If we had met at a party, for instance, unaware of the big connection, it might well have been different. But, as with Esther, if we had sat down as strangers and spoken at any length we'd have found miles of common ground. It opened out before us on that Saturday afternoon. And I kept seeing other versions of myself in them.

Their eyes looked like mine. It's an extremely disconcerting place, the hall of mirrors.

They told me about their upbringing and, of course, our mutual friend – their dad, our father – his faults and foibles. His flaws and failures. He could have really made something of his life if he hadn't been so lazy but was a very good cop. He'd been a wild man but was an intelligent and voracious reader. He was knowledgeable, charismatic and charming. There in the sitting room – three life stories, two glasses of wine and one pregnant woman with a cup of tea and a piece of cake. Joseph Junior, who was in no danger of painting a rosy picture about his relationship with the man who fathered us all, stopped at one stage and reflected. He thought long and hard over his choice of words. I will never ever forget what he said. I can hear it now, in his gentle voice with its soft Irish accent.

'But you know, there is also something rather wonderful about him.'

It gave me a warm glow. I'd got the worst of my father and now I got the best of him. For all his faults there was a magic about him – a good heart and the wish ultimately to do his best by people despite his mistakes. I felt those words physically. 'Something wonderful.' All the previous negative comments had hit me close to home but narcissistically, so did that single, glowing positive. Stella had latched on to something uncannily similar when she'd been told 'there is some good in Nicky'. The search for my parents had brought out the child in me and in trying to understand who I was, my ego needed looking after. My new brother's comment did the trick.

'We nearly lost him, you know. Throat cancer,' Helen told me. Joseph Senior had told me about it himself during our long telephone conversation when I was in Scotland. She went on, 'He was such a good-looking man and had a full head of hair until the treatment.' I instinctively touched my head. I felt the need to show them a picture of my dad as they were talking about theirs. It was all so confusing. Dad was my dad. The dad I loved and always will. The finest man I ever knew. The finest man many people ever knew. Now this man – my 'father' – who seemed to be a morally complex, manipulative and roguish individual was the one looking back at me from the mirror. I stretched over to a side table and grabbed a silver-framed shot of Dad. Helen and Joseph Junior said he looked like a really nice man. I told them he was more than that. They went into raptures about their mother Mary, who of course knew none of this. I listened with fascination. She did sound remarkable and I wondered if I would ever meet her. I hoped so. We were sitting on two sofas under two bits of cherished and expensively framed Hollywood memorabilia, pictures of Sinatra and Julie Andrews (don't ask), and we were sitting opposite shelves full of my most treasured books. There were loads there on Ireland. I'd collected dozens over the years – since my first meeting with Stella back in 1991 when my interest in Irish history and politics had first ignited. They caught Helen's eye. When I explained, she said, 'And where do your sympathies lie on that score?' Checking I wasn't a member of the Orange Lodge I guess.

'I try and understand both sides.' Is that like pleading the Fifth? A bland response, yes, but also a matter of professional pride.

'Dad is very much one-way on that one,' she said. It was generational and geographical. Fate had given him little choice.

His children, my half siblings, were from the South and very distant from all that. Our father grew up in the North, surrounded by it.

We had a laugh talking about Catholicism and Protestantism. That makes a change. Being confronted with siblings of the alternative credo was interesting and strangely exotic. But we were sophisticated, secular, educated people, for God's sake. I was reminded of Jonathan Swift's Big Enders and Little Enders. Who cares which end you eat your boiled egg from? We moved on. Back to the family stuff. That was more like *Eastenders*.

They both vaguely recognized me from TV somewhere but it was very foggy. In fact, Helen had been watching the box a few weeks before, late at night. Her husband Patrick, Joseph Senior's sole confidant about 'me', had deliberately switched over to Carlton where I was presenting the talk show *Late Night London*, to gauge her reaction as she unknowingly watched her big brother on the small screen. A strangely voyeuristic experiment by the 'mad Professor' Patrick you may think – but undeniably interesting. We laughed as she told me what she'd said. 'Patrick, what the fuck are we watching him for? I want Graham Norton.' Wrong Irishman.

Just before the end of our meeting, Joe Junior went to the loo. There is a framed photo in there right in the adult male's line of vision. It makes people smile. Staring out from it are Dave Lee Travis, Simon Bates, Steve Wright, Simon Mayo, Bruno Brookes and the whole gang. It's the Radio One line-up from about 1988,

taken before the funtabulous Radio One Christmas lunch. I am in
there with the most ridiculous floppy hair and cocky expression.
'In that photo you look just like him when he was young. It's so
weird,' said my new brother. An electric charge went through me.

The girls were heading up for a bath and bed. Helen and
Joseph Junior made ready to leave and we said goodbye. It was
difficult to know whether to kiss or peck or hug or just gently
squeeze. I wasn't the only one in a quandary. There was a tentative
mixture of all of the above on display. They drove off and I stood
waving on the pavement like a matinée actor in a fog of steam.
What next? The momentum continued. I was a tiny silver ball in
an emotional pinball machine. Next I had to meet my father.
They had stolen a march on him and got there first but meeting
them had brought him tantalizingly close. Later that night I logged
on, wrote an e-mail to Joseph Junior and hit the send button. I
needed to say more as soon as I could.

> I didn't express myself very well at the end there and probably
> won't now but I found this afternoon very moving, very strange
> but also there was 'something wonderful' about it. It was incred-
> ibly special meeting you both and I now feel elated but also
> exhausted.

Two days later he replied.

> Saturday was strange without a doubt but at the same time
> intriguing, enlightening and joyful. In an odd way though, it
> wasn't as strange as I thought it would be. Spent the rest of the
> weekend chilling out – all this *Oprah* stuff is exhausting!

Too right. What an extraordinary Saturday. After they'd disappeared into the sunset, I sat down and was immediately told to get
up and help with bath time. More blue eyes to deal with. They
were tired little blue eyes now. Would my children one day sit and
discuss me with each other the way we'd all talked about our
father that afternoon? But Joseph and Helen had grown up with
him and I'd only spoken to him once on the phone. Joseph Junior
later expressed it thoughtfully if somewhat obliquely. It was in the
context of his own relationship with the man, his own perspective
on events and the unintended consequences that make life what
life is. He said, 'For me, the story began in the middle. It started
with a revelation that has sent me back into the past and forced
me to think about the future. It's a story that has made me reflect
on what's important to me.' It was an exciting thought that I had
been a catalyst for something, but worrying as to what the effects
might be. We were all shaken up.

After bath and story time I wandered downstairs to get a beer,
open a packet of dry-roasted nuts and find some Saturday-night
bubble gum for the eyes. Not hard. The telephone rang. It's true
what they say. A sign of middle age is when the phone rings on a
Saturday night and you hope it's a wrong number. Wearily, testily,
emphatically I answered.

'Hello.'

'Hello, mate, it's Mark. What a great result for you.' I was
confused for a moment. Was my friend psychic? How did he
know what had happened and how it had gone?

'What do you mean?'

'The game.' Of course. Scotland had been playing the Faeroe
Isles in that easy-peasy Euro qualifier. I told him I didn't know the

result and asked him what had happened. Disbelievingly, he continued, and with evident relish. He is English and he was gloating.

'Well done. You got a plucky draw,' he said. I knew what was coming now. It'd been another Scotland football catastrophe; this time against the minnows of the European game. You know what?

I didn't give a flying fish.

SIXTEEN

The Dancing Detective

Very soon after this, the conscientious son-in-law made contact. Patrick thinks the world of my father and my father loves him like a son. There are secrets and confidences that Joseph has shared with Patrick and Patrick alone. They have a special bond. An adept pourer of oil on troubled family waters, he was at it again. An e-mail broke the ice and then we spoke. It was one of those long telephone conversations, the duration of which you only start to realize when your left ear gets overheated and uncomfortable. If our ears were hot – Joseph's were burning.

Patrick has a darting mind, a dry wit and a good heart. He's an adroit psychologist and his instincts are all too often right on the button. We shadow boxed with quips, cracks and niceties then the bell went and he got tore in.

'He would love to meet you and your wife and children but he understands if this isn't possible.'

'Of course it's possible. There is nothing I want more. But it's – well it's a bit complicated, isn't it?' I said. The complicated bit of course being a forty-year marriage to another woman albeit after I'd been born and whisked away.

Patrick went on, 'He confided all this to me recently. Nicky, he has thought of you every day.' I thought of him thinking of me every day. It had truly never occurred to me this might be the case. And if it was the case, were his thoughts idle or painful? Did he casually wonder what I was? Who I was? Where I was? Or was he stricken with longing?

'Patrick, it's important for him to know that this is about the present. I don't give a fuck about what he did or didn't do forty-two years ago.' Patrick leapt back in, even more animated.

'I realize that. He feels guilty though. Try and put yourself in his position.' He said it as if he were talking to a ten year old. I've grown to enjoy his occasional and very endearing tone of utter exasperation.

'This shouldn't be about guilt,' I insisted. 'I don't want him to get out the rosary when we meet.'

'He won't do that,' avowed Patrick and we laughed.

My new friend regained his train of thought. 'Since he told me all of this, I've watched him cry about you. I've talked to him about you and he said, "Tell him I love him and I'm sorry I wasn't there for him." '

Love? There for me? Sorry? Stella used to say that word sometimes. 'Sorry.' I don't really think it was an apology so much as a plea for atonement. As for Joseph, surely there was more to his regret than one little boy lost. I must have been bundled up with a whole lifetime of it. For him I was a blank bit of paper. A chance to try again. A chance to be a better father.

Patrick's voice was impassioned. 'He loves all his children so much but sometimes he's not very good at expressing it. But he loves you all.'

The phrase 'you all' went like a jolt through my heart. Now I felt like a ten-year-old child. It's the 'regressional' thing as Esther calls it. You're transported to a point in time when that's just what you were. A child. Forever a child within. Was I one of his children? I realized I was – technically. I already had a daddy. But then, somewhere deep down I'd always harboured the notion of another one. A life of alternatives.

Patrick's role in all this seemed heroic to me, well over and above the call of duty. My God, I thought. How every family could do with a Patrick. I asked him why.

'How come you're the great galvanizer? The driving force in this. Why do you care so much? I can hear you do.'

'Because I love him,' he answered. That stopped me in my tracks. But there was more. 'And also because,' he paused for a second, 'I understand this better than anyone else. I know how you feel. I only found out who my real father was when I was in my early twenties. I met him. He wasn't interested.'

'Fucking hell. What happened?'

'I'll tell you sometime.' He sounded wretched. The subject was dropped. At that moment I suddenly felt close to my father Joseph. There was a man who was interested. He was desperate to meet me. I felt very lucky. Things don't always work out like that.

Since Joseph's message on the answerphone, my whole search for him had rapidly and completely transformed from something abstract to something very real and raw. These were living feeling human beings not make-believe people in the imaginary world of N. Campbell aged forty-one and a half. Patrick was rattling it all out like a Gatling gun. 'He wanted to just see you before he dies and he knows he has made mistakes.' His voice was full of protective, even fatherly, love for his father-in-law.

I changed tack. 'What's he like?'

Patrick answered without a second's pause, but his reply was still considered.

'In my book he's a brilliant man. Bright, though he's manipulative – but that's been an occupational hazard. He was a detective, for crying out loud. He's witty and is an absolute charmer.' I thought, 'yeek. Sounds like a game show host'. Then I remembered. Yeek! I was a game show host. If he is adept at wrapping people round his little finger, I wondered whether Patrick was dangling on the end of a stubby little digit. I concluded that if he was, he was perfectly aware of it. What a confusing mixture it all sounded though: manipulative, brilliant, selfish, wonderful. I wasn't about to meet the Dalai Lama that's for sure but it sounded like Joseph Leahy would be well worth getting to know.

Somehow we had to find a way to meet up. We might have to mount a clandestine operation and fly to Belfast and meet him there or maybe nip across to Dublin. I had visions of a rendezvous in the same hotel where I'd met Stella so many years before. I felt guilty now. The guilt was catching. Maybe those Irish genes had acquired some Catholic characteristics. How the hell was this going to go down with Mary, his wife? Three kids and nearly forty years of marriage – then this revelation from the past. A long festering secret whose ugly mug flitted across British network television once a week. A baby's cry which boomed out on medium-wave radio every weekday morning.

*

The next morning a brown envelope arrived containing a note from Joseph Junior. He had enclosed three photographs. The first I examined was of my father. There he was. In the uniform of the Garda Siochana. The guards. The Irish police. He must have been twenty-two or three. Not displeased with himself. Confident verging on cocky. He was standing on his own facing the camera but you could see the swagger. He looked proud as punch. He looked kind of familiar but not how I expected my father to look. Later I showed the photo to a close friend. After the briefest glance he said, 'Oh yea. He looks like your father.' I couldn't see it. All I really saw was a young Irish copper with more than a passing resemblance to the bloke who used to sing lead vocals with Depeche Mode. When I was playing their records on local radio, never something I greatly relished, I was twenty-three. If I had fathered a child with a much older and unmarriable woman back then, what would I have done? As you can imagine, I looked at the photo a few times. I put it in my wallet and showed it to a few people, some of whom didn't have an inkling I was even adopted and clearly thought me a bit odd suddenly whipping out an old picture of my dad. Even when I explained, it didn't mean much. I needed to tell people though. I had to share it. It was just all so staggering.

The second photo was of a couple – my father and his future wife – taken around Christmas 1962. They were on the steps of a building at night and there were other party goers in the background. They must have been on the steps leading into a dance hall. It looked like a jolly old time was being had by all. Everyone was in their glad rags. She was very good looking with a great figure and what looked like red hair, like Helen's. He had a half smile, and a half bottle of something was just visible, peaking out of his coat pocket. He looked confident as anything, gazing right down the barrel of the lens, and she looked carefree, laughing and tossing her head backwards and her face away from the camera. They looked boozed up, full of beans and ready to dance some more. The night looked young. So did they. The future was bright. I looked at the dog-eared photograph and I understood a little more. They were two young people with their lives ahead of them. How else could he have dealt with the news of a baby son? What else could he have done? I wondered how Mary would have reacted then if she'd known the secret he was hiding. The laughter would have died. On that very night in another part of Dublin a matron was alone in her quarters. In another country a little boy was asleep in his cot.

There was a third photograph in the envelope. It showed another couple, a stride further back in time. They were smartly dressed. He was an open-faced stocky-looking man in a smart suit. She had sharper features and fairer hair. They both looked happy in that rather austere old-fashioned way. It seemed as if they were threatening to burst into beaming happiness but a sense of formality and propriety intervened. These were my grandparents on their wedding day. It's a strange feeling staring right into those old images, right into another world. Something awakens. Some of those genes are in me. Genes from that little Catholic fellow looking dapper as a dandy in his suit, about to get married in a bitterly divided Northern Irish town. He had strikingly long eyelashes. You could see them head on. I wandered through to the living room and one of my little girls was asleep on the sofa as she recovered from the flu. She has the very blond hair her mother had when she was very small and still strives in vain to maintain. And there they were, in stark contrast to the fairest of locks, those long dark eyelashes. My grandfather was winking at me.

The emotional tsunami continued. That weekend we went round *en famille* to Helen and Patrick's and had a great Sunday. They welcomed us like family. Tina and Helen got on very well and the fact that Helen was my new-found half-sister soon became irrelevant to them both. Our children played well together, all of them sweetly ignorant they had a grandfather in common.

As we ate lunch at an Italian restaurant round the corner Patrick remarked, 'You've got his hands. Identical.' I looked down at my stubby fingers and cursed the blessed digit gene.

I remembered Stella's long slender fingers and recalled noticing them in the Dublin hotel when we'd met. I'd always laid the finger of blame on my father. When I'm on the TV Tina always implores me to keep my hands down. 'Don't wave your stubby little fingers about. People will laugh.'

After strolling back through the park on that darkening November afternoon, we had tea and chocolate in their sitting room. Out came the photo albums. More grinning relatives and more of Joseph. I saw him in his fifties at Helen's wedding to Patrick. 'He's a good-looking devil, isn't he?' said Helen with a certain emphasis on the D word. 'Although it's gone a bit now after the cancer.' The look on her face and brevity of her words betrayed a lot – the enormous love of a daughter for her father, but tinged round the edges with bitterness and resentment at the disappointments and anxieties of childhood that never quite leave us. But the sense that there really was something wonderful about Joseph emanated from both Helen and Patrick.

Within a week the game changed completely. The air was clear. Joseph had broken the news to Mary and she hadn't merely accepted it as something to be borne with stoicism, which I'd feared would be the best-case scenario, she had actually received the news with remarkable good grace. This was all the more surprising given the manner in which he broke it to her. He didn't exactly do it with the finesse of a trained counsellor. Perfunctory would be a word. 'By the way I've got a son' was about the extent of it. He blurted it out in the kitchen one day. Despite this she embraced the news. She realized it had all happened before they met. As ever, she got solid and loving support from her children too. As Joseph Junior said to me in one rapturous call, 'Mum has been just amazing.' The exciting revelation of a hitherto unknown sibling overrode any resentment towards Joseph for keeping this locked away for so long. My other sister, Joseph's third child, just put her arms round her father and sighed. 'Whatever makes you happy, Dad. If you are happy I'm happy.' With the family reconciled, the road was clear for our first meeting since the moment of conception on the couch – but you'd have to be a Vatican hardliner to count that as a meeting.

Patrick, the family facilitator, got working on a plan of action. Helen would be thirty-nine at the beginning of December, in just a couple of weeks time, in fact, and he was arranging a surprise party for her. Would we come?

'Are you sure, Patrick. You know I have just stepped into your—'

'Shut the fuck up. You are coming. And so are Joseph and Mary. They fly over from Dublin on the Friday. He comes over to your place on the Saturday, you spend the afternoon alone with each other and then later we all meet at ours. All Helen's friends will be there on Saturday night and we'll all get pissed. It'll be fantastic. You can meet Mary.' I ran it through my head.

'Joseph visits me in the afternoon – terrifying. I join a get-together of family and close friends later that night – surreal.'

I have had some pretty wild weekends in my dim and distant past but this one promised to be off the scale. Whoever wrote the script had a fertile imagination. Part of the addictive quality of the whole searching and finding process is the sheer excitement of it. It's terrifying but irresistible. For good or ill, life is never dull. The psychological extreme sport was about to move into a new league. I fastened my safety belt.

In the days leading up to the encounter, the now familiar whirlwind of nerves, excitement and a myriad confused emotions were whipping round my mind and body. In some ways it was more intense than ever before. I was about to reach the summit. No wonder it was sometimes hard to breathe. The journey, in one sense, would soon be complete. More prosaically, I was about to put the final piece in the jigsaw puzzle. Mother, sister, brother, more sisters and now my father. Saturday came. That buzzer again. Oh who is it? Which long-lost parent now?

The children were close by my side. They were protecting me like secret service spooks round the President, except my retinue didn't have a clue what their job was. In he came. He didn't look like the photos. He was older. He looked like a man who had battled cancer and was defiantly hanging on to what he once was – how he still saw himself in his mind's eye if not in the pitiless mirror. He still had a real presence but the chemotherapy and surgery had taken their toll on his neck, hair and teeth. The hair was an inch or so too long down the back and the suit and tie a tad scruffy. He was about five foot ten, an inch or two shorter than me, and initially I didn't think he looked anything like me. But then he wasn't twenty-three. He wasn't forty-two. He was sixty-five. Then another thought struck deep. This was the first time I'd seen a father whose flesh was mine. Perhaps this was me in twenty-three years' time. When Dad lay in the hospice bed dying of cancer it was a vision of Dad in the present not one of me in the future. Seeing Joseph was different. Had the grim reaper sneaked through the door and left his calling card for both of us? If you know your biological parents you know your genetic roadmap. You don't have a blank sheet in front of you. All of a sudden, neither did I.

He put his arms out. I felt my body stiffen. Just a touch of rigor mortis maybe. I glanced helplessly at Tina as he embraced me. She looked at me. Joseph looked at her. He remembers seeing the tears in her eyes. I was afraid. He wanted to hug his boy child. I wanted to shake this old man's hand. He looked at me and said, 'Sorry.' It seemed heartfelt and something he obviously thought he had to say. It was how Patrick said he felt. But it was so uncalled for. Suddenly the significance of that incredible moment fell on me like an avalanche and I froze. Months later he asked me. 'What were you afraid of when I came through the door?'

'You can't just go round hugging strange old men,' I said. We laughed. But that was much later.

'I thought it was your Protestant Edinburgh upbringing,' he joked. 'You were just being a fucking Scottish Calvinist.'

'It was predestined I was going to be afraid then, wasn't it. I couldn't help it.' Relaxed conversations and easy exchanges like that were to come and, frankly, they came quickly. We got on and it didn't take long.

My three little girls, ranging from one to four, were wondering who on earth this was. Breagha, my eldest, later suggested he looked 'a little bit like a wizard'. Lilla was two and a half at the time. She doesn't give her hugs away cheaply but when she does they're enchanting. She looked up at the stranger, her grandfather, and stretched out her arms. Tina and I looked on in amazement. He lifted her up and gave her a big cuddle. She returned it with interest. By now Tina was in floods of tears. I was completely bamboozled. Throughout the afternoon Joseph really bonded with Lilla. Of all our children she looks most like me. Was he subconsciously playing out a role he'd missed out on? Was she the little child he'd never known?

As to my initial frostiness, months later Joseph made more characteristically forthright observations. 'After the Calvinist bollocks, I soon saw the Celtic side was the dominant one. When I looked at Tina with tears in her eyes I knew this was a genuscene.' The scene moved over to the sitting area. An early-afternoon kickoff Celtic versus Rangers game was on the box in the background and I was loath to turn it off. It gave me a grip on reality and I clung on to that like a safety blanket. We cursorily talked about football. He had a passing interest in it but no more. Celtic versus

Rangers – the Glasgow derby – is sectarian tribal rivalry funnelled into a fast and furious football match. He understood all that only too well given where he came from but said that Gaelic football was more his thing.

'I played representative Under Nineteen but gave it up because I kept getting clattered by the big fellas. I was skilful enough but not the right build.'

'I was like that with rugby at school,' I said. 'I loved taking the kicks. Hated getting the knocks.'

'Exactly.' He nodded. This chit-chat about the games we played was rich in subtext. I noticed his body. He was like me physically. We had the same build. I was his son. It was rather like that superb scene in *Annie Hall* when Woody Allen and Diane Keaton are exchanging pleasantries but the real meaning and agenda of all they say is spelt out in the subtitles that appear on the screen. The one that kept coming up for me was, 'Fucking hell. This man is my father.'

We talked more about his family and his background.

'I've got two sisters up North still. I told them about you.'

'What did they say?'

Well, I said to Evangeline, you heard of a guy called Nicky Campbell on British radio and sometimes the telly over there? BBC? She said yes she had. "I've been following his career for years," she said. "There is something I like about him you know. I've always felt a connection to him. Why do you ask?" I said, "Well, you're his auntie."'

Before long the auntie with the dubious taste and I were corresponding. Soon after that we would meet.

'How does it feel to be a Paddy then?' It sounded like one he'd thought of earlier. I looked across at his quizzical expression and devilish twinkle. I think a pair of invisible half-moon spectacles grew on my nose and my reply blew back on the draught of a Scottish East Coast winter chill. 'I'm from Edinburgh,' I said. Miss Jean Brodie had made an appearance. It was all very well discovering a brand-new past but I had to hang on to myself. Who I was. Who I had always been.

'I adore Scotland,' I continued. 'We have a little place in the north-west and one day we'd like to live there all the time. Get away from this unrelenting madness.' I felt a bit precious as I said that, given that the house we were sitting in and the rustic bolthole were effectively purchased thanks to the unrelenting madness I was decrying. Joseph engaged with the idea though.

'I can see you doing that. You are a mountain man at heart. I love looking after the horses back home and after all that time as a cop you know what my greatest pleasure would be?'

'What would that be?'

'My greatest pleasure,' he said, enunciating slowly, 'is standing in a green field and looking all around me as I pirouette.'

I imagined him pirouetting. Free of the cares of the world – that magisterial Leahy nose taking in all the scents on the wind.

He looked at me. Hansen, Lineker and Lawrenson were summing up the first half in the background but the volume was so low, their Wildean repartee was barely audible.

Then he said in his soft Northern Irish brogue, 'Tell me, Nicky, did you ever look at yourself in the mirror and wonder, What does my old fella look like?'

'I did.' I looked at him again. Every time felt like the first. His eyes were moist.

'These days I look in the mirror sometimes and don't recognize what I see.'

Tina came in from the kitchen. 'Do you want tea or coffee?'

I know the situation was extraordinary. I know I'm biased. But Joseph struck me as one of the most intriguing and remarkable people I'd ever met. There was a mystery about him. Patrick had mentioned his manipulative nature being part and parcel of his job as a cop but in a way this sense of a double life, this complex and unresolved internal world is the very thing that makes him wonderful. There are struggles going on in that head of his. Conflicts. Troubles. He is a man trying to come to terms with his life and make sense of it as we all should do sooner or later. But he has a wicked sense of humour, a passionate interest in the world around him and a deep insight into the world he grew up in. Of course, for Joseph and me there's no baggage. Ours is a relationship unencumbered by the past. I never grew up with him. It's easier for me. It's easier for him. We have ears for each other. We have time for each other. If we'd known each other for more than forty years it might be different. But I've come to know that a conversation with Joseph will always add something to life. I don't agree with everything he says but he's too smart to be a zealot and he understands the world all the more because he knows he's made mistakes.

The second half of the football was under way. As the Celtic–Rangers game roared on in the background we got on to politics and religion. In microcosm it was there before us on the small screen. It was in the faces of the baying and hysterical supporters willing their heroes to give them a Saturday-night superiority over the other lot.

I glanced at the TV. I remembered my boyhood passion for

Celtic and thought of the irony that they represented my father's tribe. Was that in the genes? Was there a Celtic FC gene embedded deep within the recesses of my Celtic consciousness? I could hear the common sense Anglo-Saxon voice of my late adoptive grandpa: 'Bunkum and balderdash.'

As Rangers were mounting an attack, Joseph did too.

'That fucking Lambeg drum the Protestants had. We could never understand why it was necessary to beat those fucking drums. The badoom badoom badoom constantly there.'

'You had your drums too, didn't you?'

'Not like their fucking drums. I'm talking about sectarianism – I remember the dole queues in my home town and the ones in the queues were all your own people. Very few of the opposite number. They had all the municipal jobs – post offices, library. If you were a Catholic you would just have to stand – they would get served first – you'd wait like a black man in Alabama. They knew you were a Catholic from your name and where you lived. All these positions were controlled and held by the Unionist people and there was a sort of nepotism there in the sense that no way would you get a job where a Protestant had one before you.'

'Did that fill you with resentment? Give you a sense of inferiority?'

'It did. You've got to put yourself in that position. I had a very definite sense of inferiority – absolutely – because of what I saw around me. That and when I used to go out at night to go to a dance – or get into my father's car and go to a dance – in those days it was traditional to get into your car and drive forty, fifty, sixty, a hundred miles to a dance because there were big marquees all over the country. I used to come South. I remember one occasion

I drove to Roscommon to a dance – 112 miles to a dance – crowd of guys in the car, get a few jars – into the dance and the dances at that time would last from 6 o'clock at night till three in the morning. Crazy. And at that time in the fifties when you went about in the car you'd be stopped by the B specials – and you were treated like fucking dirt. I remember being stopped by a neighbour of mine. He lived about four doors from where we lived. We were friendly. One of his sisters went nursing with my sister. We were stopped by Alec-Alec Pettigrew – good Irish name that.' Joseph laughed at his sarcastic aside. He went on. 'Alec stopped me in the car – I'll never forget this – and said, "Where are you going?"'

' "Hello, Alec, how are you?"'

' "Where are you going?"'

' "I'm going home."'

' "Where's your driving license?"'

' "Alec! It's me." I used to be friendly with him. We were fucking neighbours.'

'Can you understand why they were like that?'

'I can. I understand their attitude. They had a siege mentality.'

'And if you'd been one of them you would have had a siege mentality.'

'You're probably right. But that's my perspective. My father – your grandfather – could never quite understand it. None of the big families would have us Catholics working inside the house. We did the menial stuff in the grounds. My father used to pick one girl up in his car and take her to Mass and she was a rare exception. She was allowed to work as a maid. He'd despair at it all. He was such a kind and gentle man.'

Joseph was desperate to explain to me. I was eager to hear. 'Put it this way – there is a difference between bigotry and sectarianism. Bigotry is more religious intolerance and it can be eradicated with a bit of education.

'Sectarianism has an element of bigotry in it, but also an abiding racial and political hatred. I've met bigoted Protestants – you can deal with them, their siege mentality apart. They're always looking over the gate with a pike or gun. The sectarian is another matter. As far as they see it, a Fenian is a Fenian is a Fenian. You will always be a croppy boy.'

'What's that?' I not unreasonably asked. 'A croppy boy?'

'Back in 1798. They were supporters of Emmet. They cut their hair short. The women wore green ribbons in their ankles and in their hair. There's an old ballad. My grandmother used to sing it to me with tears streaming down her face.'

> And as I mounted the platform high
> My aged father was standing by;
> My aged father did me deny
> And the name he gave me was the Croppy Boy.
>
> It was in Dungannon this young man died
> And in Dungannon his body lies.
> And you good people that do pass by.
> Oh shed a tear for the Croppy Boy.

Another astonishing Saturday afternoon. Hearing him talk was fascinating for me. It was straight out of one of my treasured books, but better. This was from my father's lips. He was a man with theories, ideas and thought-provoking conversation. Moving away from the North and joining the police down South was the best thing he ever did. He got away from the stifling atmosphere of hatred and, as he saw it, zero prospects. He told me how liberating it was to go South where nobody ever mentioned another man's religion. Maybe that was because the vast majority were of the same religion. His own children grew up a long way from the suffocating sectarianism of his youth. They knew a very different life. I knew a different world.

I changed the tune. 'You like to dance then. Going miles to all those dances.'

'I love dancing,' he said. I'd found a genetic anomaly here. A real mismatch. Where were my dancing genes? I am the world's worst. Whenever my wife wants an instant belly laugh she switches on the radio and gets me to shake my funkless booty. I've got a pretty good sense of rhythm but just can't translate it to the feet or body or wherever you're meant to transfer it to. Maybe it is that Calvinist reserve.

'There is a difference you know,' Joseph returned to his main theme. 'And there is a physical difference – it is not in my imagination. I can identify the Celtic side by their actions – if they talk – and a lot of times the Protestants haven't got Irish features.'

'What about me? My features?' I queried. He answered without looking.

'You've got them. The shape of your face and the shape of your eyes – if you visited the west of Ireland you would see your prototype everywhere.' A Calvinist croppy boy – that's me.

The door buzzer went. The already surreal afternoon was about to enter the realms of *Alice in Wonderland*. A friend of Tina's had turned up on spec with her husband and kids in tow. They live in the country and Tina was loath to despatch them straight back into their people carrier. She invited them in. All of a sudden there seemed to be people everywhere. They're what might be described as probable subscribers to *The Field* – a little bit county. And we're not talking County Fermanagh.

In they trooped like a pack of Labradors. It was a bad call by Tina on the day I met my father but as she reminds me, when it comes to the overall bad call tally I'm still in a commanding lead. Celtic–Rangers had finished. Now we had Celtic–Sloane Rangers. I could have done without them on that afternoon. As Joseph later told me, so could he.

At the time I just apologized for the mayhem. Eventually Tina's friends left and we all began to gear up for the second leg of the incredible day – Helen's surprise party that evening. Joseph said his goodbyes to the girls and we put him in a minicab back over the river to North London. We just about had time to catch our breath, get ourselves ready and whizz up to Patrick and Helen's for the revelries. Before we left I downed a very large Malt – I badly needed some Scotch courage.

'What will we say if people ask us who we are? Helen's friends? If they say how do you know Helen?' Tina wondered as we approached their house.

'Sod it. I'll just say I'm her long-lost brother.' We went with that plan. It was a great conversation stopper and it was a happy if drunken evening. There were loads of people there.

'I recognize you,' said a charmingly well-oiled blonde. 'How do you know Helen?'

'I'm her brother,' said the by now slightly pissed brother.

'But you're Scottish,' she pointed out.

'I'm adopted,' I announced with finality, and I swigged from my Michelob.

'Why the hell are you behaving like Clint Eastwood?' asked Tina.

There was a band playing sixties classics in the halls. They were good. As we mingled we could detect the whiff of expensive perfumes and aftershaves intermingling with the occasional blast of a Silk Cut. Women in their late thirties, forties and fifties were squeezed into very tight dresses. Joseph had said it that afternoon – when we look in the mirror, the older we get, the less we recognize what we see. Having children we rarely get out any more anyway – certainly not to parties – so this was a most unusual affair for us on even the most mundane level.

I made a beeline for Joseph's wife Mary and spoke to her for a long time. She is a good woman. The red hair has turned to white and the carefree laughter has been tempered by forty years. But there was a lively sense of humour still thriving.

'I can see you're like Helen.' She smiled.

'What do you mean?'

'You're both so bossy.' We had one jarring moment though. She asked me how my mum was and I told her all the news from Edinburgh. She looked blankly at me.

'No. Your mum!' Mary had meant Stella. I only thought of Mum. My only mum. For a minute I felt alone.

At the end of the night as I was thinking about getting back home to bed I glanced through to the living room where a crowd of people were still dancing. There, right in the thick of it was Joseph, dancing with my wife. He was nimble, light on his feet and he was charming her. She was tossing her head back in laughter. I thought of the picture of the young couple outside the dance hall in Dublin in 1962. I thought of the dances he'd travelled miles and miles to attend when he was young; he'd come a hell of a long way for this one. And then I remembered something he'd said to me earlier in that extraordinary day.

'My greatest pleasure is standing in a green field and looking all around me as I pirouette.'

SEVENTEEN

Joseph and Stella

Joseph loved to dance. But Stella, the older woman he met outside the police station in Dublin, was never keen. It's not that she didn't like to dance. She adored taking to the floor and tripping the light fantastic in one of those flamboyant outfits of hers that categorically stated 'there's more to me than meets the eye'. It just that she didn't want to go dancing with him. Perhaps she thought he was a bit young to be seen out with. It might look unseemly for a woman in her position. Maybe she recognized the other problem – the irresolvable religious difference that doomed their relationship. It's possible he just wasn't a young man for going out with. He was one for staying in with.

All the action was at her place, he remembers. And how.

'I used to go to the side door in her digs in the hospital. She'd cycle down and meet me at the gate. It was a little wrought-iron gate at the side of the hospital with an old lock. I've got a vivid vision of her on her bike one particular time. I can see her now – the shape of her. She was wearing a polo neck and skirt just above the knee. That sight has never left me.'

I was transported by this image of a nurse and a policeman in

1960 Dublin carrying on their clandestine affair. Him arriving at dusk and her meeting him in the gathering gloom for an evening of candle-lit romance. They didn't seem like my parents. They were actors in my film. Suddenly it got a PG certificate.

'You know, Nicky . . .' I could tell the confessor father was on the point of significant disclosure. 'Every time I met your mother the switch went on. I couldn't wait to get into bed with her.'

'Amazing,' I lamely replied, not knowing what to say but thinking of the girls and women I'd known since I was about seventeen who'd affected me like that. When there'd been a volcanic chemistry. When we couldn't wait to rip each other's clothes off. They were few and far between but I remembered every moment. I thought of the face of one. Staring at me. Burning through me. Is that what it was like for him? Then I thought of Stella now. Frail and elderly. He was thinking of another Stella.

'There wasn't a time I met her I didn't have sex with her. I couldn't pass her without wanting her.'

It was through such frank and astonishing conversations that Joseph and I became close. As we got closer our conversations became franker. The relationship quickly fell into place. We were comfortable with each other and found a genuine rapport. Over the years Stella had hinted at what I later found to be the case.

'He was intelligent. Easy to get along with, I would say.' Now he was also a man who thought that after 'forty years in the dark' I had a right to know. The more we talked over the next few months, the more he told me, the more I realized that having faced and beaten cancer he didn't care any more for the dark corners of the vault. I was helping him shine a light on his own life.

There was none of Stella's instinctive reticence. Mind you, he hadn't been through what she had. But for the last ten years he's been a chronic insomniac and the wee small hours of the morning can be pitiless. His whole life tumbles down on him every night. Who he knew, what he did, what he got right, what he got wrong. What he wished he'd done. What he told me was related with dignity, and a paternal imperative to explain. Sometimes he laughed. Sometimes he cringed. Occasionally he was astonishingly candid. Mostly he was his garrulous confident self but at times his voice dropped to a miserable forlorn whisper.

He'd love to have danced with Stella more but Joseph does remember going to one function – one of her famous dos. It was a Saturday tea dance at the hospital. Stella, the famous party organizer, was rushed off her frantic feet though; far too busy to spend any time talking to him.

'I said, "I'll buzz off then and see you later." She said, "Yes. Nice to see you here, Joseph. I'll see you sometime." It was a private relationship. I used to say let's go here or there but she never wanted to.'

When Stella and Joseph did step out together it was to classical concerts or museums, where idle tongues were less likely to jump to the correct conclusion. Once, maybe twice, they sat in a dark nook of a quiet pub. A couple of times they went to the pictures. Stella remembers the films – Bergman's *Wild Strawberries* being one. Joseph doesn't. His mind must have been on other things. He was kept well away from her family. He'd heard of Stella's brother John as he cycled for Ireland but had never met him. Stella's sister had no idea about Joseph. He was none of her family's business. She was unknown to his. They were in their own bubble. They found their common ground and that's where they danced. Nothing else and no one else mattered, least of all the problems strewn in their path. But they weren't looking around or ahead. Only at each other. How long did this secret affair last? 'Certainly for one whole summer,' said Joseph. 'A year all in all.'

'At the weekends I'd head back North again.' She was the first relationship he had since leaving Northern Ireland, 'apart from the casual ones'. I can well understand how seeing this relatively important and singularly impressive older woman chimed with the wonderful new sense of freedom he found south of the border. She was a symptom and a cause of it. It was the freedom of a young man starting his career in new places having broken free of the sectarianism, prejudice and perils of his own home town. I remember leaving Edinburgh at seventeen to go to university in Aberdeen. I might as well have been going to a different continent. That's how it felt. Life was fresh and exciting. There were amazing discoveries at every turn and a thrilling feeling of empowerment. I was in control. This new life was all the sweeter for Joseph because of what he left behind.

What were his first impressions of my birth mother? A fellow policeman introduced him to Stella and the three of them stood there chatting about this, that and the other outside the station. While passing the time of day, chewing the cud with banter and bonhomie, two of the crowd were already thinking beyond the moment. 'We were all laughing a lot. And I would say there was an instant affection' said Joseph.

'Is this your usual beat?' she asked.

'Well it is for the next week or two.'

'Drop by for a coffee.'

'I will.' On went the switch.

Joseph was flattered that an older woman like Stella was taking an interest in a 'punk' like him. 'She was stimulating. She was interesting. The conversation down the police station wasn't up to fucking much, I tell you.' This young man was an avid reader with an interest in culture and music instilled in him by his mother. He'd left the North to better himself and he had ambitions and aspirations. He also had letters after his name, according to the M183 adoption form Stella had to complete at the time of my birth. At the very least he was, in Stella's words, 'doing this degree thing. Doing extra university study – kind of extra mural – nighttimes.'

I asked Joseph about all this. I heard hesitancy. He sounded defensive.

'I was going to before I got promoted to detective. I was intending to. But it didn't work out. I'd gone through all the formalities. I'd made representations.' He'd embroidered to Stella, she'd embellished further to the aoption aency and in time a boy with dreams became a man of letters. The sixty-six-year-old man sounded full of regret that those dreams never came true. Finding his confident voice again, he looked back in vindication.

'I considered myself better educated than the rest of them. More alive. More appreciative of life. I couldn't wait to get out of uniform.'

'You'd like to have been an academic, wouldn't you?' I said.

'I would. I really really would.' I could hear the longing of a twenty-three year old. 'There were no opportunities for a beatendown Republican like me. But all my children went to university and got degrees. I'm proud of that. All four of them.' He included me. I thought of Dad's beaming smile at my graduation in Aberdeen. We went for a sumptuous lunch, then he and Mum drove home to Edinburgh and I shot up to the local radio station with my guitar to record a jingle. I was twenty-one.

> Shopping is simplicity
> So easy to feed your family
> There's a whole new world of shopping to enter
> In your local Farm Food Freezer Centre.

I can understand why he wanted to impress Stella. She impressed him tremendously. Her mother considered herself 'a cut above the buttermilk' and Stella was cut from the very same cloth. She was the boss and she knew it. 'She was aware of her status, all right. Didn't seem that concerned or nervous that I was there. She knew no one would bother us. They left her to her own devices,' recalled Joseph. He'd admired her blue uniform and matron's hat and examined the badges she'd earned and wore with pride. He compared them with those of his sister Evangeline who'd trained as a nurse. Stella was top of the tree – quite a catch. And as for her private rooms in the hospital, Joseph remembers them in great detail. They were impressively spacious. 'There was a record player and a lot of records by Puccini, Verdi and John McCormack the Irish tenor. I was geared up for all that stuff with my mother being so musical.'

I remembered the first time I'd seen my father's name on that adoption form alongside as much detail as Stella knew or cared to give. One passing comment, hurriedly and officiously scribbled down by the pen-pushing social worker, came back to me. 'Father's mother very musical.'

These were the rooms where the love duet from *Madame Butterfly* filled the air.

There was a huge living room with cream drapes, a large bathroom and a third room where she kept all her clothes. The floors were 'monastic', according to Joseph. 'Pure wooden floors and big brown leather chairs and a huge brown sofa. I remember that particularly well.'

'Why's that?' I asked.

'Why do you think, you bollox?'

What was it about that particular entanglement that stuck in both their minds? Stella had rather shocked me once by precisely identifying the occasion. 'You just know' she'd explained with a mixture of impatience and coyness.

Joseph has a vivid memory of the making of me. Nothing too coy about him. 'Jeez. That dark brown leather sofa with its sunken buttons. I remember everything about it. She was wearing her uniform. She had a badge. It was annoying me so I took the uniform off.' Not so taken with the badge on this occasion. 'I remember her laughing. I was unbuttoning it and she was laughing her head off.'

As Stella once said to Esther, 'Some people are more passionate than others.'

It was very strange picturing my biological parents in the throes of this erotic frenzy. The scene of the crime. The very altar on which the sacrament was proffered and sacrifice made. Have you asked either of your parents about that sublime or awkward moment? The where and when of your conception? And if you were so bold could they even remember? That split second. That one in many millions. Every time a man ejaculates there is enough sperm there to inseminate every woman in Western Europe, I've read but never counted. One was enough for one woman in Dublin. And just their luck that the product of that microscopic swimming feat ends up writing it down. But why did it happen? How could they possibly have let me be conceived? It's a question a lot of people have demanded the answer to.

Rubber Jonnies? 'You couldn't get them unless you were linked to organized crime or the mafia or something. I was a good Catholic boy.'

'How did it happen, Joseph? What on earth were you thinking?' I realized what I was saying and immediately rowed back – right to the other side of the shore. 'And thank goodness you were so irresponsible. What a great gift for modern man I've been.'

'You're right,' he deadpanned back. 'I performed a great service for human civilization, didn't I?' Conversations with Joseph seldom pause and never lull. I was thinking what a good rapport we had when he picked up in a very different tone: 'You know,' he said, having carefully weighed up whether or not to say what he was about to say, 'I've often thought it must have been a deliberate act on her part.'

'Go on.'

'These thoughts have come to me over the years. And at the time if I'm honest.

'I was surprised Stella wasn't more aware, what with her profession and experience. She must have known whether she was, you know . . .'

'At the right point of the cycle?' I suggested.

'Precisely.'

Joseph continued elucidating the conspiracy theory. 'Maybe it was deliberate. I've often thought that. If she didn't know the risk she was stupid and she certainly wasn't that.'

It takes two to tango – the dancing detective should know that – but I didn't reject his theory out of hand as the chauvinistic abdication of responsibility it at first seemed. And the reason I didn't is the manner in which he told me. It wasn't defiant or accusatory. It was quiet and pensive. It gnawed at him every so often. The idea suggested itself to him and he entertained it fleetingly before thinking better of it and ushering it off into the long dark night. But it would come back. And there was the balance of power in their affair to consider. He'd looked up to her. She was an education to him. She called the shots in their relationship. She was in charge. He'd thought she still was.

'Some people are just more passionate than others,' said Stella. It was a passion – or to put it bluntly a sex drive – that overrode sense and reason. Maybe she did want a baby badly and didn't even realize it. A subconscious yearning to have another life inside her after the torturous agony of giving away her baby daughter to total strangers. Like a junkie craving for the next fix despite the inevitable crash, withdrawal and misery to follow.

When evening fell, the night was for passion and yearning but by the time morning had broken the world was a very different place. The efficient and imperturbable matron put on her face, went to the hospital, rang for tea and sorted her underlings out. Days later she disappeared on the scheduled holiday with her sister. Joseph carried on policing the streets of Dublin, blissfully unaware there was a new life growing inside the fascinating woman. A few weeks later he'd been visiting her again and was on the point getting back to the station when she said, 'By the way, Joseph, I'm pregnant.'

Just like that. Like she was telling him her shift pattern for the next week or so.

'She never put any pressure on me – not one ounce. She told me about it and maybe she wanted me to respond. What with my age and situation I explained it to her. I set out my position.'

'That must have been a bad day.'

'It was.' His voice fell. He was right back there in front of the cream drapes – a young man standing beside the big brown sofa in a big old mess. As he recalled the moment, all the thoughts of shock and confusion revisited him. Stella had described him as having appeared 'discomfited'. It's not a bad word for how he sounded to me right then. It's Stella-speak for 'completely shell shocked'. She never was one for hyperbole. After saying his piece he said goodbye and left her rooms to seek the meretricious comfort of alcohol. A bottle of gin beckoned. She was having his baby. Maybe she'd done it deliberately. What price freedom now? Have another drink.

Stella knew what she had to do. She was in control. He knew she would deal with it. Joseph appealed for my understanding. He didn't need to.

'Put yourself in my shoes. Think of the insurmountable problems – keep my shoes on and put yourself back in these times. Social, religious, job prospects for the future. All these problems impacting on a twenty-four year old.'

I asked him if he had told anyone. His parents? 'No.'

His sisters? 'No.' I could hardly hear what he was saying as he went on.

'I mentioned you to other people. Confided in some.' There was a long pause.

'I lost contact with Stella . . . wasn't able to . . . find out where she went.' He then plucked a philosophical nugget from the jaws of guilt. Remorse turned to reason. It was like the progression from the Reformation to the Enlightenment. A hundred years in a split second.

'I could have come out of the situation with a fucking terrible guilt complex, you know. But all it was was just humanity at work.' He repeated the word like he was saying amen.

'Humanity.'

He is right and he was right to absolve himself. As I once said to Stella. If it wasn't for this very human mistake, my wonderful little girls wouldn't exist. So, here's to humanity. Here's to life. Here's to brown leather sofas.

In time she went to Edinburgh and he went on with his life. One of Stella's most surprising revelations had come in a long late-night telephone call two or three years before I began tracing Joseph. When I asked her if there had been passion between them after I was born – after she had returned to Dublin and gone back to the job that had been kept open for her while she recovered from her 'bronchitis'. The answer from Stella was a self-flagellating 'yes'. Joseph had no idea of this conversation. He knew nothing of what she told me. I wondered what he'd say. I asked him.

'Did you have sex after I'd been born and adopted?'

The answer was a mildly diffident 'yes'.

'Really.' I said this as if he'd told a moderately interesting fact about horses.

'It was a dominant feature of our relationship.'

'What about the baby?' I asked, immediately dissociating myself from the mucky triangle. It just sounded less pathetic than 'What about me?' He picked up the signal.

'The baby was a matter of fact – over and done. Stella had put it in another department. She was good at that. And so had I.'

Never mind the G spot. What about the G word?

'Did you feel guilty about that – after what had happened?' I felt like the Archbishop of Hypocrisy – as if I didn't know what became of guilt when the switch went on. It hid in the corner, averting its beady little eyes. It might try and get a look in later but not right now. Joseph took my question right on his Catholic chin.

'There was a religious pressure on me – from way back in my youth. The Catholic ethic seemed to bear down. It was right in a physical and natural way; wrong in a religious and theological one.'

'Humanity at work? What you said?'

'Just so.'

'And here I am. Your penance.'

'You're a sweet penance, Nicky. A sweet penance.' He meant it and I felt his love.

'Did you love Stella?'

If I was expecting a definitive yes or no answer I hadn't reckoned on his elliptical Celtic mind.

'Yes. I was very much flattered to have an older woman take such an interest.'

'But did you love her?' Hark at me. Paxman. The dancing detective's verbal jig continued.

'I was fascinated by her. We enjoyed each other physically and intellectually. It was the first time I could relate to someone on those two levels. Now that can easily be misconstrued as love. Some guys think it is and they are wrong. Some think it is and they're right.'

After Stella he met and fell in love with the beautiful red-haired girl I'd first seen in the photo on the steps of the dance and most recently encountered at Helen's surprise birthday party. My existence wasn't the kind of thing to be telling a fiancée. I stayed in the vault. They married. He made it out of uniform and they had a family. He made the grade. He lost touch with Stella. She'd moved to England to marry her poisoned gnome of a wife-beating husband John Newton and Joseph was climbing the ranks. He began thinking about me more and more when he had his own family. He never thought I'd find him because he never thought I'd want to.

At the end of one long call I asked him what he would say to Stella now if he saw her. His answer was tender. It was full of affection for mother and baby.

'I'd say, "How are ye, Stella? I'm glad it happened the way it happened. I met Nicky. It's come full circle. I'm glad the gap closed."'

What about the book? I suddenly thought. The bloody book of poetry Stella was always going on about.

'Do you remember one, Joseph?'

'The whole relationship was a real education for me. It was culture and music and museums. It wasn't just banging on the bed, you know.' He was indignant. I persevered.

'Yes, but a specific book. A book of poetry.' The lovely book of poetry and quotations. I could hear Stella's voice now: 'And if you see him you might ask for it back. He borrowed it and never returned it.'

'I was always borrowing books from her and vice versa. I'd take one and put it back on the shelf. That was very much the way of it.'

'Do you still have her book?'

'I can't remember the book she means.'

'Quotations and poetry. Do you still have it?'

He thought long and hard. He squeezed the last megabyte from his memory. His brain was on the rack. Then he said, 'No.' He said it like he'd wanted so much to say yes. I'd wanted him to say yes. I really needed this particular piece to effortlessly slot into my jigsaw puzzle. I wanted him to say yes, that he had it. Yes, that he still dipped into it. Or even just yes that he remembered it. I was batting for Stella here. This special book had always seemed so important to her and the fact that Joseph might still have it meant something after all this time. Never mind the baby you had. Forget about me, what about the book. The only thing she would regularly and consistently mention of their relationship was the only thing he seemed to have forgotten. He'd consigned it to oblivion. She had elevated it to something powerfully symbolic. It was something he'd taken away from her. It was something she wanted back.

EIGHTEEN

The Bones of the Past

'Your grandfather was in the IRA at the time of Collins,' said Joseph as he smeared an unfeasibly thick layer of butter on to his toast. He munched on it and continued in an off-handed manner. 'It was before the treaty. Do you want more toast?'

We were going off to play golf – just the three of us: Joseph, Patrick and me. It was a stunning June morning and we were in the sleepy heart of rural Ireland, miles from my life. Miles from my past. We'd been talking about politics all morning, sitting in the stone cottage that Patrick had renovated. Breakfast had gone on and on. The teas and coffees kept on coming as Joseph and I got more and more animated. Our interest gelled; his from sometimes bitter experience and mine from a kind of dilettante fascination. We reached each other in a way I never managed to reach Stella.

Patrick was tidying up around us. He knew all this anyway. Whilst I know that any family in Ireland can weave their way back to some involvement in the struggles for independence, and at the time of Michael Collins, many of the future statesmen of the Republic were IRA men. I knew that even Bertie Ahern's father had been an IRA man then. But the implications of my Irish heritage really cranked up a gear. Not only was my grandfather of a different religion, culture and national identity, but he had fought for it against the Brits. I even felt a sense of pride. What a paradox. Pride in those three despicable initials. Those three letters – IRA – had been right up there with KGB and the Child Catcher in the dark forest of my childhood years. Some of that revulsion sticks, however much your understanding deepens. But this man was my grandfather. A man with a pike who wanted his country back. That's how he saw it.

I had to tell someone. Doug is a close friend and brilliant journalist. He is bright and wise. I sent him a surreptitious text as I sat in the back of the car on the way to the golf course. It felt really subversive doing it while the other two chatted in the front. 'Fucking Hell. Grandfather was in the IRA.' He replied with Rod Steiger's wonderful line as the camp hairdresser in *No Way to Treat a Lady*: 'It doesn't mean you're a bad person.'

This was only the second time I had met Joseph face to face. Patrick was busy collecting our arms cache for the afternoon's operation: three golf bags, three half sets and enough balls to fill a lough with. So, I checked out the scorecard. Grandfather Leahy was a man who had fought for something, like Grandpa on the Somme and Dad in the jungles of Burma. But his war was in the lanes and fields of Fermanagh and South Armagh.

To be honest this was just another piece of information in the clamorous assembly of feelings, facts and findings that were screaming at me and queuing up to get inside my head. When Joseph added, 'I was involved a bit when I was younger with all that stuff,' I was still thinking about my grandfather. I knew Joseph's politics and I just filed it away as something to consider later. I was more immediately concerned with whether I'd get my golf swing back after so long without playing.

The barrage of experience and information had started the very moment I landed. I'd flown into Belfast so that Joseph could take me to meet his sisters who still lived in the North. After that we faced the long drive to the south-west. When I walked into the baggage hall, the Glasgow Celtic football manager Martin O' Neill, who'd been on the same flight, had waited for me there to say hello. It's a bit like having Frank Sinatra shout your name from the other side of a restaurant. Meeting Martin is what they call the old one-two in football. It was a reminder of who I was profession-ally – we'd done a show together years before on Sky TV. But it was also an uncanny acknowledgement of the legacy I'd discovered. I remember Martin telling me what it felt like being a Catholic playing for Northern Ireland and receiving for that very reason the jeers of his home crowd when his place in the starting line-up was announced. This was also the manager of the club I had supported before I knew any better. This was the manager of the club that represented, as fate would have it, my father's tribe.

The omens for the weekend were propitious. I walked into the entrance area and there was Joseph, waiting for me, smiling and slightly nervous. As he was paying at the machine for the short-stay parking ticket I stood back as he got chatting to and turbo-charming a pretty red-headed air stewardess whom he had clearly bumped into on the way in. When she'd gone he twinkled, 'Jesus. A few years ago I'd have been in there.' I thought, Ditto. We travelled through rolling countryside and strange cold stone towns where every day is a flag day and the bunting of bigotry screams its presence. Eventually we came to the place of his birth. His sisters still live near there. I met them in order of seniority at their two different houses. Evangeline, the eldest, was our first stop. She had laid the beautifully white sheathed table with cakes and sandwiches and even offered me champagne. This was a big day for her. I don't much like the stuff so I sank into a soft chair and said that a far greater treat would be a Guinness from the fridge. She obliged. That's what I call looking after family. Evangeline's the one who had been following my career for years, unaware that I was her nephew.

'I am so glad we've found you at last.' I didn't point out that I'd found them. There were tears in her eyes. She already had photographs I had sent her of the children in a neat frame on the table. Joseph was sitting there with the slightly chastened air of a little brother who has been very naughty for not telling them about this for so long, but ultimately forgiven. The two of them even had words about it. The exchange was restrained but heartfelt. She was definitely chiding him.

'What a shame we missed out on so much, Joseph.'

'Leave it alone, Evie,' he wearily insisted. She sounded like she despaired of him but yielded to her love for him. And love won the day. I swallowed some more black nectar and shuddered to think what this would have been like if I'd been twenty. It would have completely screwed me up. Thank God I'd waited. I had another slug of stout and wolfed down some chicken sandwiches. There were more photographs of my grandfather and grandmother to see. She was slender and birdlike. He was stocky and open faced. I was dazed and confused.

A couple of hours and a couple of life stories later we went to see Bernadette, aunt number two, where a full house was waiting. A Riverdance of teenage relatives trooped in to have a look. Winsome blue eyes peered at me with unsettling curiosity. A man they'd occasionally seen on the telly was sitting in the living room drinking a whiskey and was apparently the long-lost son of their great uncle. A welcome break from GCSE revision anyway.

By now I was beginning to lose myself a little. When I met Esther and she came to my flat in Hampstead, I panicked because Tina wasn't home but at least it was on home turf and all my things were around me. My guitar, my papers, my mess. All the bits of myself. When I met Joseph Junior and Helen, and after that Joseph himself, I had Tina. I had the kids. I had me and mine everywhere to remind me who I was. Now it was different. I had waves of the feeling I'd experienced when I first met Stella twelve years before. It's one of alienation and confusion. You do lose yourself. You wonder, when confronted by this alternative family and brand-new past, if you are the person you think you are any more. They are all so different from me but all so similar. They are my own flesh and blood but to them I'm a stranger. All the certainties about the self you've become are seriously challenged. The past I know and the me I think I am are confronted by something totally new.

I needed to sleep. Just like Dublin 1991. I needed to just curl up and go to what Dad called the land of Hinkum, Dinkum and Nod. We said our goodbyes and took our leave, concurring with an aunt and a cousin that the whole thing was a most peculiar business. I was relieved to escape into Joseph's little car and head off on the long journey South. I phoned Tina just to hear her voice but the signal was awful. Pointless. We proceeded through yet more places where the tribal drum beats were emblazoned on flagpoles, lampposts and gable ends. An alien with an archaic vocabulary would reckon them a 'gay lot'. He'd be wrong on every count. Then we slipped over the border. It just happens. Like going from England to Scotland. The next thing you know the atmosphere has relented. Two tribes have become one. I noticed the gardens were different. The topiary had changed. Less fastidious. Less of it. Sleepily, I asked Joseph about that. Gardeners' question time.

'You noticed, did you?' answered the sage. He explained. 'Well, the Protestants would manicure their hedgerows more than the Gaelic side of the situation. And the gateposts are very different. They come from a different work ethic. The Scots came in here to work the land. I got the impression that those who came in regarded the native Irish as something of a subculture.'

It was one of those conversations that, heard on the verge of sleep, seems unreal, part of the spell Morpheus casts as you slip through the threshold and leave reality. I wasn't sure whether I had gone or not but he was still talking.

From horticulture to subculture. A long way from home. A long way from Edinburgh. A bloody long way from Alan Titchmarsh. I snuggled into my car seat, gripped my proxy teddy – my mobile phone – and drifted off with Daddy at the wheel. A very long way from my other daddy. I snoozed on and off for the rest of the long journey to the south-west of Ireland.

Patrick met us at the cottage and we all had a drink and a good meal. Then it was straight to bed. I'd been up since three thirty for the breakfast programme on Five Live that morning and all the emotional claustrophobia I'd been feeling was made worse by tiredness. You need to be strong for this stuff.

It was billed as a golfing weekend. Joseph's neck and shoulder had been badly affected by the operation on his throat cancer but he still has a good swing. Very good in fact. I get by. Patrick is pretty useful. The three of us played twelve holes on both days. The club we were at was a wonderfully relaxed place deep in rural Ireland – a world away from the class-ridden monstrosities you get in Britain. The golf itself was hugely symbolic for me. I never played anything with Dad. Never even kicked a ball with him. We just didn't. He always saw himself as old although he was only the age I am now when I was adopted. So, swinging a club with Joseph was an entirely new father–son experience. Joseph was outrageously competitive but was proud when I hit a good one. I started playing as much for him as for me. I wanted to show him I could do it. I was a little boy trying to please. It's par for the course really – remember Esther's phrase? – 'the regressionary thing'.

As we were all about to tee up at the sixth my pal Robert phoned. I thought I'd turned the mobile off. He has excellent comic timing has Rob. So he should, he's the script editor of the comedy programme *Smack the Pony*. He was also the school friend who, when we were fourteen, asked me, out of the blue, if I knew why my eyes were blue? Well, nearly thirty years on, the reason for my blue eyes was standing behind me about to deploy his fearsome Three Wood and smack the ball a couple of hundred yards – again. Robert had also been my boyhood golfing companion. When we were youngsters we loved hacking our way round Edinburgh Braid Hills Number Two Course. Another cue for regression.

Robert had phoned to ask my views on the day's big event: Scotland v Germany at Hampden. I'd forgotten all about it.

'What you think, wee man?' he said, assuming the patois of the central Scottish football fan. *Trainspotting* meets Rab C. Nesbitt. The 'wee', by the way, is a relative term. He is six foot five.

'What about, big man?' I asked, slipping into character.

'Where are you?' He was himself now.

'I'm in Ireland,' I was whispering conspiratorially. Golf etiquette and self-consciousness conspired. 'Playing golf with my father.'

'It's this weekend? He'll have realized how crap you are then. We're playing Germany. That is presuming you haven't changed nationalities like you change football clubs.' He was a pal during my 'Celtic' period. 'We kick off in forty minutes.'

I signed off. 'I'll ring you at half-time.'

Joseph cracked another one down the middle and punctuated it by turning round and berating Patrick and me.

'You two and your fucking phones.'

Scotland football matches had stalked me throughout my search for my natural parents. The time I unwittingly met Esther in 1978 at a friend's house, we were beating Holland; the day Helen and Joseph Junior first came to my house, Scotland were drawing with the Faeroes, and now it was home to Germany. The father of all Euro-qualifying battles. But right then I was in a different place internally and externally. I was having a distinctly Irish weekend. Maybe God was Scottish after all and he was telling me to stay true to the faith and Rob was his only son sent to tell me. Mysterious ways and all that.

As for the golf, we were just three boys out there having fun. When we finished playing we drank Guinness in the laid-back bar, had a three-way snooker competition and bantered away. We forgot ourselves. I felt like a student again. No responsibilities. No worries. Just the simple pleasures of the bachelor life. Games and drinks and laughs. He wasn't my father surely? He was some cracking old fellow I'd just bumped into who had the will to win, cutting humour and piss-taking aptitude of a master. Patrick was in great form too. He savours every minute he spends with Joseph. At the tail end of our snooker session Joseph's daughter Ellie came in. Another sister. We had a drink and a good chat. 'You look like Joseph,' she said softly.

'What him?' I said mock indignantly, pointing at the old fellow.

'No. You look like my brother.' The double meaning was unintentional. She ran me back to her own cottage for a quick tour and a decent chat, gave me a framed sketch she had done of a Georgian Dublin façade and dropped me back at Patrick's place. So far then – one father, two aunts, a cousin, six second cousins, a sister. Decades of drought and then the heavens open. When the three musketeers were all back in the cottage we ate late and talked till morning. I slept like a baby. I wasn't quite sure whose.

*

It was important to Joseph that I knew and understood my 'own people'. He saw it as a long-awaited return to the fold. 'We're all of us walking on the bones of the past,' he said. 'There's no getting away from it.' Over time Joseph and his sisters, Evangeline and Bernadette individually told me about their father's life and times. Evangeline was immensely proud of her father but was keen to deny there was any continuity through to the modern-day struggle. 'You have got to remember the IRA of Daddy's time were not like the rabble now.' Joseph took a different view. He saw it as one struggle. At different historical points it merely took on different characteristics. But who was this wee man? Brendan Leahy of the IRA? Of the big blue eyes, long eyelashes and kindly face. This is what I was told.

My grandfather was born in 1904. His father Peter was a small farmer and horseman with only one eye and his mother Alice was an incurable Republican romantic. Joseph says his grandfather Peter never uttered one word to him. He'd gently lift the boy up on to the horse and hold him up there to give him confidence but that was the extent of their communication. When Joseph was staying with his grandparents they'd say the rosary in the evening and then all just sit in silence looking at the fire and listening to the relentless ticking of the clock. It was maddening. What's worse, every time it ticked grandfather Peter would roll his wooden stick and strike it on the floor. 'I can hear it now,' Joseph says. 'I thought I was in the fucking nut house.' Joseph loved and understood his grandmother though. The memory is vivid. 'She was some woman all right. Tiny she was. Salt-and-pepper hair in a bun and earrings dangling down.'

Her children's cradle songs weren't 'Hickory Dickory Dock' or 'Rock a Bye Baby'. They were Fenian ballads – songs and poems of bold Fenian men, heroes and martyrs in the murderous face of English perfidy. The folklore of Mother Ireland's struggle against evil incarnate.

> I was born on the Bogside, my boys, I hate these English laws,
> My parents they were Irish and they died for an Irish cause;
> If I ever go to visit them for thousands of miles afar,
> It will be for dear old Ireland's sake and a Fenian Man o'War.
>
> Oh, Bridget, dearest Bridget, the truth to you I'll tell,
> The English were insulted and the Irish knew it well,
> They might make me a captain instead of a common tar,
> So I'll risk my life for Ireland's rights on board the Man o'War.

Grandma Alice would tell her children and then grandchildren the story of her own grandfather, who'd been cruelly evicted by his English landlord, thrown off the land of his birthright. He'd had a stage station for the horses and coaches on the road to Dublin and with his home went his entire livelihood too. Her rebel heart thrived on the hand-me-down hurt of it all.

Grandma Alice would say to little Joseph, 'Let's go into the garden and go hunt the guns your daddy hid.' She embroidered a child's fantasy with the dark threads of revolutionary politics. She spoke excitedly of the imaginary guns as if she were telling of treasure, or a golden fleece, or a secret fairies' den. Brendan Leahy was weaned on his mother's romantic Republicanism but it was given fire and born into active service by the sectarianism he experienced and the humiliations he suffered. He'd been thrown up against a wall and frisked by the Royal Irish Constabulary and later the B Specials too many times. These were members of the community. Local farmers. They were neighbours – acquaintances of his parents. Just like the young guy who had metamorphosed from neighbour to uniformed bully and hassled Joseph decades later. *It's me, Alec!*

As Brendan's daughter told me, 'Tears were never far from Daddy's eyes. Needs must, his country came first.' He first got involved with active Republicanism through a regular route – local Gaelic Athletic Association clubs when he was twelve years old. An interest was noted. When Brendan was slightly older having access to a car was invaluable and a fast track to local promotion.

It was 1916. A pivotal year for the Republican movement. It was the year of the Easter Rising. On the weekend I met Stella in Dublin in 1991 the papers were full of articles on the seventy-fifth anniversary.

The Rising galvanized popular support for violent Republicanism not so much when it happened but in the wake of the executions of those involved. The sense of persecution and victimhood was easily felt. The sense of outrage and martyrdom was fondly nurtured. The rising tide of anger was portrayed by W. B. Yeats in his poem 'Sixteen Dead Men'.

> O but we talked at large before
> The sixteen men were shot,
> But who can talk of give and take,
> What should be and what not

While those dead men are loitering there
To stir the boiling pot?

The security situation deteriorated. Within four years the notorious Black and Tans were on the scene. They were a scabrous assortment of demobbed British soldiers, their officers and a rag-bag of mercenaries and adventurers brought in to supplement the beleaguered Royal Irish Constabulary. Even the local coppers they were there to help had mixed feelings about them. They could have used some diversity training.

In 1920 at the age of sixteen, Brendan, already an active volunteer, but for all they knew just a local lad, was picked up by the Tans, with RIC men in attendance, shoved on their open-topped tender and paraded round the perimeters of Armagh as a human shield. The volunteers wouldn't dare have a go with the little chap there. Not with a Catholic in the back. This was common practice. He also took foul mouthfuls of abuse. 'You little bog Irish Fenian bastard.' He never forgot this event. It was one of the first things Aunt Lucy told me when I asked her about those times. It reinforced all his prejudices about their prejudices.

This in turn rang my own bells of unthinking bigotry. 'Fenian this. Fenian that.' I've got good friends who used to sing that stuff at football matches. Anti-Celtic songs. Anti-Hibs songs. They are clamping down hard on it now. One mate of mine rather objects to what he sees as the political correctness of it all. He thinks it's a good release valve. You'd think with his Oxbridge degree he might get the bigger picture. When we went together as kids I sang with him. Just for a laugh you understand.

Could you go a chicken supper Bobby Sands.
Could you go a chicken supper
You filthy Fenian fucker.
Could you go a chicken supper Bobby Sands.

Joseph told me Brendan's role as armaments officer in the local IRA was to procure, accumulate, hide, distribute and transport weapons; put them in local dumps and make sure they were available when required. There was no semtex then. Gelignite nicked from local quarries did the job. Molotov cocktails served a purpose too. It was simple enough to put a kerosene-soaked rag in a bottle. 303s were the prized assets though and many of the volunteers fresh back from the trenches with the British Army could handle them brilliantly. These rifles had a vicious kickback but were deadly accurate.

Brendan Leahy's younger sister Cecilia, or Cissy, also imbibed the Republican zeal with mother's milk. She was a member of the Cumann na mBan – the women's IRA. Their role was very different from that of the sexually egalitarian Provos of recent times when women came to serve and die in active units.

The pinnacle of Brendan Leahy's involvement was the big rally in Armagh in September 1921. He was seventeen, a touch over five foot seven; a strong stocky man with a generous face. Those deep blue eyes had never seen anything like it. Armagh had never seen anything like it. Republicans had converged on the city from miles around. The police, who had lost many of their number at the hands of those marching, had a threadbare force on duty that day. It was an uneasy truce but the security forces stayed in the background so as not to antagonize the situation. They were watching closely though. This was a pivotal political moment. Given the bitterness of the preceding years, some of the by now demoralized constabulary were only too pleased to let the Fenians get on with it.

There was a ceasefire in place and Michael Collins needed to convince the reluctant Northern heartland that the impending agreement creating partition was the only way forward. He believed it was a way out of the bloodshed, would only be temporary and would ultimately lead to a free, undivided and united Ireland. The British Prime Minister, David Lloyd George, and his team were to prove shrewd players at the table. Gruelling and exacting negotiations would follow. They knew how to turn the screw. Deal or else. As Tony Blair said seventy-six years later, 'The settlement train is leaving. With or without Sinn Fein.' Clearly the political process had to be sold to a sceptical grassroots. This was about hearts and minds. It's familiar stuff. Tim Pat Coogan, the great historian of Republicanism, summed up the contemporary parallel and perennial paradox: 'Now, as with Collins, Gerry Adams is having to face both ways at the same time.'

On the big day in Armagh some of the Orange population of the city and its environs hurled stones and lobbed abuse but most merely scowled and sneered or gave that part of the town a wide berth for the day. For the men and women of the IRA and Sinn Fein, there was strength in numbers. This was about pride and dignity and defiance.

The north end of Armagh, the Catholic part of town, was 'lavishly decorated with Sinn Fein flags and bunting' according to one newspaper report. Some estimates put the crowd taking part in or observing the march at over 20,000. They made their way through the streets to the heart-stirring martial sound of pipers and fife and drum bands. It was impressive and imposing. Their day would come. They were convinced of it.

Michael Collins gave two addresses. A few words in the city hall before proceeding through town to Greenpark, and then a rousing open-air speech. He started in Gaelic and then switched to the adopted tongue. On live radio whenever we suddenly cross to Adams or McGuinness as they stand at Downing Street or on the steps of Stormont for some historic announcement, they always start in Gaelic and we always get caught out. This after the producer has been screaming, 'Go now. Now!' It says to the world, 'We are different from you. We even have a different language.' I've heard it said they don't even speak it very well. Pidgin Irish some of the purists call it. Continuous live-news channels weren't to face these problems for a good while yet.

Collins' speech was a classic mixture of the conciliatory and the hard line. Compromise was interwoven with dark threats and determination. It was a textbook example of sounding implacable to sell a compromise. This was a speech designed to prepare his people for recognition of what was for most of them the ultimate heresy: the partition of the North from the South, the north-east corner of Ireland wrenched from the motherland.

Collins took to the stage to an ear-splitting welcome. The cheering lasted for minutes. The huge audience spontaneously struck up 'The Soldier's Song'. When the tumult had calmed, he first paid tribute to those who had given their lives for the cause and said the ceasefire was thanks to them. He then went right to the heart of his audience with a plea for the prisoners. He was talking about the husbands, brothers, sons and fathers of those present. The rhetoric was both impassioned and carefully measured.

He rejected the British terms for the agreement while quoting the nineteenth-century Nationalist Parliamentarian, Charles Stewart Parnell – 'no man has the right to say thus far and no further'. In other words – implicitly – he was saying he'd accept the British terms but only because they would be a stepping stone towards the final and inevitable goal.

As for the Unionists – he implored the 'Orangemen' to join them as Irishmen. 'We can afford to be generous.' Freedom was coming and nothing could stop it. 'Our message to the North – no matter what the future may bring. We will not desert you.' He concluded and was cheered to the overcast skies.

It was 4 September 1921. The future brought an Ireland divided. The treaty was signed three months later and a year after that, Michael Collins was ambushed and killed during the civil war by former comrades, branded a traitor. For some implacable hardliners he is still a man who supped with the Devil, split the movement and paid a justifiable price. 'My father believed in him. He understood what he was trying to do,' said Joseph. 'To his dying day he said what a great man Collins was. And this peace process now. Father would have been delighted.'

That late summer Sunday in Armagh no doubt had a huge effect on all those present, not least on seventeen-year-old Brendan Leahy of the 4th Northern Division. He must have near burst with pride as he formed part of the advanced armed guard round Collins on that vast demonstration through the city. He had stood by the stage listening intently to the speeches and cheering and singing loudly with the exuberant audience. Brendan Leahy died thirty-four years before I knew he existed.

'Daddy's politics died in 1921,' said Aunt Evangeline. According to family sources he took no part in the civil war that followed the signing of the treaty with David Lloyd George. That war and the divisions it wrought upon Irish families broke his heart. Exactly when his involvement with the IRA ceased is unclear though. Brendan's brother Michael was to recall high-level army meetings in the Leahy farmhouse. Joseph remembered the family talk: 'If those walls had ears, Mick used to say.'

But for the rest of his life Brendan rarely if ever spoke about politics in the house. As Evangeline told me, 'If you'd done it you didn't discuss it.' A great raconteur, he could tell a fantastic story, carving an elegant turn of phrase and showing all his talents for mimicry. He was angered by the bigotry he encountered and the discrimination he believed was endemic in his land but as far as overt politics went, the only thing Joseph ever heard him express openly was that admiration for Michael Collins. The only other noticeable vestige of his time as a volunteer was an uncommon expertise in handling a gun.

Brendan went on to run a smallholding. Then a pub for a while and later a taxi. A decent ordinary life. He married Bridget and they had five children, two of whom died in infancy. When he passed away in 1968 his wife was approached by members of the movement asking whether she wanted military colours at the funeral. She declined the offer. He was no soldier. He was her husband.

*

As Patrick and I flew back to London on Monday morning, we were both deep in thought. I thought about this grandfather. I also thought about the grandfather I'd grown up with who lived with us in Edinburgh for half the year. Grandpa had died in 1976 and had fought in the First World War. I'd been close to him. Brendan Leahy seemed closer in one way but miles away in another. I couldn't work out which past was mine. Which legacy could I claim? If we are prisoners of history it was difficult to know which wing I was on, never mind in which prison.

And Collins? What a job leading that lot with the legacy they all claimed, revered and were enclosed by. I remembered my encounter with Gerry Adams six years previously. What a bizarre morning that had been. At the time, December 1997, I'd not long started doing a job I adored. I was hosting the morning phone-in on Five Live. Sitting in the studio with the leader of Irish Republicanism was an intense experience. He is an intense man. Gerry Adams was there to take listeners' calls. A hulking-looking security guard stood sentinel on the other side of the door. At one point he tried to prevent the travel girl from coming in to tell us about the 'sheer weight of traffic' on the M25. Quite why he thought the four foot nine blond former actress was a one-woman Loyalist death squad I don't know. Mind you, you never do.

The President of Sinn Fein was sitting opposite me. Tony Blair had been elected PM in May and the peace process immediately picked up pace. A fresh warm wind was blowing from Downing Street and the front doors of number ten had opened to Republicans for the first time. Adams was being treated like a normal constitutional politician to encourage him to continue to lead and persuade his movement into cleaving to normal constitutional politics. To abandon physical-force Republicanism for ever.

If this was a big day for Gerry, it was a huge one for me. I had to get this one right. Securing Adams' appearance on the programme to take calls for an hour, en route to see the PM, was a major coup. There is a local radio cliché – 'the phone lines are lighting up like Christmas trees' – well, they were. And the reception wasn't the uncritical and adulatory one he'd get at a New York fundraiser. For the most part people were quite the opposite. Water off a duck's back to Adams though. He is a self-assured man. He has handled a few troublesome council meetings in his time. He has skilfully negotiated a treacherous career path.

Whenever interviewing Adams or McGuinness certain thoughts are inevitable. Whose blood is on your hands? What did you do in the war? What orders did you give? I wondered if I could detect the sliver of ice in his heart. I tested the temperature at the earliest opportunity. A programme trail played out at nine fifteen. I had forty seconds off the air. I hit him with a big one.

'I am getting married on Saturday.'

'Congratulations. Whereabouts?'

'Here in London.'

I took every available opportunity to make small talk, partly to fill the gaps but also to improve the atmosphere and perhaps even relax the deadly stern subject into a chink of on-air revelation. Some hope. Apart from that, it's not every day you chew the cud with G. Adams.

During the nine-thirty news and sport bulletin I unleashed what I reckoned was my Libyan arms cache. My Tet offensive.

I wanted to tell him that since I'd met my mother, and had my Irish roots confirmed and personalized, Ireland had lurked in my life like a ghost. It had become an obsession. It had challenged every notion I had ever had about who I was and what I was, and of course back in 1997 I still didn't know the half of it. This was five years prior to tracing Joseph.

All this would have taken some explaining though so I kept it simple.

'My mother comes from Dublin.'

'Really. Is that right? Whereabouts in Dublin?'

I couldn't remember. He had answers to all my questions and now he asks me one and I'm stuffed. He was polite though. He's a versatile operator. The White House is a long way from the Falls Road. He was polite but so uninterested. Why should he be anything else? Straight out of the studio what was he going to do? Lunge for his mobile?

'Martin – the guy who interviewed me this morning. Radio Five Live. You'll never believe it. Get this. His mother, yea? His mother is from Dublin!'

For goodness sake, dozens of people have mothers from Dublin. He perked up rather more when Ken Livingstone's voice popped up in the bulletin.

'I thought I recognized those nasal tones,' he intoned, nasally.

On the air it was going all right. I had worked really hard to prepare for it, poring over books, articles and briefing notes for days, talking to those in the know and searching for areas on which he would be less confident and more exposed. People with Adams' level of belief and self-belief are never going to suddenly buckle and exclaim, 'Golly! You got me there. You know, I never thought of it like that. I think you may just have a point!' But you live in hope and work hard on leading them into moments of consideration and concession. An off-guard acknowledgement that there is no monopoly on truth. A slippery denial or tenuous rebuttal that speaks volumes. A deft but discernable wriggle. A human moment. A new angle. Or, the perennial wish of the editor and BBC press office – a new line.

I made no real headway. Nice build-up play but no penetration in the penalty area.

'Come on,' I proclaimed, 'a Catholic in West Belfast who watches *Coronation Street* and *Eastenders*, supports Man United and whose kids love the Spice Girls. What are you saying to them? Let me liberate you? They are wrapped up in the culture of these islands.'

He shot back, 'I don't know about *Coronation Street*. On their street there are British tanks.' Nice try, N. Campbell. Bring in another caller.

A little later I attempted to remind him of the bloody legacy of Collins. He had tried to strike a deal. To some, any deal is a sell-out. I went for it. 'Michael Collins stopped short of the ultimate Republican goals. He was murdered by Republicans. Mr Adams, you've seen enough death in your time. Are you worried you'll be history?' I remember vividly his vulpine stare. Straight ahead. Not at me. His voice defied his expression. Cold as that December morning, he patted it away with one of his trusty off-the-peg numbers, delivered with a tone of weary frustration. 'We need to address all the causes of conflict.' That's a favourite.

On that Monday-morning flight from Dublin to London in summer 2003, I stared out at the clouds. I wondered how he would have reacted if I'd known then what I know now.

I could have told him that my grandfather was armaments officer for the 4th Northern Division of the IRA in 1921 and formed part of the armed guard for one of Collins' big rallies. He might have raised one of his dark brooding eyebrows at that.

If yet again he had asked 'whereabouts?' I could have said, without missing a beat, 'Armagh.' I could even have told him the route of that march – from the City Hall via Lower Irish Street, English Street and on to College Grounds. As it was, the mind of Gerry Adams was on the place where IRA mortar bombs had landed in 1991 – Downing Street. He was due there in an hour's time.

There was a thrill about my latest discovery but all the IRA history never really answered the question, who was my grandfather? Only what he was. A product of his life and times and circumstances. He was also a great dad. He was tender, loving, soft spoken and was always for giving his kids a big hug. He could be a real showman and joker. One time on the farm he told the kids he'd hypnotized the chickens. Ten of them. He'd put their heads under their wings and was talking chicken language to them. Of course if you put a chicken's head under its wing it can't move but the children didn't know that. He was prancing up and down clucking at them and all the birds were apparently under his amazing spell. His children were laughing till the tears ran down their cheeks. When he recounts it, his son is still laughing till he cries.

I'd had a wonderful weekend. It was one of the most memorable weekends of my life. It was full of wonder. I was far removed from the normal contours of my life and times and I felt renewed by it. I'd been a baby, a little boy, a young man. I'd also had a great time with 'the lads'. One of them happened to be my father. Now I needed to see Tina and the girls and beam back up to planet reality. I also learned a little more about where these genes had been before. We are all treading on the bones of the past. I was looking both ways at once. I wanted to make sense of the future too. The skeletons had flesh, and the flesh was mine.

> And death shall have no dominion.
> Dead men naked they shall be one
> With the man in the wind and the west moon;
> When their bones are picked clean and the clean bones gone,
> They shall have stars at elbow and foot;
> Though they go mad they shall be sane,
> Though they sink through the sea they shall rise again;
> Though lovers be lost love shall not;
> And death shall have no dominion.

NINETEEN

The Vault

The vault is where we hide our secrets. I had mine and Joseph had his. I'd been one of his. No longer though. I'd known him for eight months. As far as my mum and sister Fiona were concerned none of my searching and finding had happened. They weren't in denial. They were in total ignorance. They knew nothing about Esther. As to the intense months of discovery and revelation and the joyous disorientation and emotional turbulence of finding my father and his family – they were oblivious. To tell them, and I was convinced of this, would be to hurt them and they would see me differently. They would start to see me as someone else in the way I'd started to see myself. I was essentially finding out who I was and if they were in on it everything might change. The bedrock plates of my life would irreversibly shift. Mum and Fiona might not acknowledge it. They might totally dismiss it. But I was worried they'd be subconsciously affected by it. And then? Then I'd be cast adrift. A wretched orphan with a forest of family trees. Truly alone.

Just as Joseph had become real to me in life, Dad's memory in death was ever more vivid. I was dreaming about him frequently and he was holding on to me with both arms. Some of those dreams were desperate. All of them were full of love and longing: the funny songs he sang when shaving, the smell of his freshly shaven face as he picked me up to kiss me, the exotic snatches of Hindi learned during his time in the Indian army.

By guarding the contents of the vault so zealously, I was protecting myself. For now, it stayed firmly shut. Joseph kept his secrets deep in a dark vault. The son he had lost and the tangled past, personal and political, he'd only ever confessed to his son-in-law Patrick at the point in his battle with throat cancer when he thought he was near the end. There was another vault – a vault under Armagh Cathedral. This was back in the mid fifties. It was used as an IRA arms cache. The entrance was a trapdoor in the grounds in the tangled shrubbery. It was concealed under a carpet of leaves and a mass of brambles and laurels. Inside the murky breathless space below were fuse wires, detonators and primers. All the paraphernalia of subversion.

I flew to Dublin and motored south to see Joseph on my own. I love driving in Ireland. There is a part of me that feels a part of it. In the light of everything I'd discovered, it was like the excitement of a new romance. I'd known her for years, admired her from afar and now she was staring at me with a look I could feel in my heart. On the golfing weekend Joseph had begun to open the trapdoor on his own secrets. He'd told me about his father and he'd casually mentioned something else. I remembered the very words. 'I was involved a bit when I was younger with all that stuff.' I needed to find out more and when I said I was coming over, it was clear he was going to tell me. I was both intrigued and excited. It fired up the journalist in me and I had an urge – an instinct from somewhere – to record it all. Not so long ago all I'd had of him was that precious message on my answerphone. With my Dictaphone in my briefcase, now I was going to keep him for ever.

When I eventually arrived, Joseph and I sat together in the front room of his bungalow. For some reason I still expected to see the fresh-faced young policeman whose photograph had provided my first glimpse of him. We'd both changed in forty-two years though. 'I'm an old hag now,' he sometimes says. Yes, and I'm a middle-aged man. I put my dictaphone on the table and fiddled around trying to attach the mic to make sure it was working. Writing this now, I can see that I was the one who was working. I was in full professional mode, about to conduct an interview. Yes, I was preserving a record of his voice and story but more than that, it was also my way of coping with what was to come. This way it wouldn't be terrifying unknown terrain. I knew what to do. I knew how to react. I could be objective. I didn't have my children beside me. I didn't have Tina. I didn't have the football on the telly. But I had the me that could deal with it best. In this most intense situation with my father, the professional and the personal were vying for control and mostly indivisible.

'Do you mind the machine, Joseph?'

'Don't give a fuck. You've got a right to know. Forty-two years in the dark. And to use that horrible word – it's like closure for me, you know what I mean?'

He didn't beat about the bush. He ripped up the shrubbery, hacked through the brambles, pushed the detonator and blew the trapdoor wide open.

'1955–57. During the border campaign. I was in the IRA at that time.' The shrapnel hit me.

'And what did you have to do?'

'The new volunteers would be put into a section to get intelligence. Just peripheral stuff. Even at that stage they were organizing units into small groups.'

'Are you OK talking about this?' I was taken aback and had to check again.

'I told you. It's your right to know.' Opening his heart like this was an act of love. His voice was trembling. 'There was long enough I wasn't there for you.' He was gifting me his most cherished belongings. We were sharing his past.

'I joined with Jamesie, Patrick and Seamus.' These were lads like himself from families like his own, with beliefs and traditions chiselled from the same stone. Their paths in life were to diverge from his though. He went on to become a policeman in the South. As I later found out, for some of these young men the path was either to prison or lifelong activism, or both. I thought of myself at seventeen. I was a rebel, yes. But on a slightly different scale and in a very different context. Getting high. Getting into trouble. Getting into Punk. My only armed struggle was the constant urge to exercise my left wrist. The only 45s I was interested in were by the Sex Pistols, the Buzzcocks and Ian Dury.

Joseph carried on with his story. 'I was doing the intelligence stuff and Liam was armaments officer. Cormac and Liam came up to me one evening – "Come on, we're going. We're going to get some stuff." So I got my father's car and we drove all the way to Monaghan and into this farmyard. A guy called Sean South was there and this old man. We were brought in and we were given a drink and we sat chatting for a while. Sean South said we are planning some operations in Armagh. So I looked out of the window and they were loading the car with stuff and I thought, Jeez. My father's car! A blue Ford Zephyr 6. If it's seized now I'm in trouble. So I went out and figured how could we hide this stuff: under the back seat or should we just throw it in the boot? And there was the cortex and gelignite and a couple of 45s and 38s and ammunition.' Sean South is a Republican hero. He was killed at the tail end of 1956 after a bungled attack on Brookborough RUC barracks and is celebrated in poetry and song.

> They have gone to join that gallant band, of Plunkett, Pearce,
>   and Tone
> Another martyr for old Ireland, Sean South from Garryowen

Joseph carried on talking. I was just listening. The tape machine was whirring. So was his mind. The number of times this experience must have played in that mind of his. Now I was privy to it. I felt touched that he'd taken me into his confidence but I was afraid of what he was going to tell me. I was ready for the worst. Someone was going to get blown up.

'And this was for a specific operation?' I could hear my voice. It was dispassionate. Journalistic. His face was taut with concentration. He was tense, still the young guy sitting with the big guys in a Monaghan farmhouse. I had a flash of Dad in 1956, married to Mum and sitting in one of his beloved Edinburgh pubs, sucking on his pipe and chatting. Chuckling. He had a baby daughter at home, my sister Fiona. He was the happiest man on earth. It was light years from South Armagh. And he was forty-one. I was forty-two.

Joseph continued. 'It was for a series of operations. To restock the supplies really, though I remember one of the jobs that came from it months later, long after Sean's death. It was a plan to blow up Irish Street barracks in Armagh. Anyway, when we drove down over the border to get the stuff there was this guy there, an English fellow who had a wooden leg. He stopped us. He knew me a bit because I drove over the border regularly to dances and he knew my father and he said, "Young Leahy, how are you?" On the way down the boys had loaded two guns and given one to me. I said, "I can't use this. I'm driving the fucking car." I was sweating a bit at this stage I remember well. We stopped at the border on the way back and Peg Leg came out and said, "You weren't in there long, lads. You weren't South long." '

They told him they had just nipped south to say goodbye to a girl who was off on the boat to England that night. 'No problem,' said Peg Leg. 'Off you go, lads.'

'So we went into Armagh. I don't know Armagh too well but they directed me to drive down near the Catholic cathedral and Cormac said we have a place here in the vault. So we pulled into the side of the cathedral gate and all the stuff was in a plastic bag. Cormac got out of the car and as he got out he bent over and a gun dropped out of his waistband. There was this guy – a bread man – on a bike who saw what happened and kept staring as he cycled past, but Cormac picked up his gun, looked straight at him and said, "quiet." '

Joseph put his finger up to his mouth in the hush sign Cormac made. Be quiet or else. Although it was rather like a scene in an

Ealing comedy, the bread man clearly knew what 'or else' meant. Carry on cycling.

'So they took the stuff up and hid it and it was some time after that they blew the wall out of the police station. I had nothing to do with that end of it.'

Months later Joseph was back in Armagh at a dance when that end of it did happen. When it 'blew'. He saw Cormac and Davey sneaking out of the dance hall just when things were in full swing. Everybody heard the blast. What the hell was that? The device went off shortly after twelve thirty. A hole was blown in the barracks wall. There was rubble dust and smoke everywhere. A brief exchange of gunfire had followed but the IRA men disappeared into the night. No one was hurt. Joseph and his mates went up to the station to have a look at the damage. 'I remember stepping over the rubble and there was panic everywhere and an RUC man was shouting us all to go away.' They were ushered away, drove out of Armagh and headed back to their homes. In a report on the bombing the *Ulster Gazette and Armagh Standard* of the following Thursday explained the ease with which the perpetrators escaped.

> There was a considerable traffic at the time due to an RC dance and no particular vehicle was noted.

I read that out to Joseph. He railed against, as he saw it, the derogatory use of the initials RC. 'That would be typical of the attitude.' It was as if he was pointing me to reasons for the act itself. Within a few hours house-to-house searches were under way all over the county. A large number of likely candidates were hauled in. Joseph was one of them. This report appeared in the *Unionist Armagh Guardian* the following Friday. When I showed it to Joseph it made him even more angry. He mocked it for mocking the IRA operation and playing up the gritty professional RUC response to it. 'Bollocks' was his operative word.

> Irish Street barracks in Armagh were bombed at 12.35 a.m. on 30 September 1957. In the finest traditions of 19th-century Irish republican bombing, there was minimal damage to the barracks but most of the adjacent houses were destroyed or badly damaged. They placed a mine or bomb on the gable wall in Callan St. When the mine went off, there was a gunner in Vicars Hill who shot at the sentry position in Irish St with a Thompson sub-machine gun to allow the bombers to escape up Callan St. The machine gunner appears either brave or badly informed as Charles Nesbitt, the Sub District Commander of Armagh USC, lived in Vicars Hill but he didn't see anything.
>
> The newspapers reported a quick response from the RUC but they didn't catch anyone on the day, although they did appear to round up the usual suspects.
>
> The cost of the damage was estimated the following week at £15,000, most of which was to the Cathedral's stained glass windows (13 in all).

Joseph had already been under observation. A few weeks previously he had been in the back of a van coming back from an IRA training session with their football gear as cover, and was stopped by the police. The van had clearly been watched and their names were taken. It was no surprise they picked him up again when there was a wide sweep in the hours following the blast. This time it was nasty. A knock on the door in the wee small hours. Dragged out of bed. His mother crying her eyes out and his father sick with the fear his son had been dragged into the unwinnable war he'd left behind in 1921.

Young Joseph was taken to Armagh Station for questioning. He says they screamed at him, 'You stinking fuckin Fenian bastard.' He says he got a 'hiding'. They shoved his head into a bucket of water. When he could see the wall, he stared at a point on it and tried to block out everything else.

The District Police Inspector of the time was John Gorman. He is Sir John Gorman now. Until his recent retirement he was the Ulster Unionist Assembly member for North Down. He was decorated for his bravery in the Second War Two and for many years served the RUC with great distinction. He is also a Catholic.

Like a hack chasing a buck I spoke to him about the whole story of the vault when I found reference to it in his book, *The Times of My Life*. There I was again with notebook and pen. I wanted to check the two accounts against each other. My friend, the Northern Irish writer and journalist Chris Ryder, acted as go-between and Sir John became my latest interviewee. He reminded me so much of Dad. He is a gentleman of the old school. He was helpful, courteous to a tee and only too pleased to talk at length about the whole sorry saga. The irony of his being like Dad hit me. The personification of my father's enemy was a man so like my dad. Which way was I meant to look?

I let Sir John in on what Joseph had told me.

'My contact says he was given pretty rough treatment when he was picked up after the 'fifty-seven barracks bombing. His head shoved into a bucket?'

'Bucket? I don't remember that. I couldn't be there all the time. Sounds a bit unlikely. If someone wanted to ingratiate himself to us all he had to do was give us bum information.'

'Would you have been around when these people were brought in?'

'I was very hands on, certainly.'

'And what would the approach have been to a young suspect?'

Forty-six years later the gentle and distinguished elderly man scoured his memory.

'I would say there was fairly strong verbal abuse, yes, but in my day there were none of the sophisticated methods like stopping people sleeping. Those cruel but shall we say, robust methods of interrogation weren't really introduced until the sixties.'

I tried to explain to the man who sounded like my dad that the 'contact' was my father. I explained I was adopted and was trying to piece the whole story together.

'My word!' He sounded genuinely surprised and absolutely fascinated. 'And does he still believe in all that?'

'It's at his very core. He is an idealist I suppose.'

'Well there's an idealism there. Misguided and misplaced. But an idealism.'

'Jesus I'd like to talk to that shit,' snarled Joseph when I reported the conversation back to him. 'I'd like to tell him a thing or two.

Idealism? It's a knowledge of history – what's been going on in this country for the last thousand years. Idealism! Fuck that.'

I calmed him down and almost ticked him off. In a sense I was defending Dad and his kind here. Sir John didn't just sound like him but said the sort of things he would have said in the way he would have said them. There was a storm going on inside me. Who I was and how I grew up was raging against who I'd found and what I might have been.

'Sir John was a real gentleman. Fascinating to talk to,' I insisted to Joseph, defending the old world.

Joseph reigned back. 'I respect that. I respect that. Just operating within his position.' We had a ceasefire.

'Another place, another time, Joseph, you could have been him and he could have been you. The difference is you'd really have beaten the shit out of your prisoner.'

Joseph told me about being in the cell. 'Paddy was singing rebel songs in the room next door and I remember thinking, Shut the fuck up or we'll end up on the prison ship in Belfast.'

'What was your father doing throughout all this?'

'He came to get me at the station after getting help from an Irish senator who was also a solicitor.' After two nights in the cells Joseph came back home.

'Father closed the door – put his two arms round me and just held me,' I could barely hear what Joseph was saying at this point. His voice sounded frail. It was choking with emotion. My so-called journalistic veneer just crumbled. I thought of the dreams I'd been having: Dad with his two arms round me. Holding on to me and never wanting to let go. Keeping me safe.

Joseph's father knew his son had to get away and start afresh.

'I remember Father looking right into my eyes and there were tears in his. Right at me saying to me, "I am glad you are going. The way things are going you'll end up in jail like a lot of your buddies will." And a lot of them did.'

This idea that there was no other path didn't square with me.

'They didn't have to though, did they? They didn't have to become rebels.'

'Listen, I wasn't rebelling. I was conforming. Father understood it was necessary that I be like that. He'd be disappointed if I wasn't. He never voiced it. When I was picked up, he never said, "What were you doing? Who were you with?" Just, "It's time for you to get out of here now."'

'Why did he understand it was necessary to be like that? To be in the IRA? To help in a bombing operation?'

'In those communities you had to be. It's inside you.'

'It's still a choice.'

Joseph took a long loaded pause and set out the manifesto in his heart. What he saw as the gospel truth.

'It was something that had to be done.' He seemed to emphasize every second word when he said that. 'It was the way your tribe went. The way you went – it was just a matter of degree as to what level you were prepared to serve at. One friend of mine was in an active-service unit on Antrim. Only three in the unit there in the Glens of Antrim. But they had fantastic support and they'd create havoc.

'Support from whom?'

'From everyone. Transport, safe houses, food – through and down to "shut mouth": see nothing, hear nothing, say fucking nothing. Look at your toes.'

I asked, 'Is that from fear or allegiance?'

He shot back with clarity, force and total conviction. 'Allegiance.' My question and his answer had overlapped and the word 'allegiance' stood to attention the second it came out of his mouth. It marched on ahead. The unit followed.

'There was a road to travel on if you had the courage to do it. It was recognized that at any given period there was always an element who would be at the vanguard of it all.'

Joseph told me a story to illustrate the sense of allegiance people felt. 'When I was a cop in the seventies, I went up to the North to visit my mother while I was on an undercover job in Dundalk, just south of the border. And I used the undercover car to drive into the town and street where my mother lived. It was late when I arrived and I pushed the front door and it opened. I walked in and shouted, my mother got up and made some tea, and eventually I went to bed. The next morning having breakfast I said, "By the way, Mum, your front door was open last night."

'"Yes," she said, "I leave it open for the boys – for the IRA to escape through the house if there's any problem." And this was a woman who in my estimation was no more Republican than that chair you are sitting in. But I know for a fact that many people up there who would say 'IRA no no no' would vote Sinn Fein when it came to the vote.'

From his mother and his father there was a big push to get Joseph out of the situation after his arrest. He was sent to the North of England for a while to stay with his sister Evangeline, who was studying there to become a nurse. He applied to join the Garda, the Southern police force. His mother knew the wife of the Commissioner who himself was a Northerner. Joseph even had occasion to meet the man. He sailed through the exams and the coordination between Southern and Northern constabularies on such a minor matter as an application was nonexistent. Even if it had been scrupulous, he'd never actually been charged with anything. There was no record. Joseph remembers, 'The commissioner would know that coming from the North some loose connection with Republicanism was inevitable but if he'd known there was a firmer connection I'd never have got in. It was completely haphazard. I went south to Monaghan and applied from a station there anyway.' A new beginning and new life in the South beckoned. He grabbed it with both hands.

Blue eyes stared back at me from all the photo frames in Joseph's front room where we sat. His children and grandchildren. I listened to his relative values.

I then asked him a question that I attempted to frame and phrase as subtly and tactfully as I could. It came out as a long-winded dissertation.

'The reactions to atrocities – now every right-minded person says that is a terrible terrible thing and lots of innocent people have been killed and it's awful, but there is still, by degrees, as you have hinted, a different reaction to the atrocities between the English and the Unionists on one hand and those people who would be broadly speaking Republican on the other. What would those differences be?'

Since we'd met he'd teased me about adopting my 'radio/TV persona' with him. The professional me again. He was right. It was back. He let it pass though. He answered thoughtfully.

'Hard to put your finger on it because the attitudes would vary within the Republican community. At the sharp end the view would be that it had to be done – the human factor in it wouldn't be considered at all because of the long-term gain. And the policy was to sicken the British with atrocities.'

I asked him about Enniskillen, where on Remembrance Day 1987 a bomb blew eleven Protestants to pieces at the Cenotaph. One of the IRA's worst atrocities of the troubles, it horrified him. It sickened him. He went on.

'I questioned how the IRA could do that. I got a question in my mind – I didn't want to believe that it was a headquarters' staff decision. Immediately I said to myself, Jesus, something went wrong.'

Something went wrong? What would something going right have meant? There was a completely different moral calibration going on here.

'What about something like Mountbatten's murder?'

He came straight back with dismissive confidence. 'Oh that was quite justified. I wouldn't have any qualms about Mountbatten going down.' He sniffed casually. 'I'd have no qualms about him.' The 'him' was dispassionate.

'What about the young lads and women?' I reminded him.

'That was ancillary stuff. It's a pity but – you know – collateral. That was an awful shame, his wife there losing a leg – one of the ladies there lost a leg – badly maimed. But, he was a beautiful target to hit because it would have a reaction. A reaction in Britain – the British people would turn round and say Jesus get out of here. Get out of this. Get away from it. But the British people saying that is one thing, convincing the Unionists . . . is another.' His voice tailed off, beaten down by frustration.

I shuddered. The emotional force of this moment was profound.

I knew these attitudes. The politicians would normally dissemble better and moderate them for public consumption, but this wasn't just some slippery customer from over there I was interviewing. From that place that has seen so much bloodshed and misery for generations. For a thousand years, according to Joseph. This man was my father. And I wasn't just an interviewer either. I was his son. His little boy. And Mountbatten was a beautiful target.

The only brief I held for Mountbatten was his humanity and the fact that Dad admired him and thought his murder senseless and evil. Here was my own flesh and blood with a mindset so far removed from my parents' and my own background that he might as well have beamed down from another planet. But he was from the same set of islands. Over the years, when doing stuff on Ireland on the radio and TV of course I've tried to burrow into the Republican mindset to seek to understand it – as I did with the Loyalism. As I sought to do with Nationalism and Unionism. This is no great philosophical accomplishment, it is merely a basic of broadcast journalism. Know where they're coming from. But here it was staring back at me with its blue eyes and a certainty that struck deep. It looked like me.

On the same day as the Mountbatten carnage, 27 August 1979, eighteen British soldiers had been killed near Warrenpoint in County Down. What did he think of that?

'I would have no problems with that. No problems at all. But being a cop, if it happened south of the border, to Irish soldiers or Irish police, I couldn't accept that at all.'

'What about a seventeen-year-old British squaddy on the street – hit in a drive-by, something like that?'

'I had a cousin shot by the British. He was going up the street and he was shot in the back. He was prominent in the IRA and they shot him in cold blood.' He told me our cousin's name.

I thought just two clearly enunciated words to myself: Fucking hell.

Long after I was back in London, the conversation in Joseph's front room played over and over in my mind. There were things I wished I'd said. Questions I still wanted to ask. One of those came to me in the endorphin rush of a six-mile run. I was mulling over what he'd said about British soldiers killed in the Troubles. 'I would have no problems with that. No problems at all.' He'd justified his stance, or as he saw it, explained his position by pointing to our dead cousin. One of our own clan, gunned down by the Brits. When I got in from the jog I hauled myself upstairs and quickly showered, needing to be as clean as possible to ask it. I rang him. He wasn't long back from the dentist and he'd been having forty winks by the fire.

'Can I ask you something?'

'Go ahead, Nick.'

'If an intermediary had traced you and said, "I knew your son who was adopted and he would have wanted you to know about him. He joined the army and was murdered by the IRA at Warrenpoint in 1979 when he was eighteen. It broke his mum and dad's heart. How would you have felt?'

He thought. He didn't kick it away. That's not in his character. He tried to answer. 'I'd . . . Jesus – I'm just back from the dentist and you're asking me these difficult questions.' He gathered himself. 'It would be a double tragedy. Losing a son and losing him again. That is a difficult question, Nicky.'

'But you said a British soldier was a legitimate target?'

'I'd . . . it . . . would accentuate the tragedy. The political tragedy. The sheer fucking stupidity of the whole situation. Would it shift my political position? No. It would make me think of the tragedy and how it could have been avoided if the peace had got together. It was a price that had to be paid by many mothers' sons. What a fucking question.'

'What's the fucking answer?'

'They didn't represent humanity.' There was such unshakeable belief in his voice. This is, of course, a familiar technique of warfare. De-humanize the enemy. They didn't represent humanity.

'Just the Empire. What it was doing. What had been done. I couldn't see them as mothers' sons.' It was an attitude just as unappeasable and unappealing as that of one former British Army officer I encountered at a Kent dinner party and heard talking about bog-Irish murdering psychopaths. The attitude is the same. The total opposite. But the exact same thing.

'Joseph, if that had been me – one of those soldiers – would my death have been worthwhile?'

'From a military point of view, yes.' I gulped. Then his voice went into the whisper that appears when his emotions get the better of him and that certainty of his blinks.

'When I got home to bed at night, what my conscience might say . . . I don't know. I would have to deal with that myself. But I wouldn't have been confronted by the living flesh of him. He – you – would have been in the abstract.'

'Were any of the murders worth it? The killing of innocent people? The lives devastated? What did it all achieve?'

His voice was loaded with emotion. The full force of his deep-seated convictions came pumping back up. If there'd been a table handy he would have been thumping it. 'We wouldn't have got here to this point. Without it the Unionist people would never have accepted any political movement to take us here. It needed the Unionist people to cry for help with their hands up and the message to get through to their political leaders in Belfast. *Unfor*-tunately. In 1969 you couldn't get a house. You couldn't get a fucking job. You couldn't get fucking nothing. Bigotry begets vio-lence. The boil needed to be lanced. *Un*fortunately. Without all the maiming and bombing and, *un*fortunately, yes, all the mistakes, the Protestant mindset would not have shifted one fucking inch.'

I wondered if his position had shifted one inch in his whole adult life. One inch since he sat on his grandmother's knees and rocked to the soothing lullabies of her rebel heart. I stretched across and turned off the dictaphone.

Once I asked Joseph another 'what if'. It was a bit of a clumsy one that got off to a bad start and sounded really pretentious. I asked him what his reaction to me would have been if I'd not been on radio and television and hadn't amounted to anything much. He came right back (and quite right too, I hear you say): 'What makes you think you're anything fucking special?'

'I don't mean that. That came out wrong.' I tried again. 'What if I had been some useless, dysfunctional, nasty lump of worthless-ness? I don't know – a crack head. A convicted sex offender.

Whatever?' I was snatching examples from the ether to try and justify my ugly value judgements.

'Would have made no difference to me at all,' said Joseph defiantly. 'I'd have tried to understand and make amends for not being there for you. I'd have no right to judge you. Just a duty to understand.'

He meant it with all his heart. I felt it too. Whatever I think of his politics, his prejudices or his past, I have no right to judge him. Just a duty to understand. He is my father.

TWENTY

Three Armies, Three Funerals

Back in London I was still getting to grips with Joseph's long confessional. He said the conflict had been awful but necessary. Bloody but inevitable. And what of the young lads who joined the British Army for a glamorous, thrill-a-minute life and ended up in the Bogside and West Belfast? His justification for their deaths had been swift and certain. His words again: 'I had a cousin shot by the British. He was going up the street and he was shot in the back. He was prominent in the IRA and they shot him in cold blood.' So who was this boy? What of my cousin killed by the British Army? I found his entry in David McKittrick's salutary commemoration of the dead, *Lost Lives*. This is the tragic inventory of all the victims of the Troubles, in which the human cost is laid bare, page after shocking page. And what about the collateral tragedies? The families left behind. These aren't statistics. More than three and a half thousand souls. Civilians, paramilitaries, policemen, soldiers, fathers, mothers, children. Lovers. All lost lives.

When I'd read about my cousin I looked at countless other entries. Inevitably I thought about the lives I'd lost and what I might still be feeling now if they'd been blown to pieces while shopping or mown down while pruning the roses. I still grieve for Dad but thankfully he died peacefully and I was fortunate enough to be able to say goodbye. Dad was the greatest loss I'd experienced but he was still there in so many ways. The more I got to know Joseph, the more I thought and dreamt of Dad. Have I two-timed him through finding another father? Have I been disloyal? I don't know, but I do know that his death was the saddest day of my life.

At his farewell I attempted to give a funeral oration. Well, it was an oration of sorts. I tried to say a few words. Unlike the funeral of my IRA cousin and those of his ilk the oration was rhetoric free. I didn't rage against oppression. I didn't rail against compromise. I made no mention of his politics – for the record he was a tribal Tory. I merely tried to do justice to his bountiful beautiful humanity. His was a life to celebrate and a death to mourn but he had no cause to glorify save one of gentle decency.

I can replay the funeral in my head. It's November 1995. There are fifty or sixty people in attendance at the main chapel in Mortonhall crematorium. We are some two miles up the road from my parents' house in Edinburgh. Now it's just Mum's house. Dad stopped off at home one final time on his way from hospital to the hospice. He asked to spend a quiet few minutes in every room and was so pleased the bathroom redecoration was complete. Piped organ music oozes through the speakers – 'Dear Lord and Father of Mankind forgive our foolish ways.' After the poignant hymn, I go up to the lectern and say my piece to the assemblage of retired doctors, bank managers, Murrayfield debenture holders, Scottish Curling Association office bearers, fading widows and handsome wives. They're all so much less imposing than I remember them from my childhood. Softened by this intimation of their own mortality. I break down and weep. I've lost control. It happens when I look up at them looking at me in my helplessness. Any semblance of restraint just buckles.

My shoulders are heaving. I know I won't get the next word out, that I'll lose the power of speech. I'll crumple at what I'm saying. Can I get it together again and read the next bit from my little piece of paper? It's crumpled too. I want to mention that one of Dad's favourite expressions was 'The sun's over the yardarm'. Time for a drink I think. When I relate this and am about to say that the sun now truly is over the yardarm, I look up and see one of his old buddies gently nodding. I crumple again. I see my school friend Iain's dad crying. When we were all kids, he was quite the most intimidating father of any of my pals. JR we called him. Now there he is. Older and softer. More human. Sitting in row six, quietly weeping. I understand why. He is seeing a contemporary of his own son, remembering a father just like him. Funerals make people think like that. I make it to the end of my little bit of paper and go to sit down. We pray.

There was no wailing or ululating in the congregation. Theirs was a quiet unassuming grief. Tears here and there. The wailing was within or trumpeted into white handkerchiefs which signified surrender to the grief inside. But, my Celtic display aside, the Edinburgh reserve kept everything within the cordon sanitaire of Edinburgh decorum.

We walked out of the church to the sound of his favourite old song, 'Paper Doll'. That was his Requiem. No Mozart. No Bach. No lone piper and lament. He liked catchy tunes and he liked catchy tunes in pubs, preferably played on pianos while beer was being served by brassy blonde barmaids. The service over, it's back home for the booze, food and the beginning of an ever-lengthening road away from his life towards the dominion of memories.

One incident lightened the funereal gloom and still makes us chuckle. I say 'chuckle' because that's what Dad used to do. He didn't laugh or giggle. He chuckled. When we'd been hastened into the hearse to take us up to the crematorium earlier that day, the ever so 'umble but ever so scrupulously professional funeral directors had allocated specific cars to everyone in the family group decreeing that Mum, my sister Fiona, cousin Philip and I go with Dad. Phil was the last to get in. He is a very big lad. When he was through the door and his full weight was applying itself to the gravity of the situation, the car sank down by what seemed about three feet. I had to stop myself guffawing. I am sure we all silently worried for the big black Bentley's suspension. It was extraordinary. Phil was coolly unfazed. We still chuckle because Dad would have chuckled. He would have found it hilarious. I can see him getting his hanky out to wipe the tears of laughter from his eyes. There are tears in mine as I write this.

That was Dad's funeral. His army was the Indian army. He started in the Gordon Highlanders when he bunked out of his medical degree at Cambridge at the outset of the Second World War. A year or two later he got a transfer, making it to the rank of major in the Rajput Regiment by the end of the war. He fought against the Japanese empire in the jungles of Burma.

'Ever kill anyone, Dad?' I asked him once.

'I don't know. They shot at us from the jungle and we shot back into the dark. There was thick canopy.' He didn't want to tell me much. He did talk about the friends who fell, and to his dying day he corresponded with old Indian soldiers he'd befriended sixty years before. He had a love affair with India and the Indians. Any film or documentary about the subcontinent and he was glued to the telly. Anything featuring Japanese cruelty like that old Clive James clip show of their sadistic game shows, and he'd leave the room muttering politically incorrect but empirically accurate imprecations. That was his prejudice. Born of his experience. Just like Joseph, I suppose.

After the war, his medical degree out of the window, he went into publishing and settled in Edinburgh. Maps were his passion. He had a rare knack with them and preternatural understanding of them. Even the simplest A to Z looks like a secret Aramaic code to me.

Dad was a popular man and could mix with and talk to anyone. People immediately warmed to him and liked him. It's a trait I missed out on. 'You can do it,' says Tina, 'with effort.' Dad didn't need to try. Mum had been especially touched when the daughters of the local paper shop came to the house with flowers and wearing their beautiful traditional Indian dresses to convey their sympathies and return the respect the dear and mannerly gentleman had shown to them. That would have meant so much to him.

Dad's father was a life I never knew. He was the grandfather I never had. He cast a stern shadow on Dad's world for all Dad's life. James Argyll Campbell was born in Australia of Scottish parentage. An eminent doctor, he appeared in the bible of the British establishment, *Who's Who*, in 1916. Here is the entry.

CAMPBELL, James Argyll, M.D.; Professor of Physiology, Government School of Medecine, Singapore since 1913; b. Brisbane, Queensland, 30 Mar.1884; s of late James Campbell,

M.D. Brisbane; Educ. Brisbane Grammar School; Edinburgh University, Aitken Carlyle Bursar; Vans Dunlop scholar, 1905 and again 1906; Carnegie Scholar, 1911; Crichton scholar, 1912; M.B., Ch.b., with Honours, 1909. M.D. [Theses Highly commended], 1912; D.Sc [Physiology], Edin in absentia. Assistant to Professor Schafer, University of Edinburgh, 1911–1913. Publications. Several papers on Physiological Subjects. Recreations: cricket, swimming, tennis, golf. Address: Government School of Medicine, Singapore. Clubs: Golf, Cricket, Singapore.

Far too much to live up to. As far as his father was concerned, anything less than the above was failure. So there he was – James Argyll Campbell: academic, cricketer and true scion of the old Empire, cracking the leather on willow at the going down of the sun, in one of her far-flung outposts.

Another funeral further back in time from Dad's. Twenty years further back. There I am at Mortonhall crematorium's smallest departure lounge. I am fourteen. Me, Mum, Dad, Fiona and Mum's sister Lorna and that's all. I'm sobbing. I'm wailing. The rest of the family have tears but theirs are more restrained. Silent. It was my first death or the first human death that mattered like this. Granny had gone before but I never knew her like I knew Grandpa, my mum's dad. When I was eleven my dog Candy died and I was churned up by it. I kept a lock of hair for a long time. I demanded Mum announce the tragic and untimely death in the *Scotsman*. You'll be relieved to know she refused.

The funereal muzak is making its insidious presence felt. I am sobbing uncontrollably and a boy – an assistant – a sable-clad lad is staring and staring and staring at me. Looking away and staring.

Looking away and staring. Am I the first person he has ever seen crying at a funeral? Maybe this is his first funeral too? Whatever happened to professional discretion? He has become my *bête noir*. Fuck off, I think. Just fuck off.

When he died it hit me very hard. I was so devastated I had to take three days off school. I remember lying face down on my bed, my fists pummelling the pillow in grief. I loved him very much. He was the son of a chicken farmer. His parents moved from Scotland to Cumbria where he was born. In his final ten years, the long winter of widowhood before he died, he lived with us half the year and our cousins in Surrey the other half. When he did pass away he was with us. He died in Edinburgh Royal Infirmary flying on morphine. What dreams came before he shuffled off this mortal coil? I visited him every day and watched his delirium. I wrote a derivative and pretentious adolescent poem that was published in the school magazine. John Lennon's book of poetry *In his Own Write* had made its mark.

> Ever ready dave
> As the wind glows ever ready where
> And the rain pours drown.
> I have nothing to save
> Except how are you?
> Pure old man.

Grandpa was full of quips and gags and boiled sweets, but like *Hamlet*'s Yorick: 'Where be your gibes now? Your gambols? Your songs? Your flashes of merriment that were wont to set the table on a roar.'

Where be your bloody boiled sweets? I haven't been able to find them from that day to this but you always had some in your pocket. They looked like they came out of an old glass sweet jar, high on a shelf in a Victorian confectioner's. I could see the dark polished wood and a moustachioed chap in a white apron, standing on a roll-along ladder stretching up to the multi-coloured delicacies on display. The blackcurrant-flavoured ones were so delicious. I wanted them to last forever. But there were other flavours in there too. They can't all be blackcurrant.

We once went for a walk to the slate factory down the road, got some coloured crayons and on the way back I counted to a hundred. When we got home he proudly recounted my feat to Mum. I loved him for that. The slate factory is a housing development now. They sold the show home years ago. Grandpa would also do this trick with his false teeth and his gums. He'd dislodge the dentures, suck on his gums and screw his face up like a gurning monster while his spectacles teetered in comical Eric Morecambesque disarray.

He made me laugh whenever he wanted to. I still copy some of his silly faces and his jokes and gibes and gambols for my little girls. His spirit's so often inside me when I make them roar with delight as he so often used to do with me.

I wanted him to last for ever but one terrible day he never got up. A few weeks later he was taken to hospital. The bookies lost a friend. The bridge club lost a member. The unknown confectioner lost a valued customer. We lost Grandpa. He was one of the significant figures in my life and still is.

During the First World War Grandpa – a milliner and a gambler in peacetime – had seen action on the Somme with the Royal Artillery. 'Did you ever kill anyone, Grandpa?'

'I don't know. We just fired back at them.'

Not only was he sweet, funny, charming and affectionate, especially to his grandchildren, but he was also the most self-centred, difficult man his daughter, my mum, had ever known. Like my dad, she kept many of her paternal resentments deep within her. Typically though, the grandchildren got only the best of him. It's a little like my relationship with Joseph. He has another chance. In the two years before Grandpa died he wrote his memoirs in painstaking longhand in four-lined jotters. I have only recently read them for the first time and found myself utterly engrossed. An incident in June 1915 particularly stands out.

I saw a sentry with his rifle standing beside a wooden hut. As I approached I saw a small boyish looking chap standing at the open door.

I thought he was a prisoner for some offence, as I was passing he asked me in a broad Lancashire accent, 'Got a fag, mate?'

I had about five in my packet. I said, 'You have these.'

He said thank you and smiled. When I got back to our HQ I said what had occurred to Sgt Major Grimes and he said, 'Oh he's for it tomorrow.'

I said, 'Is he being tried by court martial?'

He said, 'No, he's for the firing squad.'

I didn't grasp the matter at first and let it pass. Well I had a small bivouac in the field, close to a small coppice, and my bivouac was near the path that led through the coppice. The following morning I was half asleep about 5.30 a.m. and I hear voices. Sgt Major giving orders. I thought this most unusual at such an hour.

I listened and sat up in my small tent. Looked through the flap. It was broad light and I saw several soldiers lined up. Then the order quick march.

I saw they were marching towards my tent to enter the coppice. I got the shock of my life. Leading were two officers followed by a Sgt Major, two or three other NCOs and about 8 or 10 soldiers at the back. Most with rifles. One was carrying what I saw later must have been a stretcher.

Walking in the middle of the party smoking a cigarette and out of step was my little prisoner of yesterday, smoking as a last privilege what I hoped was one of my cigarettes but I expect the poor soul must have smoked all he could get knowing what was ahead for him.

I was really shocked to think he was to be shot by his own countrymen. They marched off into the coppice. I sat up in my tent and listened about 8 or 10 minutes later. I heard one loud distant crack of rifle fire and that would be the end of that poor boyish looking lad who, because he could not face up to killing others, had lost his own life.

This soldier – this boyish-looking prisoner – was about eighteen. With a bit of research I established who he was. One Private Chase. He was found cowering and terrified in a ditch after a gas attack on the Lancashire fusiliers. Chase was shot at dawn *pour encourager les autres*. A volley of gunfire echoed against the St Sixtus Monastery wall. A little boy who had heard the early-morning commotion looked on.

Round about the same time as Grandpa's last farewell there was another funeral only one hundred and fifty miles away as the raven flies. There was another crack of rifle fire, as deafening as the one that killed Private Chase, but this time it's a volley into the late-afternoon sky and there is no monastery near by. There's a church. A priest is about to deliver the funeral rites. As he begins a pungent incense pervades the cold air. It's cordite. The gunfire didn't cause the loss of a boy's life, it marked it. It was celebrating his sacrifice and recognizing the cause for which he gave it. Three days before, bullets had peppered his body. Like Chase he was shot by British soldiers. This was my cousin.

Dad and Grandpa. These were the men I knew and grew up with. These were the men I loved. Their send-offs were low-key affairs marked by a few sombre lines in the births, marriages and death column of the *Scotsman*. For my cousin shot by the British Army there are photos and articles and dozens of death and sympathy notices. 'Soldier of the people. He died in the service of the people', 'From the graves of patriot dead spring living nations', 'You can kill the revolutionary but you can't kill the nation'. These are set on pages beside trite adverts for local shops: 'Good news for home furnishers', 'Scot Free to Scotland. Just bring your car and three friends'. Maybe my cousin should have taken that advice. It makes for surreal reading. The unsettling and threatening beside the reassuringly banal. There's even the radio listings column tantalizingly close to the name of my dead relative. And there it is, the section with the Radio One line-up for the day. Banal at its best. 7.00–9.00. Tony Blackburn. A lifeline back to something I understand. The station I was to work for in years to come. A litany of DJs' names – people who became colleagues, people I know, right next to a dead revolutionary relative I didn't.

How did he die? A British Army patrol came across some men loading weapons into a car. The Army claimed the men took up firing position. The family and Republican groups conceded there were guns in the car but maintained the men were unarmed. One man fell and the rest fled. The British soldiers put a jacket over my cousin's body and were attacked by a screaming mob of mainly women. Two days before this incident two British soldiers had been blown up and hours after that another young IRA volunteer had been shot near his home.

Why did he die? My cousin's death was yet another entry into the ledger, the true circumstances of which will forever be in dispute. The rights and wrongs; the fact, fiction and fallacy all bound up in a barbed-wire tangle of allegation and counter claim. The shape of it changes all the time though. It depends on your view. Loading weapons into a car. Back in 1956 Joseph was doing just that for the same cause. But he was undetected by any patrol and he kept his life. A life he went on to change.

A cortège of 5,000 mourners, including leading Republicans, set off from my cousin's home. A lone piper plays a lament. The primal notes stir together grieving and grievance, hurt and hatred and all the history Joseph keeps coming back to. Stirred together in cauldrons of tribal blood flowing in the hearts of the bereft. The piper plays on. *Pour encourager les autres.*

I see from the press photos that some faces are expressionless. Others express sorrow as if that's all they've ever done and ever known. Pinched, gaunt and gimlet eyed. All are as grey as the day.

The procession halts at the point where he was shot. Eight uniformed men wearing green camouflage jackets and black berets are walking beside the hearse in open defiance and open grief. A British Army helicopter is buzzing around at an indiscreet distance overhead but that's the extent of the security presence in the immediate area. Women and children carry wreaths. Everyone carries this latest grief now added to whatever other baggage they haul through their lives. The Tricolour-draped coffin makes its way to the cathedral. The vault is now long disused and the entrance undetectable. As dark as eternal night.

It's both a family funeral and a highly charged political event. For the broken hearted and the hard hearted. Men from his army, the IRA, are gathered there with his old school friends. Some are both. Another cousin – the dead man's younger brother – has been released on eight hours' parole from prison to attend. He is best friend, sibling and brother in arms. There is weeping and gnashing of teeth. There is bitterness. There is resolve. The uniformed guard fire into the sky. An unholy crack of fire at a holy site. The sacred and the secular. The pious and profane combined in the hearts and minds of the faithful. There is a graveside oration for this twenty-year-old boy. My cousin was prominent, deemed worthy of an address by the wary man in the duffle coat with the darting eyes, who'd slipped through the security cordon. The leader condemns the 'cold-blooded murder' of the young man while saluting his sacrifice. He intones solemnly, with passion and with clear purpose. He knew the unstinting belief of his martyred acolyte. Those present stare into the grave and gain strength from the past. The fact that two British soldiers have recently been blown to pieces is, for

some who are there, scant consolation. In that emotive and politically motivated oration the leader ignores the promises of compromise currently on offer. 'Stand firm in the struggle.'

After the gunfire, the coffin is lowered to the signs of the cross
and prayers for the dead man's soul. I'm related to this stranger in
the earth. He's a cousin. Like the Windsors and the Romanovs.
I'm not related to Dad, nor to Grandpa. I am related to this other
soldier. We share those things called genes. Some of my flesh and
blood lies within him. Mutated, diluted and modified, but there.
My own flesh and blood in that grave. Same blood, different
universe.

I used to watch these occasions on the TV news and wonder
at the bloody nerve of those mourners. I shared Dad's anger. I
shared his view. They were sick. They kill us and in their deluded
logic they claim the moral high ground in a mockery of truth.
They kill British soldiers and they maim and bomb and mutilate
and still thousands line the streets to grieve for the murderers. Old
men and women. Mothers. Children. We didn't ask any deeper
questions. And neither did they. We just confirm all our prejudices
about each other's prejudices.

My Grandpa had fought proudly. He was a British soldier. And
he knew about death. He knew about senseless carnage. He'd seen
so much all around him during the Great War. In his notebooks
he described the aftermath of the British Army's bloodiest day. The
Somme.

I knew the infantry would have had a good rum ration before
they went over. That was the custom. As I passed through

Bertrancourt on this beautiful summer's day, the skylarks were singing as they flew heavenwards and thousands of our troops were unknown to them on their way there too.

I left the guns about 11 returning to the wagon lines as I passed through the village of Bertrancourt again. I was surprised to see a casualty clearing station had been established there and wounded were arriving. I came up to guns again the following day and what a sight Bertrancourt was. In an orchard they were operating on barn doors on trestles and about 30 men of the Labour Corps were digging graves.

There were already about 150 wooden crosses showing in the field next to the orchard. The wall had been knocked down to make it all one. There were dozens of wounded soldiers lying round the orchard awaiting the doctors who were working full out. Near my battery another battery was entrenched amongst an avenue of trees. And about an hour earlier they had been heavily shelled and had heavy casualties. I saw 15 of their men rolled into one large hole. Their boots and uniforms were buried with them – only their belongings were kept. These were sent to echelons who dealt with personal belongings.

Our battery was in the same place a week later and when I passed through Bertrancourt I asked the NCO of the Labour Corps how many he had buried in the field. He said he didn't know. They kept the records in the farmhouse [the medical corps] but he said, 'I suppose 14 to 15 hundred are buried there so far.' That was only one of dozens of casualty clearing stations.

What if I had never known Grandpa? What if there'd been a different twist of fate? What if Grandpa had died on the Somme instead of surviving and he'd been one of those corpses under one of those endless little wooden crosses? Dad would have married someone else and he would have been a stranger for ever. I'd have been adopted by another family and would have become someone else. There but for the grace of Kaiser Bill and something greater still go any of us. Grandpa's survival made me what I am. But whatever the outcome for Grandpa of the stuttering rifles rapid rattle, the boy in the ground sixty years later would still have been my cousin.

TWENTY-ONE

The Forest

Eighty-six summers have passed since the Battle of the Somme. We're in the Western Highlands in our cottage a mile and a half from the touching village war memorial that marks the sacrifice so many local men made for King and country. The vestigial clan traditions of loyalty and service to their chieftain, like the pipes themselves, led Highlanders into unquestioned battle for their king. I jog past the monument every morning when we're there. It fascinates me. It holds such dignity and nobility. In a cynical moment I might be struck by the naivety of another age. They believed it was a struggle for right against wrong. Wasn't it more a struggle for dominance by one military industrial complex against another? The romantic in me prefers to believe they died that we might be free. The truth is in the eye of the beholder. Look at Ireland.

The tales that monument tells are endless. Listed first are the officer class with their sometimes precious and often double-barrel surnames and then, further down, come the Highland soldiery. Chisholm, Cameron, Macdonald, Maclean. Names redolent of failed Highland rebellions and tragic land clearances. Names that fill the latest local phone directory. We're all treading on the bones of the past.

Helen and Patrick are staying with us in the cottage. Their kids and ours are running through the fields together, along the beaches, climbing rocks and splashing in the sea. These are cousins playing. All I can hear is the laughter of our children. All I can taste is a beautiful cold beer slipping down my throat as I gaze out at the sparkling ocean and faraway islands. I watch the little ones in their carefree worlds, happy as skylarks. I'm so envious of that innocence. They don't even really know they're related to each other. We've sort of explained it but what does that mean to a five year old? Related? You've got the same grandfather? I might as well explain the structure of DNA – if someone could first explain it to me. A cousin is just a friend you see and play with a lot. It means nothing to them but finding people I was related to came to mean everything to me. I hadn't realized how important it was until I'd completed the jigsaw.

These children know none of that inner angst, the unsettling mystery over who you are and what you are that adopted children can feel. And we are always adopted children, never adopted adults. When I was their age I knew I was chosen but my real mummy and daddy were as untouchable and unreal as the tooth fairy and the sandman. As I grew, so too did the need to know. Now they're real people. As flawed, complex and contradictory as all real people are.

We have been having a wonderful time while Helen, Patrick and family have been staying with us. Patrick and I go running every morning and find a mountain waterfall to shower under. To get to the most magical spot of all we have to walk a mile and a half from the single-track road down towards the sea and then make our way through a spectacular forest of Scots pine. At eight o'clock on an August morning with the early promise of a scorching summer afternoon, the sights, smells and sounds all around are breathtaking. As we make our way down through the forest, we look up at the pockets of blue above and shards of sunlight playing on the tops of the trees. The gentle dappled hints of sun on the forest floor belie the thunderous sound we're approaching. The roar of the waterfall gets ever louder. When we've negotiated the route to our vantage point by its spectacular side, we have to yell at each other to be heard.

'Its amazing, isn't it?'

'What?'

'Incredible.'

'Are you going in?'

'What?'

'I'm going in. Life's too short.'

'Are you going in?'

'What?'

I've been three thousand feet further up near the top of the mountain and seen the marshy spring where this force of nature begins. To be under that black rock shelf with the primeval power of the peat-stained water thundering on to your head and gushing down your body is the most incredible feeling. You have to hold on tight. Then you step out of the deluge and into the warm morning rays feeling so alive. It's cleansing, thrilling and the elemental power of it is almost threatening. The journey to find who I am has been all of those.

Patrick understands the force of nature that lead me to the source of my life. He understands the need to erase the question mark and the desire to fulfil the quest but he's honest enough to admit he can't fully appreciate how it feels. He isn't me. Tina sort of gets it. She's a journalist too and completely identifies with the urge to satisfy my curiosity. Likewise, she understands the motivations to write about it, which in all honesty has helped me make some sense of it. But what Tina doesn't quite see is the overwhelming emotional importance of it. The addictive driven necessity of it. She isn't adopted. Maybe you need to be a bundle of one mother's sadness that became another mother's joy really to understand. As we enjoyed the Highland heatwave, the person I know who understands all this most of all is far away and has been for a long while. We grew in the same womb. We both became the same poor woman's bundles of sadness. I was thinking about Esther.

I hadn't spoken to her for so long. We'd become disconnected. I'd been too immersed in the cascading power of all this Leahy stuff. The elemental power of it all – a father, new siblings, a fascinating (to me) political and historical backdrop and a whole new national, cultural and religious heritage. I was drenched in the experience of the new family like a naked man under a huge waterfall. My senses were overwhelmed. I'd edged myself along a slippery ledge, hanging on to a few treacherous branches for grim life, teetered on the rocks and stood in a place I never thought I'd reach. Then I let the roaring, ineluctable force of the experience engulf me. But Esther? She was still there, wasn't she? When I'd dried myself down I'd give her a ring. Right now I was immersed and she was alone.

Then as I stared out on that glorious day at the heat haze that had settled over the glassy sea, clouds began to cluster inside me. And like the slate-grey storm that you can watch looming in the far distance, my atmosphere darkened. It was a feeling of profound unease. I realized how much Esther meant to me and I realized how much I'd abandoned her. We used to have long funny stimulating conversations with moments of instinctive empathy and almost telepathic understanding. I could sometimes speak to her in a way I spoke to no one else. I couldn't remember the last decent conversation we'd had that hadn't been about my new father and brother and sisters and aunts. She has her husband and kids, I've got Tina and the girls, but in addition I'd found this treasure trove of relations, with Joseph as the big prize. With the exception of Stella, I was the only one Esther had. While I was brim full of Joseph, her natural father was dead. While I was revelling in the endless thrills of discovery I was neglecting the fact that this was something she could never have. I'd treated her like a staging post on my journey that was now miles behind me. She didn't deserve that. She had been there for me at the start, standing in my kitchen trying subtly to counsel caution to her impulsive brother. She understood what a strange place the hall of mirrors is.

We are alike. It's hardly surprising. We shared a mother and had similar middle-class Edinburgh upbringings. We're both quick, confident and assertive but we also share that nagging fear of being rejected. Of being second choice, second best and second rate. The irrational unwarranted terror of not being the child our parents really wanted.

It isn't obvious. Esther always seems to be so in control. I'd focused on the professional woman and forgotten that she was also a little girl lost. I'd forgotten how much I missed Esther. I'd forgotten how much I'd come to rely on her.

Esther, it turns out, was missing me too. She was that lonely little girl again, wondering if I was going to abandon her in favour of my new siblings. She puts it so much better than I could:

What did I make of all these new developments in Nicky's life? Well, it made me realize for the first time that Nicky was very special to me. So when this special person started finding other special people – his other birth relatives – I sort of panicked and started to feel all strange and alone.

This relationship was like the horse on the dining table. It was there, and it was significant, but it was not acknowledged. There was a particular bond which I think we both felt, but didn't talk about at all – not to each other, and not to anyone else. You don't when you're from Edinburgh. It's all a bit Californian to discuss your feelings. We had got along fine up until then without getting all soppy about it.

There were obstacles to being open about our relationship of course. Nicky didn't tell his mum or his sister Fiona anything about me for fear of upsetting them. He didn't even tell them that I existed. Tina was on strict instructions not to mention it. That felt quite odd – as if I was a dark and embarrassing secret. As for me, I reported the raw facts of both Stella's and Nicky's existence to my adoptive dad and brother, but played down the emotional significance of it all. They were both grateful that I had told them about my searching and finding, but didn't feel the need to know more. It was easier for them not to ask, and for me not to tell. If you don't *talk* about something like that, it never really becomes reality. It stays in a heat-sealed unit and never sees the light of day.

When Nicky started searching, yes I became needy. I admit

it. I needed reassurance that the relationship was special for him too. Just like a child with their best friend. Are you my best friend? No, I'm someone else's best friend. I looked for positive signals – I didn't want to be hanging around if there was nothing on offer. The nearest Nicky ever got to saying anything remotely affectionate was, 'Tina really likes you.' It was better than nothing.

Did I tell him how I felt? Are you kidding? I couldn't possibly say anything to his face. And I didn't really know how to put it. Couldn't quite find the words. I did try an e-mail – OK it's a bit formal, but give me a break, I was doing my best here. But the response was as expected – a wisecrack. His deft forehand topspin outsmarted my weak lob. Back to the serving line.

From: Esther Cameron
To: Nicky Campbell
Sent: 07 October 2002 11:25 AM

Nicky

Thanks for keeping me in the picture with what's going on for you with your new relatives.

I feel a little bit voyeuristic in this process of yours. The other sensation is one of envy/jealousy.

I suppose I hadn't realized that this relationship between you and me is quite important to me, and I feel a bit envious of and slightly threatened by this thrilling, emotion-laden stuff that's going on for you now. Is this birth sibling rivalry?

Speak soon.

Esther

From: Nicky Campbell
To: Esther Cameron
Sent: 07 October 2002 4:14 PM

Thanks for that e-mail.
NX

PS – when I met you I didn't have e-mail so I couldn't send you one but I did grant you quite a few telephone conversations I seem to remember.

From: Esther Cameron
To: Nicky Campbell
Sent: 07 October 2002 5:15 PM
Subject: RE:

Nicky

I'm not saying this feeling is rational. You can throw logic at it if you like, but it won't work.

Esther

P.S. I have no complaints. You granted me all the airtime I needed.

From: Nicky Campbell
To: Esther Cameron
Sent: 07 October 2002 5:32PM

Getting to know you has been one of the best things in my life. What is your name again?

Nicky's searching and finding was like some peculiar form of torture. He talked to me about it all, and to begin with I was interested and found myself carried along by his excitement. He's a very entertaining storyteller, and the story was fascinating. He was enthralled by the physical similarities, as anyone would be, and seduced by the good looks and the sophistication of his half siblings, Helen and Joseph Junior. Helen sounded especially lovely – great fun, beautiful, gentle with the kids, slim, amazing hair, didn't reveal much about herself, an enigma . . .

Then they suddenly started to become real, which was quite threatening for me. Tina told me in passing that they had invited Patrick, Helen and the kids up to stay with them in their cottage in Scotland. She might as well have kicked me in the stomach. My God – these new relationships were serious. I felt strangely alone at this point. I couldn't even tell my husband Duncan until a week later. I was so churned up. Later, when I was brave enough to tell Nicky how I felt, I asked plaintively: 'How could you do that? How could you invite them to your most special place in the Highlands? You never invited me there'. It seems so childish, but it was how I felt. I was hypersensitive.

'It's not my bloody tree house in the garden, Esther. It's not just for my best friends. It's not my special little den. I invite all sorts of people up there. It's not that big a deal. You always had something else on anyway.'

The sudden realization that I had overplayed the invitation made me laugh out loud. The tension was released. To celebrate, I entered the phone number of the cottage under Tree House on my mobile. Now it pops up if he should call me from the Glens. It reminds me that I love the way he can make me laugh even at the most difficult moments. But the jealousy still lingered, and was ready to pop up too, even at the most unexpected moments.

I managed to stay away from the new relatives. I didn't ask to meet them or look at photos of them. It was easier that way. But one evening when I was looking through an envelope of recent family photos that Tina had sent me I came across this photo of Tina and Nicky and Helen and Patrick – and excuse me, but isn't that Paul McCartney in the middle?

'You never asked me to come to a bloody Paul McCartney concert, let alone to meet the man himself!' I railed in an e-mail a few days later. The jealous child was awakened from her brief snooze. Nicky replied quickly with an oblique e-mail apology. Then innocently tacked on the end: 'P.S. Would you like to come to a Chris De Burgh concert. Perhaps we could meet him?'

Incensed, I stormed through to the kitchen. Chris de Burgh? What an insult! But lucky for me my husband is a very wise man. 'It's a joke, Est,' Duncan said, gently giving me a hug. 'It's just a joke. Calm down.' I didn't laugh until the next day. Funny guy.

I was really disturbed by my reactions because they seemed so out of proportion. I guess I was in a fairly muddled emotional state at the time. This searching business had been a series of closed doors for me. I had found my birth mother, Stella, which was initially a great joy. But she was so damaged by the trauma of giving up two babies for adoption that she couldn't really talk to me about anything important.

I had said goodbye to a baby too, and this had been the

starting point for my search. But my goodbye had been different. My baby was dead. Memories of the loss of my daughter Iona were, and still are, terribly vivid and piercingly raw. Iona, our little daughter, was stillborn in October 1994, just four weeks before her due date. She was a dark-haired, serene, silent, beautiful 7lb 12oz stillborn angel who came and went before she even started her life – warm enough to cuddle. She was buried in a tiny white coffin. No mother should ever be separated from her baby. I never had a chance to talk about the loss of Iona with my own mother. She died two months before Iona died. And I loved my mother with my whole heart and soul and I miss her daily.

My birth father was another closed door. Stella told me he had been an alcoholic all his adult life. She had lost touch. He would either be a terrible mess by now or be dead and gone. There was little hope of finding out what happened to him. I mourned him without ever knowing him at all. Then around the time Nicky was seeking – and finding – his father, my lovely adoptive dad who brought me up and gave me everything was dying of leukaemia in a hospital in Spain. It was a bad year.

I sought refuge in a metaphor to explain these muddled feelings to myself. It sort of helped to make sense of it all. Why was I having such trouble absorbing Nicky's new-found father and sisters and brother and aunts? Why couldn't I just be happy for him? He'd found this lovely family, who were all smiles and welcomes. It was making him happy. He had really come home to his Irish roots. But I was full of resentment and uncertainty.

My picture is this. I see a big stone house; a welcoming house with three steps up to the front door. There are plenty of rooms, lots of space, friends can come and stay. It's warm and open and there are like-minded people to talk to, people in the same boat as you. I call it the *orphanage*. It's not a real place – it's a virtual place. It's a place associated with that nagging idea of abandonment. The people there are not really orphans. Most of us have parents, some of whom have passed away. We are not really abandoned – because we're grown-ups, and the notion of abandonment doesn't affect us day to day. We live with it. But now and again it's good to know that there are others you can talk to about being apart from your natural parents, and never really being able to experience your natural mum or your natural dad as a *parent*. We can never do that. After a time we stop wanting to do that.

I'm there and Nicky's there. There are other adopted people there. Maybe some of you reading this book are there too. Nicky's colleague Jack is peering through the windows. My dearest old friend Mary is there. Although she'd rather play sport than discuss all this damn fool nonsense about abandonment.

Nicky and I have recently taken to the habit of sitting together on the steps of the orphanage – and we can talk for hours. He's the charmer – always with a smile and a joke, flashing his blue eyes and his winning look. He's the one you would expect to be chosen when the nervous, eager families come and visit, looking to give one of us a home. I particularly like him because I can talk to him in this easy, familiar way. I also like him because he's rather like me. As fate would have it, we were grown in the same womb. We share a natural musicality, a fluid creativity, a quick dark sense of humour, a vulnerability, a speed with the things that interest us, butterfly minds, an ability to feel tremendous emotions without always expressing them the right way, a need for reassurance, an outer confidence, a sensitivity, an impatience, a searching . . . a mother.

Nicky is sitting on the steps telling me that he has found a lovely family. He acts out all the characters and his eyes light up with the tempting possibility that this family really loves him. Part of me wants him to be happy, because I care for him, but I am worried that I will lose him to them. Will our nice chats on the steps become less and less frequent as he spends more and more time in the company of the alluring, open-armed, ruddy-cheeked family? First it will be weekends, then holidays, and then the killer – Christmas. I fear the isolation this might bring.

I will never find another companion like him. Helen, Patrick, Joseph Junior and Joseph Senior seem like aliens to me but they share so much with him too – things I don't even know about, things we have never discussed. As fate would have it, Joseph Senior is Nicky's natural father. Yes, that counts for a lot. That's quite something to be close to your father in this way. I am very moved by that and it's a really wonderful relationship that blossoms a little more every day.

Despite all this connection, I still can't really understand why Nicky needs to go and get a family. He'll grow up soon, so there's hardly any point. It's nice here in the orphanage. We support each other. We have fun. Stay here. Don't go. I'm not going anywhere.

Esther wrote this after things were not only reconnected and fixed but were getting better and better. We'd got right back on the same bit of yellow brick road and we were skipping along together.

But I was like one of those old-style Variety plate spinners who was obsessed with just a couple of poles on one side of the stage while the rest of the crockery crashed to the ground. But relationships need tender care and they need to be nurtured. People that matter need to be reassured. I know I do. I should have realized how she felt. Once it was: 'So you are a sister. Yea, I like you. You're bright and funny and good company when I can be bothered seeing you.' Now it was: 'Right. Half siblings we may be. God, or maybe just Stella, saw to that. But let's take control. Let's have a lasting friendship. Now I think we're getting it right.'

The long slow turning point was when our mutual birth-mother, Stella, took ill. It gave us a new base camp from which to climb. Stella had a stroke and was clearly no longer able to live in her sheltered-housing project. She had to move to a nursing-home. We thought she was going to die. I'd spoken to her a fair bit about having found Joseph and she'd of course been interested. She'd even expressed a desire to meet him again. What a thought being at that meeting.

When Stella fell ill I didn't really know what to feel. I didn't feel much. That made me feel dreadful. I phoned Esther and suggested that if the worst happened and Stella didn't pull through, we both go over for the funeral. Esther did the verbal equivalent of putting two hands round my neck and wringing it. I think her knee was involved too. Tartly, sharply, she snapped back at me, 'What's the point of seeing her when she's bloody dead?'

That shook me out off my complacency over our relationship; and made me realize how important it was to go and see Stella, something I hadn't done for years.

We chose the weekend, booked the flights and, after a taxi ride with a great character who had the broadest, loudest Dublin accent we had ever heard, soon we were checking in to a hotel a couple of miles from the home. We decided to walk and promptly got lost. Neither of us had a clue, but the more we got lost, the more we began to find each other again. Eventually we got our bearings and located the place.

Walking into the home we went past the old souls just sitting and staring at nothing. It was all a long lifetime away from the joyful laughter of children on a West Highland beach. Stella was thrilled to see us and she'd had her hair done specially but she was frail and forgetful. Esther was so caring and attentive with her. I wondered where that came from. She carried such disappointment that she'd never really connected with Stella and yet there she was, so solicitous of the woman. There they were, failing mother and tender daughter. We stayed for two or three hours and conversation was difficult. It had the sad slow pace of a funeral march. I was screaming inside. I wanted my mummy. My proper mummy. The other one – the woman who gave birth to me was fading before my eyes and I wasn't distraught. I was sad and reflective. I was depressed by it all. But this wasn't like the times when I visited Grandpa in hospital and I'd been inconsolable, when I could barely cope with the sight of him lying there after all we had had together. But that was the key to it. Stella and I had had nothing together. Not when it mattered.

There were photos of Esther's kid on Stella's bedside table. Where are my kids? I thought. It was a childish thought. I was momentarily jealous that Esther's were on display and mine weren't. It made me think that Esther meant more to her than I did – as if that mattered. What strange emotions. Then in an instant I was appeased. I saw a framed picture on the wall above Stella's head. It was of me when I was a little boy. I clocked it for a second or two and thought I'd absorbed the information. I was about eleven or twelve. I was looking a little bit coy and unsure, standing outside a cottage squinting into the sun. I recognized that look from so many of Mum's photos of me. I felt angry Stella had it. That was Mum's photo. Mum or Dad must have actually taken it. She had no right to my childhood. Why did she have it? Then in another instant I saw it wasn't me. That was no cottage door I knew. It was a picture of Stella's dear departed heroic brother John. I'd made an astonishing mistake. A surreal moment of epiphany.

I stared and stared at the picture. I got it off the wall and talked with Stella about how much he reminded me of myself at that age. She smiled sweetly. So many times John had tried to rescue her from herself. There he was, looking down on her. Still looking out for her. A few days later her nephew Robert sent me a copy which I now treasure.

Stella was so pleased we were there and through the after-effects of the stroke and her advanced Parkinson's disease her delight was evident. When she tired and her supper arrived, we took our leave. We kissed her and held her hand. We wondered if it was the last time we'd see her. As we stepped into the light outside I wanted to run and run and run. Instead we went back to the hotel for a few pints of Guinness and a good chat. As Stella was slowly approaching her end, Esther and I had been given a new beginning.

While I was in Dublin, possibly at the very moment I was calling out for her in my heart, Mum phoned Tina at home. Near the beginning of the conversation, in other words after around twenty minutes, she asked, 'Where's Nicky?'

'He's . . . er . . . in . . . he's in Dublin,' Tina stuttered.

'Why has he gone there?'

'Work. He's on a weekend away with Five Live.'

'Well, tell him I phoned and send all my love.'

When I got back from Dublin Tina launched her attack.

'I am sick of covering up for you. You have got to tell your family about everything.'

'I can't. I don't want to hurt them.'

'But you are causing infinitely more damage by keeping it all hidden away.'

'I can't.'

'You've got to do it. Secrets are bad things in families.' She was imploring me.

She is right. Secrets are corrosive. When she said that it hit home. It had taken Joseph years to open the vault on his own secrets. Was I going to hide, conceal and dissemble like he had done? Was I just a chip off that cunning old block? I'd forgotten Mum and Fiona too. I'd taken them for granted as well. It was all very well having all these sisters but what about my sister Fiona? I love her very much. I was hurting her and she didn't even know it. I remembered our play fights and our real fights. I remembered our Highland summers when, like my children now, we ran through the fields together, along the beaches, climbed rocks and splashed in the rivers and the sea. When we were little ones in our carefree little worlds. Happy as skylarks. We weren't related to each other but we were brother and sister all right.

When we were on holiday in my parents' run-down little cottage with its oil lamps and outside loo, we had our own magical forest track. It led down to what Fiona called a fairy pond where we used to swim. I recalled the unique sibling solidarity you can develop when you grow up with someone. We have it. We found it early. As we sat on those holidays, fobbed off with Coke and crisps in the back of the car while Mum and Dad spent hours in the Highland village pub. It got dark outside so we couldn't play any more. This didn't happen more that twice perhaps. But it happened. And we both remember. One time a local man climbed into the car with us and we both sensed the danger though we didn't understand it.

I remembered Fern village, a special hiding place we made in a forest of bracken one long summer night. I remember her first boyfriends and the pain of her first rejections. I thought of her unconditional love for her severely autistic baby Jamie. Now he is a young man. She loves him just the same. Would she love me just the same?

And Mum? She knew I'd traced Stella but she knew little more. I never discussed it with her. She picked up what scraps she could from my first wife Linda and now from Tina. How to tell her I have found a father without undermining Dad? How to tell her all this without her thinking that my family, her family, the family I grew up in, counts any less to me? Without her thinking about me differently?

'Do it at the weekend,' Tina hollered.

'Tina,'

'No. You have got to. It will come out sooner or later. One of the kids will let slip. Fucking do it.'

She meant it. She wanted me to open the vault and say, 'Hey, everybody, guess what? I've got something to show you. Have a look at this.'

The thought of lifting the lid of the vault – or more literally the phone – and telling Mum everything – from meeting Esther and on through the years to Helen and Patrick and Joseph Junior and Joseph Senior and Ellie and telling her all the background – was petrifying. I though and thought. Tina was busying herself with something else. Deliberately. She was clearly intensely irritated. At the end of her pretty long tether.

'Tina?'

'What?' she barked in the certainty that I was about to trot out some new and ever more ingenious delaying tactic. I surprised her.

'I'll do it.'

TWENTY-TWO

Opening the Vault

'Hello, Mum.' *Hello, Mum?* That's the easy bit.

Tina and the girls were away. I was home alone. Tina had been pressing and pressing me to call Mum: 'Call your mother. Your mother. Call her. Call your mother. You must call your mother.' There were echoes of long ago. Fourteen years previously my then wife Linda had shown a similar persistence and insistence. She'd wanted me to call Stella, my birth mother. We had the number and were about to enter the unknown. Her words were pummelling me into submission like Tyson in his prime laying into some big white lump of lard. 'Go on. Phone her. Phone her tonight. Do it now. Phone her.' I ducked it. Eventually Linda had taken the initiative. This time it was up to me. There was no avoiding it and the call was every bit as terrifying. Different wife. Different mother. Different century. The same quaking fear of the unknown.

How was I going to drive this particular stake through Mum's heart? Gradually, while twisting it, or in a frenzied fit of stabbing and jabbing? 'I have found all these relations. It's been thrilling. It's dominated my life for months. I have met my father. I've met four siblings including Stella's other daughter. I have become particularly close to her and to one of the other sisters too. One on either side, which is nice. How are you?' I was on the verge of committing emotional matricide. I was Anthony Perkins in *Psycho* – cold eyed and preparing to kill. Soon she'd be a corpse in a chair. 'Mother. My mother, She isn't quite herself today,' said Norman Bates.

Tina and the girls were in the Highlands and every time I rang to see how they were I got all the variations on the usual theme.

'Have you done it yet?'

'Not yet but I will.'

'Promise me.'

'OK.'

'You have got to do it, Nicky.'

I knew I needed to tell Mum everything. Tina was right. Secrets are bad things in families. That was her refrain. Secrets are corrosive. Mum had been so candid with me from my earliest years and it could have been so different. I've a friend who found out she's adopted when she was nineteen. She is forty-two now and I don't think she has ever really recovered from the shock. Her relationship with her mother was never the same again. Before I went to Dublin to meet Stella, my mummy had touchingly given me her written account of the circumstances surrounding my adoption. It was what she'd told me, as soon as I was old enough to understand.

I got it out of my special box and read it again.

Once upon a time there was a mummy and a daddy who had a little girl called Fiona and all of them wanted a brother or sister for the little girl but Mummy couldn't grow any more babies and that made them sad.

One day they talked to the doctor about it and he said he knew someone who had a baby and wanted it adopted. The lady was very nice, he said, and would like to have kept the baby herself but was very wise and very courageous and wanted the baby to have a proper mummy and daddy and a good settled home which she was unable to provide so she put the baby into a special baby home and that is where your mummy and daddy first saw you at a few days old.

'Come along,' said the nurse as we walked past a row of cots. Mummy kept stopping and looking and in one cot a dear little baby actually seemed to smile at her. 'Look, nurse,' said Mummy. 'Isn't that one cute? I wish I could have more than one baby so I could take that one home too.' 'But Mrs Campbell,' said the nurse, 'that is Nicholas, your very own adopted baby!!'

So of course Mummy and Daddy were delighted and wrapped you up and took you home and an excited Fiona helped to look after you when you were a little baby. Now you will soon be big enough to look after her! And Mummy and Daddy love you both very, very, much.

So there I was on that Sunday morning. Even in these trying circumstances it was too early for a drink but I needed some kind of a kick-start so I went for a five-mile run. When I came back I got under a beautiful hot shower and then to augment the high and keep those endorphins buzzing I had a strong cup of real coffee. Then I sat down at the kitchen table and casually picked up the

Sunday Telegraph. There was plenty to read. That would delay things. A double-page spread on the Iraqi weapons inspectors' perpetual game of cat and mouse would provide a suitable diversion for a while but my efforts to get the sense of it were as futile as finding anthrax in the desert. I think I reached the third or fourth paragraph when I gave up, lunged at the phone and dialled Mum's number. I stood up and started pacing up and down. It rang and rang. Where was she? My heart was racing and my mouth was already bone dry. She answered with that slow, quizzical but welcoming voice.

'Hello?'

My mum is a phenomenon. She's indefatigable. She has boundless energy and a boundless capacity for love. Since Dad died she has kept herself busy by scooting off on adventures with her friends Elmer and Joanna. They fly away on cheap breaks to Venice and Saga holidays to South Africa and wherever she is, she'll take more photos in one afternoon than David Bailey has in his entire career. Her career was impressive. She was a professional, much admired in her field. Mental health and family breakdown was the world of her work and for a long time her work was her world. She was strong and capable for others but she wasn't there when I got home. The school fees had to be paid, didn't they? She has a vulnerability too. Despite all her bluster and a telephone voice you can hear for miles, I can still see the little girl who ran away from boarding-school when she was eleven. The miserable and lonely child who'd wanted her parents. When she arrived home, and her parents lived in the same town as the school, she was promptly placed in a taxi and sent right back again. The headmistress dealt with her. She was put to bed for a few days on a diet of bread and milk and presented with sanitary towels.

There's something inside Mum that needs to be loved as much as she can love, which is a hell of a lot – something that's in all of us but is manifest in Mum. She's an extraordinary woman. Infuriating and selfish, but more often wise and strong and always so loving. And these days, always there when I go home.

'Hello.'

She sounded bright and cheerful and so pleased to hear from me. She asked me how everybody was. 'Fine. Missing them. House empty without them. Won't be long now. See them soon.' I was going through the motions while I got ready the lethal syringe.

When I spoke I felt breathless. I thought about the mum I was about to hurt and the little girl inside her I was going to devastate. 'Get in that taxi at once. You are going back to school now.'

'What other news?' said the old lady who used to bounce me up and down on her knee and cuddle me with all the love in the world.

'I have got a lot of news, Mum.'

I was staring deep into the heart of who I am and what that meant to both of us.

'A lot of news? Really?'

She sounded excited and frankly pretty taken aback; she was set for an unexpected big blast of lovely news. All the latest on me, Tina, the girls, this, that and the other. What a change from the usual monosyllabic mumbles. It was indeed a rare event for me to invest so much time in sharing news. Normally it was a case of 'Here's Tina.' She does the talking. Well, Tina wasn't here.

'I have got something to tell you, Mum.'

'What's that, love?' she asked with anticipation.

I swallowed and jumped over the edge. 'I've been meaning to tell you for a while but a few months ago I traced my biological father.' I took such care to emphasize the clinically correct defining word: *bio-logical.* I was really saying, 'He is a father in a strictly technical sense but not in any real or fundamental way, Mum. Nothing changes.' My heart was leaping like a frog on mescaline.

'Really?' She sounded surprised but not unpleasantly. She was interested, receptive. She didn't break down. She was her strong and confident self and even had a touch of wonder in the voice. And she was just delighted we were communicating about something so important. All of sudden, after that one word 'really', and all that word conveyed in feeling and tone, I felt strong again. I wasn't falling. I was flying. The fear went. I was so relieved. The vault was open and a big dark festering secret was withering before my astonished eyes like a Hammer Horror vampire in the sunlight.

'How interesting,' she said, eager for more. 'Have you met him yet?'

I told her he'd come over to London and I had been over to south-west Ireland to play golf and I explained all this in the context of collecting information for the book I felt I needed to write. Perhaps I was being slightly protective in reassuring her it was more functional than emotional but it was so far so good. I didn't want to rock the boat. She was being incredibly grown up and I was a child again. The rational and cognitive gave way to the primitive and emotional. I was clinging on to her hand in the supermarket as I didn't want to experience that dreadful moment of panic when I turned round and she was nowhere to be seen.

And Mum is so important to me. My relationships with the people I'd traced and found were works in progress. They might be ephemeral, they might not. But Mum was my rock of ages.

I explained how I'd never really clicked with Stella but how Joseph was much more on my wavelength. Mum listened. It was then that I came back into the bosom of the family I knew, the family I'd always known, and asked Mum to send me copies of the memoir Grandpa had written before he died. Maybe on one level I was trying to tell her that his history mattered more than all the new history I'd discovered. I needed her to know that the family heritage I'd grown up with was the one that really mattered. At that moment it was.

Her inquisitive mind was at full pelt so I explained Joseph's background – the roots, the politics, his life story. I explained the surprise at uncovering it and the challenge in confronting it. Mum was enthralled but she wasn't detached like someone listening to a stranger's story. She was fully engaged. She had emotion in her voice but was strong and most of all was pleased for me. Esther's dad hadn't been able to express interest when she'd told him about finding Stella. He didn't want to face it for all sorts of reasons. Mum was embracing it and was probably aided in doing so by all the resources of her professional persona. People's inner feelings had been her livelihood. That put her at a distinct advantage.

At that point though she said something that struck me to the quick. She didn't mean it. In these high-wire emotional situations, tripping up is easy. The terminology itself is a lion's den. She made an innocent enquiry.

'And when are you seeing your father again?' I was momentarily poleaxed. Utterly confused. For all my life up until that moment, when she'd uttered the expression 'your father' it had meant only one man. My dear departed and painfully missed Dad. I had that feeling of being alone. Wanted by no one. Rejected by everyone. It's akin to the creeping freeze of a general anaesthetic. You are numb outside and dead within. She didn't mean it. What did I expect? The standard and obligatory insertion of the word 'biological' or 'genetic' before any utterance of the F word in relation to the aforementioned newly found progenitor Joseph?

I reacted quickly. I needed to make everything all right for me again. I needed reassurance that our bond was still there and still as strong as ever and to do that I had to say things to make her feel as positive as possible. I'd been a clingy child and was clinging on again. 'I didn't tell you this until now because I didn't want to upset you. I love you and I love Dad. You are my mum and dad and that underpins all of this. Nothing changes that.' I wanted to cry when I said that but knew I couldn't. Once I'd started I wouldn't have stopped. Now she had a break in her voice.

'I know that, darling one. We go back so far together. We have so much history together.'

It's more than that though. I thought that as she was saying it. It's the bond that was there all along. The bond I'd just taken for granted. The bond I need now more than ever.

Then Mum said, 'How is Stella? Have you seen her recently?'

She was behaving as if this conversation was the most normal thing in the world. She had never ever asked me that before. What was going on? It felt as if the world had turned upside down. One of the reasons I never discussed Stella with Mum is that I didn't want my mother asking me about my mother. I didn't want Mum to feel like some kind of understudy and I didn't what to talk about Stella while we were connecting like this. But, it was her natural curiosity. I am the last person to condemn someone for that. And she was signally more interested in Stella than she was in Joseph. That told me something.

'Stella? She's poorly. She had a bad stroke.'

'Oh I am sorry.'

Sorry? Why did she say that? Why did she sympathize? Sorry for me? I don't want her to think that I need her sympathy for someone who gave birth to me but with whom I never connected. Mum and I were Fred and Ginger on an eggshell floor.

I explained my feelings of guilt over Stella to Mum, the fact that I felt no affinity. I tried to tell her what it's like. I was pleased to be telling her this and should have done it years before.

'Mum, you meet an old person you have never known and it's just impossible to really grasp the fact that they're a parent – your birth mother or biological father. The brain just won't take it in. When I think of you or Dad I remember every stage of our lives together. You're nearly eighty now but ageless in a sense. In the mind and memory you're thirty-eight, forty-eight, fifty-eight, sixty-eight, seventy-eight – a life-long collage if you know what I mean.' She knew.

'Mum, I feel like a traitor sometimes.'

'Don't be silly. It is perfectly natural to want to do all this and I am so glad you have. I love you so much and Tina and your wonderful family. They are just lovely.'

She did it again. More eggshells cracked underfoot. What did she mean 'your family'? I dragged through her every utterance with a mental nit comb. It's her family too. She's their Granny. I do wish she'd said 'the family'.

Don't reject me, I thought. Don't reject me. Adopt me again. She didn't mean it. The eggshell shuffle was in my mind not hers.

She asked all about Helen and Joseph Junior and Ellie and I gave her the run-down. Who they were, what they were like and where they lived. I rushed through it. More like a shopping list than an inventory of newly discovered siblings. He is in advertising and she has four kids. It's a coincidence they live in London. The other sister is in Ireland and is a very good artist. Was a beauty contestant once.' As I said it I was anxious about Fiona. The sister I grew up with. I broke as quickly as I could into the Leahy litany and asked, 'How is Fiona?'

Then I took another deep breath and told Mum all about Esther and how we'd become soulmates through all of this madness and how she'd helped and supported me.

By this stage in the conversation nothing would have surprised Mum. She was in full-on acceptance mode.

'It would be lovely to meet her some time,' said Mum. The thought seemed fanciful. What would it be like for both of them? What about me? All my competing realities would come together in the most bizarre denouement. That wouldn't be an emotional journey. That'd be an acid trip.

'What about Fiona, Mum? How will she take it?' I quickly asked.

'I am sure she'll understand, love, as long as she doesn't feel undermined.'

'Undermined by what?'

'By the fact that you have found these other people. Other siblings.'

Mum was really worried about that. In a way this was encouraging because she was saying that although Fiona might have a real problem with this, she didn't. She'd cracked it. She assumed a position of strength and then, slyly, she took control.

'I want you to phone Fiona and tell her today. Do it now.'

'I'll phone her in the week. One conversation like this is enough for one day.'

'No,' she said. 'Next week is no good as she is really busy with work.'

'I might.'

'Phone her this morning.'

There she was – another woman nagging on at me to phone someone about something incredibly frightening and sensitive. She grandly decreed she'd only send me Grandpa's memoirs once I had made that call. It was a regressive bit of blackmail – or cajolery, depending on your point of view. She was the frustrated mother; I was the recalcitrant teenager. She was telling me to do my homework and I couldn't go out until I had. Having laid myself bare I'd made myself weak. I slipped back through the time tunnel. Adulthood dissolved. I don't like feeling exposed and there I was – a gawky gangling teenager in a battle of wills. Mum knows the buttons to press. She knows because we have so much history. Whatever adult relationship we have, there's always a level that is forever stuck in another time.

I promised I would phone Fiona. I told Mum I loved her. That made the fifteen-year-old me blush but it felt good to the rest of me.

'I love you.' It felt librating and cleansing. Like a Hail Mary. The stain of the secret washed away like a sin. She said she loved me too. I could tell she really did. As if I didn't know; but this was deep unconditional love. The love of a mother for her only son. When I put the phone down I felt like a new me. I rushed up to my computer immediately and e-mailed her photos of Helen, Patrick, Tina and myself backstage with Paul McCartney at Earls Court. She mailed straight back to say she had them. The Dowager Duchess of Cyber Space had downloaded.

I sat back exhausted, rubbed my face in my hands and I felt spiritually calm. A warm feeling of elation took me over. Such a relief. Every conversation we had from now on would be totally open. No hiding. No fibbing. No spinning. No impromptu alibis or aliases. The vault was open. Just as I was wallowing in the relief of it all, I seized the moment and picked up the phone again, this time to call Fiona. I was emboldened and wanted another snort of this drug called honesty. It was such a good feeling.

'Fiona?'

'Hi, you? How are things?'

I went straight into it: 'I've just spoken to Mum and I've got something to tell you.'

As I told her about the secret underground network of sisters, I felt like one of those men you read about who has had two wives and two families in two different places for years and nobody's been any the wiser about each other. I felt like a hero of the trailer park speaking to the bespectacled host with the cynical bouffant while the screen caption reads: *I am a liar.* We'd only ever had each other and now I was telling her she wasn't the only one. But she was the only one. She is my sister. How could I explain?

I told her the lot. I tipped it all out of the trailer and on to her lap. Joseph senior; Helen and Ellie and Joseph Junior. And Esther. Then came her Jerry Springer bombshell. You know? The bit where the bad guy gets trumped.

'I knew about Esther,' she quietly replied.

'What? How come?'

'I heard a hint of her from Tina years ago.'

I was flabbergasted. All this time she'd known. All this time it had been a cold spot on her heart. Gnawing away.

She told me how she knew. It happened when our oldest was born five years before and Fiona had been down from Scotland to see us.

'Tina was chatting away and casually mentioned Esther in reference to something or other and I put two and two together. Then when the two of you were upstairs together I heard you raising your voice telling Tina never to mention her in front of me.'

I felt ashamed on every front. 'Why didn't you talk to me about it, Fi?' I felt wretched. 'You lived with it all that time and said nothing?'

'I wanted to mention it,' she said. 'I nearly did a few times.'

'You should have.'

'The time never seemed right and – well, the opportunity comes and then it's gone.'

'Fiona, you know I love you.'

'And I love you. The thing is . . .' She gathered her thoughts meticulously, 'You chose to keep things separate. You felt you were protecting people. The irony is that none of us *knows* what really hurts other people and I was more hurt by not knowing.'

The tears came like Highland rain. I repeated myself. I wanted her to hear it again. 'I love you. You are my sister.' She was my sister. Talking to me. We hadn't spoken properly for years. Well, we'd spoken but we hadn't said anything to each other. But there we were back in the back seat of our parents' car. Through the time tunnel again. There in the maroon Ford Cortina. ESF 255C. I wanted Dad to get a Ford Capri – the height of style and elegance, I reckoned. There wasn't enough room in the back though and Dad had to have a company car anyway. There we were in our childhood home in Edinburgh. There we were in Cobble Cottage, the two-room bothy in the middle of a Highland peat bog. It had an outside loo and no electricity. It was the magical place we spent our summer holidays.

'Do you remember the loo getting knocked down by the cows once?' I said.

'I can see Dad now,' she remembered, 'laughing about it.' Other images rushed to her mind. 'I can visualize him right now on one of those long summer days, scything the grass, pipe in mouth. And at night you and me lying in bed with the sounds of Mum's radio echoing through the silence; the reception coming and going and the two of us talking into the night.'

'And we could sometimes hear the old colonel up the Glen playing the pipes and the sound wafting over the hills.'

'Colonel Musker,' she added as a point of impressive detail.

Then I mentioned one of Mum's peculiarities. Her UFO fixation.

'Remember when we were outside the cottage on the most incredible starry night, all gazing up at the sky, wrapped up to the nines, with Mum looking for flying saucers. She was convinced we saw one. Flashing pink. In years to come the more she told the story the pinker it flashed. Like a fucking pink elephant.'

We were laughing our heads off now.

The memories came flashing through our minds like gin-powered UFOs in the sky at night.

'Remember Matilda? My tortoise that disappeared?' I said. 'I was devastated.' Something inside me still yearns for that reptile. We never found her.

'God, Nicky. After that you and Mum came to my school's end of the year concert in the Usher Hall. When the song "Waltzing Matilda" started you dissolved into racking sobs about the tortoise. You were seated right at the front and Mum had to take you out.'

Where have these moments all gone? They're light years away but we can still see them in a clear and starry sky. More than that, if we clear our hearts and minds of all the clutter and crap, we can feel them. We can feel those moments as if they've only just passed.

There were sad times too. Fiona had a hellish experience when she was sixteen, working as a child minder-cum-au pair for a German family living in Holland. The mother, Hella, had done the same in our house when she had been a student and little blond me had been the *apfel* of her eye. But as an adult she was cruel to Fiona, making outrageous demands of her. Matilda still makes me sad. Hella still makes me angry. What my sister remembered moved me deeply.

'You wrote to me.'

'Did I?'

'I've still got the letter. It meant a lot, as did the care and concern you showed when I returned to Inverness and you all met me off the plane.' I was floored by this. It was a *me* I'd forgotten. A *me* that was once there and had become long since buried in the peat bog of life. A *me* that would go out of my way to show love for my sister because I cared so much and didn't want her to be hurt. By not telling her about Esther I'd hurt her again. More maybe than even Hella did. That is something I should never have done.

Fiona went on. 'And when Mum's mum died. Nana. I remember coming back from school and you were sitting on Mum's knee trying to comfort her. You were very distressed and sobbing at Mum's upset. You must have been about seven.'

We carried on summoning up memories like a Shaman invoking the spirits of the dead. Inevitably we came to the magic of Christmas when we shared the fantastic tingling uncontainable excitement of it all. The times when we wound each other into paroxysms of delight. We were doing it again.

Fiona loves Christmas and the child in me still feels it inside. It's a distillation and annual fix of the innocent wonder of childhood. Fiona was wallowing in it.

'It seemed best when we shared a bedroom and the whole build-up. Things were so magical. Remember standing in the playroom with huge snowflakes billowing outside? Sitting on the stairs absorbing the atmosphere and the music from the telly? Counting and feeling and prodding and poking the pressies?'

Most of all I remembered the love. Mum and Dad's all-embracing and protecting love. I remember Mum still in bed and

Dad singing in the bathroom whilst shaving and playing the toilet paper and comb. And Fiona and Nicky.

We'd banished the misunderstandings of the last five years. We remembered the late-night horror films we'd watch when she'd make me stay up and cling on to her during the scary bits. 'Sometimes you would fall asleep but it was still crucial company in support of scary viewing. Then we'd have a mad race to leave the sitting room as last out had to lock up.' We were there for each other again. And we always will be.

After the call to Fiona, I wandered round the empty house and sporadically picked up the phone to call Tina and tell her what an extraordinary morning I'd had. There was no reply. It just rang and rang. She wouldn't have her mobile with her, not walking on a West Highland beach with the kids – talk about the sacred and profane. I looked around and got my guitar out of its case. I hadn't played for ages. The tips of my fingers hurt on the steel strings when I pressed them down to shape a chord. Then I played the tune I'd once played Esther. I had let her hear it the first time she came to my flat in Hampstead back in 1996. It was the song I had written about Dad after he'd died. She said she liked it. I'd love to play it for you now but the written page has its limitations. The music is very minor-league Hoagy Carmichael and the lyrics are hardly Cole Porter but I meant them.

> I remember hearing – your songs of morning joy
> Gentle and endearing, to this little boy.

Love is all I bring you – best that I can do
I am here to sing you, a lullaby in blue.

Dreams are getting stronger
Colours glowing bright
Echoes getting longer
Tender is the night

Sun's over the yardarm.
Have a drink or two.
And I'll be here to bring you.
A lullaby in blue.

See the stars as they float in the sky
See the moon with that fly look in his eye.
I don't blame them for gloating on high
Pretty soon you'll be – dropping by.

Now the light is fading.
Shadows growing long.
Birds are demonstrating
Sweetest even' song.

Now you've no more troubles
Peace is flowing through.
And I will always sing you,
This lullaby in blue.
I am here to bring you
A lullaby in – blue.

What a Sunday. All alone in the house. Normally, without Tina and the girls, I'd have been moping about. Speaking to Mum and

Fiona though – the two lynchpins of my life for as long as I've been alive – and telling them everything did more than just ease my guilty conscience. I felt redeemed, although I'd done nothing bad. I felt forgiven for the betrayal, although there'd been no treachery. Now they knew our bond was stronger than ever. It was strong because it was about me and them and history and now it was fortified with honesty. The experience also reawakened me. The pell-mell nature of discovery and revelation is an astounding and ceaselessly stimulating journey, but rediscoveries are just as important as new discoveries. I'd found my family again. I'd also discovered a lot about myself. I was certainly more grounded than I'd been in 1990 when I first found Stella but by at last being honest, I was more open to loving and to being loved. I thought, I can still do this. I can still meet and know and form relationships with these new people and Mum and Fiona will still love me and know I'll still love them. Of course there are challenges for all of us in this – but they don't need cosseting from it. Wrapping them in cotton wool is the worst thing to do. But I'm maybe lucky they are who they are. And it's because of that, I'm me.

Sitting thinking in the Sunday-afternoon silence, I needed to hear Esther's voice and tell her everything. I rang her. When I told her what had transpired, I could feel her relief. She was thrilled for me and I felt close to her. Later that afternoon she sent me an e-mail which I'll always keep.

Nicky

Just so pleased about your conversation with Fiona. Hold on to it like a raft in the madness.

Just reading a book on mid-life crisis (for executive coaching purposes) and here's an excellent quote for you . . .
'We shall not cease from exploring. And the end of all our exploring will be to arrive where we started and know the place for the first time.'

T. S. Eliot

TWENTY-THREE

Return to the Emerald City

Before the birth of Kirsty, our third little girl, I picked up the newly released DVD version of *The Wizard of Oz* on a therapy shopping trip down Oxford Street. I watched it again and again with my children. They loved it and it enthralled, captivated and amazed me all over again. I even ordered up a book from Amazon about the making of the film. If I get interested in something I tend to go the whole hog. It's an extraordinary piece of cinema and an enchanting story, which awakens the inner child in all of us.

It's a good metaphor for my journey too. I left home during the storm of my first marriage and set off on that yellow brick road to find my birth mother. The fourteen-year journey – a journey that is in so many ways still going on – was an experience that brought out the child in me and forced me to face who that child was. It was fantastic and frightening. It was thrilling and terrifying. There were lions and tigers and bears. There were dark forests and strange other-worldly places. The real adventure took place in a wondrous Technicolor landscape far away from the monochrome world of reality. There were faces I'd never seen before that were instantly recognizable. There were faces I'd known all my life but didn't recognize. There were places I knew, but had never been. And I was searching for something over the rainbow, and someone who might be there: someone I'd projected on to a huge screen in my mind, someone who could answer all my questions and give me what I thought I never had. But ultimately he was just a man. She was just a woman. We are all just little men and little women in little booths trying to be bigger than we are. We may all be extraordinary but none of us is anything special.

All the while I'd been at home I'd yearned to go and find the answers. All the time I was seeking, there was a part of me that yearned for home. Then when you do eventually go home – everyone's different. Nothing is ever the same again. You wouldn't want it to be.

'Who's Dorothy then?' I said to Esther as we were playing the *Wizard of Oz* game. We never had a childhood together so we'd a bit of catching up to do. This was fun.

'I am,' she said like a big sister.

'Who the fuck am I then? A friend of Dorothy? Thanks a lot.'

'No,' she said. 'Don't you see? You're the Tin Man.'

'What? I don't have a heart?'

'That's the point. Of course you have a heart. It was there all along. Didn't you rediscover your heart through your conversations with Fiona and your mum? Fiona reminded you of that caring little boy who wrote her a letter to make her feel better. It's as if you had hidden your heart away somewhere underneath your professional armour, and maybe that was making you sad without you knowing it.' Esther was right. I'd opened my heart to Mum as well and I'd felt stronger for it.

And as Esther and I skipped along the road holding hands, we met people, made discoveries and had adventures that gave us a shared past. We came to see and understand the child in each other that we'd never had a chance to know. As I started to write this book to work it through, work it out and try and analyse what was happening, Esther and I talked and talked about things we'd never normally have discussed. We explored feelings and fears that I certainly wouldn't normally recognize, let alone express. It's been good. There are parts of us so alike and parts so different. They say that some blind people's sense of hearing, smell, taste and touch can be far keener than that of the sighted. Maybe adopted people who have traced their siblings have a stronger sense of mutual empathy. Esther and I had achieved a real ease with each other and a sometimes instinctive understanding perhaps because of what we never had.

The fact that we grew in the same womb gave us the impetus, but the whole complex journey offered both of us the means and the context to get to the heart of a very special relationship. The trips we made together to Dublin, Edinburgh and elsewhere weren't just about finding out about our adoptions and revisiting our childhoods to jog memories and liberate thoughts and feelings. They were about finding each other. I could tell her what I was feeling and fearing, and she articulated her deep anxiety about rejection and being left 'alone' in her orphanage.

As I've already written, the trip we made together to Dublin to see Stella was a significant point for us. Another extraordinary turn in the road was the weekend in Edinburgh when we met Francesca Harris of the Scottish Adoption Association. As the coachman at the Emerald City says, 'This was a horse of a different colour.' Straight after landing at Edinburgh Airport, we picked up the hire car and drove across town to see my mum for lunch.

We saw the castle in the distance. We passed the palace by the ancient volcano. We headed for the terraced house where I grew up. Mum had initially suggested she'd like to meet Esther after I'd finally opened the vault to her in my Sunday-morning telephone confessional. Inwardly I'd recoiled in something very like horror. I couldn't get my head around it. But happening it was. Why not? Why shouldn't Stella's other child meet my mum? 'I'm not afraid,' said the cowardly Lion. 'Put em up. Put em up.' This was just the next stage in the *normalization process*. Normalization process? Sorry, but I don't know what the hell to call it. Nothing is ever going to be normal, is it? By now we were out of the dark though. Out of the forest and into the light. Why not? This was a big weekend. We were both going home to Edinburgh – a place that never leaves your heart. If you've got one.

I'd rung Mum as we left the airport.

'Hi, Mum. We are on the way.'

'Excellent. I have some soup for you both. Does Esther like minestrone?'

I have got to tell you, that's not something I ever thought I'd hear her say.

As we arrived and parked I had a surge of nerves. The jitterbugs were jumping.

I asked Esther, 'Are *you* nervous?'

'Not too bad. You?'

I came clean. 'I'm shitting myself. It's just . . .' I couldn't really find the right word. Weird was the word that did it. We rang the bell.

That little path. Those window boxes. That front door. An old woman's form materialized behind the frosted glass and the door opened. We embraced and I rather gingerly introduced Esther. Mum said how pleased she was to meet her and in we went past the hallway bookcase lined with dusty old videotapes of *The Wheel of Fortune*, *Top of the Pops* and *The Video Jukebox*, a pop quiz I'd presented on Grampian TV in 1987.

Mum offered us a drink.

'Mum, the beer better be cold.' The stroppy teenager was back in town.

Mum politely enquired about Esther's children. Then they spoke about her parents. I could see them warming to each other and felt Mum relax as she realized the world was still turning. All around were pictures of Fiona and me at every stage in our childhoods. Some of them were incredibly unflattering and as cringe-making as those old TV tapes. Not for Mum though. This was the museum of her pride. A lion's and a mother's. There were pictures of my children and of Dad. There he was, looking on benignly. What the hell would he have made of this? Meanwhile in the real world, if that is the right expression, my adoptive mother and natural half sister were chatting away while I got stuck into a cold and mercifully large bottle of Tiger Beer.

Esther excused herself and asked where the loo was. Mum got up to show her and when she sat down again she said, 'What a lovely person Esther is. You know in a way she feels like one of my own.' She'd felt a bond through me. This was Stella's other child and that wasn't to be discounted. It was a real connection for Mum. I found that really moving. And I could hear the relief in her voice. It was OK.

'What is the relationship with her like for you?' she immediately asked.

'Oh, it's not like a sister – she's more like a really good friend,' I answered protectively. Sister. It's such an emotionally loaded word.

My really good friend Esther came back in and these two women carried on engaging as I gibbered the occasional remark. They were two trained observers watching, perceiving and feeling. But communicating.

Esther later described Mum as 'expressively perceptive'. All Mum's demeanour and body language made it quite clear she was understandably and quite openly appraising Esther.

'You're very assertive,' said Mum. 'He needs constant reassurance.' She'd found her own reassuring difference. At least she thought she had. The needing constant reassurance bit is in fact a shared trait. Give Esther more time, that's all. All Mum's professional instincts and personal emotions were interlaced. Esther is inexpressively perceptive. She's inscrutable. She takes it in but you only realize quite to what extent when she says something trenchant much later.

'I found out what you do when you're nervous,' said Esther, much later.

We were talking about the meeting.

'What?'

'You interject strange comments very loudly. You just say something to say something.'

'Like what?' said Mr Indignant.

'I was talking to your mum about the plane journey and you suddenly said something about one of your girls. Totally disconnected.'

The emotional memory came back. I hadn't really known what to do or how to behave. It was new territory and I didn't have the right software installed, did I? I was sitting on that couch in a state of parlous malfunction. I didn't have the tools for the job. It wasn't a job – it was mission impossible. I'd compartmentalized these different people in different corners of my mind, heart and life for so long and there they were – together in my childhood home. The very room where we all sat every night and watched *Some Mothers*, *The Two Ronnies*, *Upstairs Downstairs* and rugby internationals, with the warming voice of Saturday afternoons by the hearth – Bill McLaren. The room still smelt the same. Same carpet. Same sofa. Same most things. But it was never meant to be like this – same mother, different sister.

My stubby fingers were taking a hell of a biting. The cuticle skin-ripping was testimony to my utter confusion. I knew how to function with Mum and I knew how to function with Esther. I was, as Esther correctly observed, interjecting strange comments very loudly.

'It's quite a nice drive that Rover we hired.' But come on, this was a mind-blowing new synthesis. We are who we are partly because of how our reactions to other individuals create a role for us.

'It's called social construction,' Esther later explained helpfully. 'There are books on it.'

'Well, there's about to be another,' I replied.

My roles with Mum and Esther were clearly defined. My role

with this challenging new synthesis of both of them together was clearly not just ill-defined but entirely nebulous. Was I to be the defiant teenager or the vulnerable victim of mid-life crisis? The certainty was sucked out of me. All I could resort to were those arbitrary comments and random responses punctuated by slugs of beer. I wasn't entirely sure who I was. Maybe I was the Straw Man now. If I'd only had a brain.

> I would not be just a nuffin'
> My head all full of stuffin'
> My heart all full of pain
> And perhaps I'd deserve you
> And be even worthy erv you
> If I only had a brain

We three would meet again the next day for a curry but for now we had to go. There were adventures ahead. Into the hired Rover – which incidentally was a *very* nice drive. And drive we did – across town, past the palace, by the castle and on to the house where Esther grew up. From my childhood home to hers. Another womb. Another cradle. As we sat in the car outside I thought, Mmmm. Much bigger than our house. I said as much to Esther.

'Are we going to go in then?' she said.

'How would you feel if you were having a nice Saturday afternoon and somebody knocked on the door and said, "Hello. We used to live here. Can we have a look around?"'

'Nothing ventured. They can only say no.'

Up the path we jolly well went.

Behind the glass panels of the front door a youngish woman's form materialized. The door opened and there she was. Curly brown shoulder-length hair, attractive face, intelligent glasses and a confident voice.

'You're a friend of Chris Main's,' she said, recognizing me. 'We know his cousin Anthony really well.' That's a certain echelon of Edinburgh society for you. I know him – he knows you. Same old school. How do you do?

'Come in,' said the lovely Kate.

We were in. By the time we'd properly explained the purpose of the visit we both had drinks in hand and were chatting to Kate and husband Rupert in the spacious and beautifully appointed elm kitchen. The Aga was enormous. The kitchen was expansive. The wine was expensive. A small boy was playing in the room next door. He'd been playing rugby for his school that morning. His school? The Edinburgh Academy. His sisters were at St George's. My old school for him. Esther's for them. Little boys and girls like we were. We had walked into the archetypical well-heeled private-schooled middle-class Edinburgh home. An Edinburgh family like both of ours had been. In the same orbit but of a different generation.

A family like ours – except they weren't. They were too perfect. Gorgeous mum, dashing dad, bright and beautiful children. Was God having a joke? Were these actors? When we got back to London I made Esther watch the Jim Carrey film – *The Truman Show*.

'I don't like him,' she'd protested.

'You'll like it,' I insisted. She loved it. She knew what I was getting at.

Something told me the whole thing had been an elaborate set-up, a cosmic gag by the Wizard of Fate. For Esther it was way beyond bizarre. This was her house – but it wasn't. She knew it intimately but she didn't. And when she'd lived there I'd been an schoolboy just round the corner. I was her little Academy-boy brother – but I wasn't. And we'd turned up on their doorstep like a pair of waifs only for them to welcome us as their own. They'd adopted us, but this time as a package. Brother and sister. Now could we get on with our lives? Take two.

Rupert's in whisky and doing very well, but what about his beautiful wife? 'What do you do, Kate?' I asked, having explained the nature of the book I was researching and seeking to write.

'I'm a journalist. I do stuff for the *Scotsman*.'

Fucking hell, I thought for a second. It's the Wicked Witch of the North.

Of all the houses in all the tree-lined avenues in Edinburgh – I walk into hers. And she moves into Esther's. Kate was fine. It was weeks before she e-mailed me about an interview. Frankly, I'm lucky anyone's interested. As Esther said as we sat in the car outside her old homestead before knocking on the door of that double-fronted stone house, 'Nothing ventured.'

Within minutes of the kitchen confab, Esther led us out, got down on her hands and knees and crawled into the cupboard under the stairs, clearly not for the first time. She joyfully pointed out some graffiti next to the electricity meter. 'Esther was here 1967.' Well, she was back. And the Beatles had split up and Harold Wilson had been replaced by a younger man. Esther and Kate disappeared upstairs to show each other round their respective homes. An hour or so later we swapped numbers and gave them our addresses in readiness for Christmas card time, which was imminent, and we kissed our goodbyes. When we were in the car Esther realized she'd forgotten her coat. She went back and Kate already had it in hand. I watched the two of them standing on the path having a conspiratorial chat. When I drove off Esther looked at me from the passenger seat.

'You know, Kate just said the strangest thing.'

'What now?'

'Well, she asked me if I'd ever seen the ghost in the house. She says she hears a child's voice in the front room upstairs. She wondered whether I knew about it.'

There are more ghosts in this town than she'll ever know.

We drove past old haunts, heading through Edinburgh in the gathering Saturday dusk and passed through the gates of the Edinburgh Academy. At least, the part of the Academy you attend until you're eleven. After walking around a bit we wandered over to the endless playing fields. What privilege. As I smelt the cold damp turf (is there a more nostalgic fragrance?) I peered through the windows of the changing rooms that had seemed obsolete when I'd been at school. I saw the chipped thirties shower tiling, filthy floor and decrepit wooden benches. Rugby after school. Blood and mud and cold and wet; carbolic soap and dark winter nights. The weary walk for the bus and a reassuring John Player Special. And then – home again.

We set Sunday morning aside to meet the ladies whose mother had run the digs where Stella stayed when she gave birth to us and regularly visited for a long time after. Mrs Blackie's daughters have vivid memories of those times. We sat in the front room with a plateful of sandwiches, a pot of strong tea and a roomful of stories. May and Ann were on great form. The last time they'd seen me in the flesh, was the traumatic day the social worker had come to take me away to the Willowbrae nursing-home. A few weeks after that I was deposited with my adoptive family. A new home and a better chance. A Campbell. I was five days old when I left Mrs Blackie's. In those precious five days Stella, Ann, May and Mrs Blackie would all take turns in holding and changing me. As I nibbled my Battenberg cake, I half thought of letting them pass me round again. I didn't need changing. Nobody offered though.

'Did she kiss me goodbye?' I asked.

May nodded. The mood changed. More ghosts – the ghosts of a wretched day momentarily stole into the room.

For the most part there was laughter and warm memories. It was a beautiful and uplifting morning with great people. They have a kindness that must have pervaded the old stone mansion round the corner where their mother used to run her boarding-house. People weren't judged. They were welcomed. I can well understand why Stella felt so at home there. They call it a vibe, don't they? There was a great vibe.

May cackled with laughter as she told a tale. Stella used to love smart clothes – no rubbish for her! She would arrive on the plane from Dublin and May wondered what the hell she'd be wearing. It was one of the wonderfully unpredictable things in life. There would be all these nuns on the plane – the Sisters of Seriousness – and there was Stella with an amazing hat with a huge feather sticking out of the top. She looked really proud, quite a show-off. She was working all the time, so May supposed coming over to

Edinburgh gave her a chance to dress up. And what a nightmare she'd been to shop with. May once went shopping with her for shoes and vowed 'never again'. Stella tried on ten or fifteen pairs, examining them at every angle for colour, shape and detail. It was an extraordinary performance. One time she went shopping in Portobello itself. She tried on a suit and told the assistant she would walk back to the house and see if Mrs Blackie liked the look of it. The assistant wasn't keen, but Stella was insistent. She just started walking. May concluded that she just had a way of going for what she wanted and getting it.

We went for a brief look round the old house – now an old folks' home – and then, after saying our goodbyes to May and her sister, Esther and I wandered down to the Portobello seafront and talked. It struck me there were two sides to May's story about Stella. Yes, it was a tenacious stand against the tragedies that beset her. But in another way the story was as cold as the late November wind that whipped off the North Sea. It led inevitably to the intrinsic sadness of her life as we, her children, stood in the freezing beachfront wind. Kids were coming in and out of a leisure centre. There was laughing and shouting. Once there'd been a *joie de vivre* in Stella that battled valiantly against the dreaded demons. She fought and fought but they they caught up with her in the end. Now she was like some of the people in the care home we'd just left. An empty shell.

'Do you want to walk on the beach?' asked Esther.

'Nah. I'm fucking freezing. Let's get in the car and drive some-where.'

'Shall we go for a drink?'

'Good idea.' Esther drove and we met a special old friend of hers in town before meeting up later with Mum for the curry. It was important for Esther to see Mary. She needed a familiar face – a reminder of who she was now. It was a well-earnt breather in the marathon of madness. This was yet another homecoming. Mary was her representative of family – a link back into the childhood past that we were exploring – part of Esther's lifelong psychological furniture. Mary was a chair right up beside the hearth. She was adopted too. When Esther was growing up they understood each other, and their friendship allowed the whole business of adoption to seem normal. They'd stuck together through thick and thin, and had a fierce friendship, like sisters. It was a friendship that seemed indestructible. It was built on firm foundations. I didn't understand at the time why Esther was so keen to touch base with Mary and for me to meet her too. You can't really appreciate somebody properly from a forty-minute conversation in a reeking, cacophonous pub, but she and Esther had such a positive energy with each other. Their mutual glances, smiles and winces were a history book.

As we drove, our memories were sparked by the streets and houses all around us. More ghosts everywhere. Esther and I realized how intertwined our lives had always been. People we knew. The circles within circles. All the families whose mums and dads were the Ruperts and Kates of their day. Warm secure homesteads filling up with children who would one day yearn to finally leave and then having left, forever dream of coming home.

After the drink with Mary we headed home in readiness for dinner with Mum. I sat down again in our front room and gave Mum a scattergun round-up of the day we'd had. Emotional. Exhausting. Incredible.

'Oh and May and Ann mentioned that they all received a beautiful bunch of flowers from you and Dad after I'd arrived on the scene. They . . .' I couldn't quite believe I was passing this on, ' . . . they asked me to thank you very much indeed.'

Mum didn't blink before saying, with total sincerity, 'Oh good. They got them. I'm so pleased.' Forty-two years – from home to home.

We went round to the local Tandoori place and I was better able to cope with the me/Mum/Esther axis than when I first arrived. I'd got more used to the concept of Mum and Esther together by then. Mum – 'expressively perceptive' in Esther's estimation, remember – having a liking for the red wine, became steadily more expressive if not necessarily more perceptive. At one point Esther and I made one of our connections when telling a story in tandem. Mum noticed the chemistry between us. I was oblivious to the nuance as all my mental efforts were still mostly geared towards coping but Esther picked something up on her dependable antennae. She saw some mild difficulty for Mum. There was clearly something for my mum to get used to here. The situation was a challenge to her emotional status quo and a temporary disruption of her family dynamic. The previous norms and certainties were no more. Everything is different now and there are challenges for all of us. It's a strange place, this hall of mirrors, Mum, but it's how we pass the day in the merry old Land of Oz.

Mum felt she'd known Esther for ages. 'It was more than her being raised in Edinburgh. I felt sorry that she couldn't find out more about her father. I really felt her sadness over it.' As for Esther; she felt strangely drawn to Mum. She said it was like meeting a kind of melange of all her friends' mothers from the past, moulded into this totally familiar sounding and looking person. Same tribe I suppose. Same 'family' – the Edinburgh middle-class mafia. But more than that, Esther was drawn to Mum's vivacious spirit, and to her wisdom. 'I could sense a kindred spirit and felt we had met before. Crazy really, but a good feeling. A really warm feeling.' Esther has plans to meet up with Mum one time in Edinburgh, and to introduce Duncan and the kids. There was a time that would have felt impossibly uncomfortable. Now more and more, it feels absolutely right and natural. All part of the crazy journey. All part of coming home and, as Dorothy said, 'There's no place like home.'

We weren't there yet though. There was one last extraordinary adventure. There was another twist in the road that neither of us would have expected in a million years.

TWENTY-FOUR

Too Much Crazy

During the emotional turbulence and euphoria of my Leahy odyssey, Esther had begun to feel a bit unsettled. She only had two contacts with the genetic underworld, two links to the ghost kingdom. The first was our mother who was emotionally unreachable, the second was me and I'd been preoccupied with my own adventure. What about her paternal puzzle? If she solved this, it wouldn't so much be sibling rivalry as sibling symmetry.

In one sense the timing of the search for her father couldn't have been worse. Her own dad had died recently. She was still grieving. The guilt of going now, of all times, to find the man who impregnated Stella would be hard to bear. But in another sense the time was right for Esther. There was a psychological gap and there was a huge great gaping blank in the picture of 'our' lives. It was on this fertile ground of 'dad disorientation' that her curiosity grew and her enthusiasm for the quest became reignited.

She knew her father had been a policeman called Frank who drank – but little beyond that. Whether wilfully or carelessly, she'd forgotten his surname so she wrote to Stella's younger friend Heather and asked if she'd try to wheedle it out of our doggedly reticent mother. Heather came up with the goods after eventually getting Stella to write it down on a bit of paper. By doing that, there was less chance of Stella changing the subject as a diversionary tactic.

'Ryan,' Esther told me. 'Frank Ryan.' She did a bit of Internet searching but Ryans in Ireland are akin to pebbles on a Highland beach.

I knew that now Esther had the name that would be it. I knew that once the shape of this man started to emerge from the mist there'd be no turning back. You can distance yourself from it all you like. You can try really hard not to think about it – but once you've dipped your toe in the water you have to jump in. And psychologically, once she had his full name, there on a piece of paper in her hand, her feet were soaking wet. As she told me his name it whet my appetite for the thrill of another case. Another chase. I also knew she had to know, like a Jehovah's Witness knocking on your door, who just knows you've got to be saved.

I was on the phone to Joseph a few days later. We were setting the world to rights when I mentioned it.

'Esther's father. He was a policeman too. His name was Frank.' I said it slowly and was about to clearly enunciate the surname. He beat me to it.

'Was it Frank Ryan?'

I was stunned.

'Yes – how did you know?'

My heart was going at it like Olga Korbut on the beam.

'Frank introduced me to Stella.'

Now I was on the floor. 'He what?'

'I came out of the station one day and a woman came towards

us and said, "Hello, Frank." She stopped to talk and Frank introduced me.' I vaguely remembered the story coming from Stella's lips. Some other policeman had introduced them, she'd said. Well, that some other policeman was my sister's father.

I couldn't wait to get off the phone so I could tell Esther but I needed to stay on the line for more information. I was Olga again – doing the splits this time. I wanted to pick up the phone to Esther right then and tell her that we had a man here. She had a father who had lived and breathed and laughed and cried. And my father knew her father well.

'What was he like, Joseph?'

'Frank was highly intelligent. From Limerick. Tall, dark, very funny guy. Highly intelligent. He was a good-looking man was Frank. Very brave too – he got in several dangerous situations – a bad one with a knife I remember. He could go into a situation and read people and calm it all down. But he *was* an alcoholic.' This confirmed what we knew. As Stella had curtly told Esther – he was a drinker.

'When he left the barracks there were bottles everywhere,' said Joseph. 'He was sent to treatment centres and was eventually dismissed because of the drink. Then he got jobs as night watchmen and security guards.'

'And might he be still alive?'

'No, he'll be dead now. He ended up on the street. Living in shelters. I remember giving him a fiver when I bumped into him in Dublin.' Joseph's voice dropped. 'Poor man. He'll be long dead will Frank.'

'Are you sure?'

'Yea, I'm sure I heard he died.'

'Did you know he was involved with Stella?'

'No, but I remember after leaving them in the street when I first met her, he carried on chatting to her like he knew her well. So, it figures. A few days later I was on the beat and bumped into her and she says, "fancy coming round for a coffee sometime?"'

I asked him if it was OK if Esther rang him. 'Of course, God love her.'

'Speak to you later, Joseph.' My heart was racing as I dialled Esther's number. She answered after a few too many rings for my liking.

'Esther Cameron.' She answered with a businesslike veneer.

'I've just spoken to Joseph. He knew him.'

'Oh my God.' Her voice was soft. She suddenly sounded vulnerable.

'I've just spoken to him and he mentioned the name unprompted.' I heard the impact this was having. I could feel it inside me.

She is a thinker. She's self-possessed, intellectually confident and analytically acute. Right then she sounded not quite there. She seemed sad. This news brought her sadness into sharp relief. She was flustered. She explained that she was having a bad day after her dad's recent death. She was in a difficult place so I offered to ring back but she wanted to hear what I knew. She had to hear it now.

I told her all the things I'd just heard. The cleverness. The heroics. The funny stories. The ultimate surrender to alcohol. The fondness of Joseph's memories. My eyes were darting over my raggedly scrawled notes as I focused on the scraps of this man's life. Then I saw the word I'd written boldly but badly.

D – E – A – D.

I said it. 'He's dead.'

'What?'

I hadn't said it loudly enough. I'd swallowed the word. I'd bottled it. I said it again. 'He's dead.'

She paused. 'That's pretty major news.' Then I realized what I was saying.

Your father is dead. For God's sake. That's two fathers' deaths she has had to contend with in two months. She said as much with a rueful smile in her voice. 'I'll do my best to get you a third by teatime,' I said. A joke was all I could offer to rescue the awful situation and bring us both back to ourselves.

'There's a challenge,' she answered. We both laughed.

I rushed on with more information so I could move away from death. I moved back to life. A tall, good-looking, funny, intelligent cop. A living being.

'He was a drinker. He was from Limerick.'

'Tall?' echoed my tall sister. That is the word she picked out. Every tiny piece of information is like a little jewel, a precious stone in the most intricate setting. A recognition of the essence of belonging and being. She saw it sparkle and had to have it. She saw her reflection in its lustre.

'He sounds like a lovely man,' she said wistfully. As my mum noted, Esther can be assertive. But now her voice was hardly there. I told her everything that I knew. I told her every word Joseph had related about his friend and colleague. 'He was six foot one, dark haired. A funny guy.'

She was the closest she has ever been to her natural father. In a way it was as if he were reaching out to her.

Is this how Crick and Watson felt when they discovered the double helix? This was better, surely. This DNA discovery was personal. Not a hill of beans for mankind but a huge step for a woman.

'Joseph doesn't think he ever married or had a family.'

'I would love to have known him,' she said as much to herself as to me. She sounded so regretful. I felt such a huge responsibility.

'Listen,' I geed her up, 'this is a breakthrough. He is bound to have relatives. A whole new world is opening up here.' I could hear she knew that another mysterious vault was creaking open. What secrets were inside?

'Joseph saw Frank in the street, on skid row, living rough about twenty years after their time in the cops together. He was on the streets living in shelters.'

She was shaken by his ignominious demise. He died a wretched drunk. She felt for him as she could feel for no other down-and-out. Your dad a down-and-out? A tramp begging for money to buy his next hit of booze?

'Are you going to phone Joseph today?'

'No. I will phone him, but not tonight.'

'What are you going to do now?'

'I need to go for a long walk. I've a lot to take in. But I will phone him.' She was thinking out loud and speaking to herself again. 'To speak to someone who knew my father.' The strength in her voice was consumed by the inner volcano of her thoughts and feelings.

She asked me about Joseph. Would he tell her what she wanted to hear? She wanted good Edinburgh realism not fey Celtic romanticism.

I reassured her that all the things he told me about Frank

being a down-and-out, begging for money, didn't exactly sound like a rose-tinted vision.

'He calls a spade a spade. Remember how honest he's been to me about himself.'

Losing her mum and then her baby Iona so close together had given Esther the impetus to trace Stella and now, nine years later, in the wake of her dad's recent death, another parent had appeared and departed in an instant. Like a brief contact from the spirit world. Maybe this man, now dead, would have more meaning for her than Stella. He somehow seemed more real.

I felt brotherly. I felt so close to Esther. We shared a lot in that phone call and the fact that my father held the key to hers was difficult to absorb but easy to believe. It was extraordinary but obvious. I was glad I'd been able to tell her and share the moment with her. I understood those emotions. I knew just how she felt. On this last turn of the road, I would go with her all the way.

She spoke to Joseph on the phone a couple of days later. He told Esther the worst of it and the best of him. He mentioned that Frank didn't crash about the place but 'moved like a cat'. She liked that. It was something she could feel and visualize, something she felt a connection with and could easily emulate given her own sleek physicality.

She was with me at our house in London two weeks later when Joseph came to stay for the weekend. Esther popped up from Bath for a couple of hours to meet the only man who knew both her parents. He was already there, playing with the girls when she arrived. She came in and he got up. As Esther and Tina kissed I noticed Joseph. I could read his expression. He had a wide smile of recognition. He could see an old comrade. Frank Ryan. As we sat and drank gin and tonics he told her all he knew of Frank. All the sad stuff was there but there were good things too. The intelligence, the bravery and the humour.

'Oh he was a terrific mimic,' said Joseph. 'We'd go out for a pint at the end of work and he was away. Into the pub and sit down and he'd do the funniest mimicry of the native Dubs.'

'*Dubs?*'

'The working-class residents of Dublin. He did their accent to a tee. And he'd imitate their outgoing attitudes – the Dubs were upfront about everything – straight to the point and that. Frank – he was a popular guy. It was later I saw what the drink did to him. I saw him dodging around town, wrecked by it.'

I went through to the kitchen to pour three more stiff gins.

Apart from the connection with Frank this was a watershed weekend. My natural half sister, having met my adoptive mother, now makes the acquaintance of my genetic father. I rang Esther after the weekend for her verdict on Joseph.

'What did you make of him?'

'He is like you.'

'What do you mean?'

'He has a similar energy. Intelligent. Likeable. Full of sparkle. He puts himself at the centre of everything. Quite a presence.'

I spoke to Joseph a few days after. He was painfully worried that he had been too frank about Frank. His wife had chided him for being so harsh about the 'poor girl's father'. Esther, though, was grateful for the truth.

But what now? What was the next step? Esther wanted to see if she had any relatives. But she was anxious about what she might or might not find. This was a whole new truth waiting to be revealed. I understood this so much. When I'd sat down and written that letter to Joseph the year before, I'd crossed the Rubicon. I knew how it was done and I wanted to help Esther. She was grateful I took the helm. She'd sit in the boat but I'd row. I phoned up my private detective Steve and gave him one absolutely definitely final job. If this man is dead, and Esther still needed absolute confirmation of that, who is left behind?

It didn't take Steve the Gumshoe long. Despite the prevalence of Ryans in the Emerald Isle, only one Frank Ryan was born on that day in that year. Esther got his date of birth from the Irish police archive and Steve got back to me within three days.

Dear Nicky

Re: Francis Ryan

Further to your instructions in this matter we have now completed our enquiries in respect of the above named, which have revealed the following information.

The last record of Mr Ryan was known to be in the Limerick area when he was an in-patient at St Joseph's Hospital until 11 October 1999. On that day Mr Ryan unfortunately passed away.

We have been advised that Mr Ryan had a brother, whose first name was Eddie and that he is still alive. [name of village supplied]

Our intelligence suggests that Eddie Ryan is a frequent visitor to his local Post Office, usually on a Friday.

> *We trust this information will be of assistance to you and*
> *accordingly we refer the matter back to yourselves in order that you*
> *are appraised [sic] of the situation.*
>
> *Yours faithfully.*

He died in 1999. Far later than we had supposed.

'Shit, I could have met him.'

'Don't think of it that way,' I said. 'You weren't ready and if you had found him, it wouldn't really have been him, would it? He was probably a wreck by then.'

Esther had the bit between her teeth now and got on the phone to the local post office. She ascertained the whereabouts of the widow of one of Frank's other brothers, stretched her long athletic legs, sprinted down the runway and raced for the finish. She phoned the number. Initially she was met with friendliness, then wariness frosting over into denial.

'I don't think my husband had a brother called Frank. Not that I know of.' The voice at the other end eventually froze her out.

Esther rang me with a heavy heart.

'What do you expect?' I said. 'To suddenly find out that Frank had a child and there you are on the other end of the phone – forty-four years later. It's a difficult one to embrace there and then, isn't it?'

'I'll write and send photographs and she'll have more of a chance to reflect and absorb it all.'

'Yeah, and explain the whole thing. Remember we're old hands at this. She won't be.'

The photographs did the trick. She was, by all their accounts, her father's daughter and his brother's niece. A cousin called

Martin called Esther within days. He was effusive. 'No DNA test necessary' became his rather comical catchphrase. Esther suddenly transformed into the euphoric tracing tripper that I'd been. All the fun of the fair. The next peak on the rollercoaster was Uncle Eddie. He was friendly and accepting but difficult to understand. His Limerick accent was as thick as the mists of time. I listened eagerly to Esther's excited voicemail messages updating me on the latest contacts with her new relatives. She would leave the messages in Esther-time, late at night, and I would pick them up on my way to work at four in the morning, travelling in for the Five Live breakfast programme. Each time I heard the excitement I knew so well, it lifted me out of the doldrums of that unearthly hour. Soon another journey to Ireland was mooted. Then we were booking the tickets and planning the trip.

'Are you sure you want to come to Limerick?' asked Esther. 'This is my story, not yours, Nicky. Do you think you'll be able to keep awake?'

I came over all McEnroe. 'You cannot be serious.'

But she was. She wasn't sure if I had the resources to put myself out and help her like this. She was wrong. The Tin Man had a heart – a bit rusty but pumping away all right. It had been my search up until now and she had been there for me – when I'd let her. As things had become more and more involved and I started to write this book, she'd become a mentor, a counsellor, a second opinion, a blast of sanity – a sister. Now it was my turn to support her. This was becoming *our* story. And I had an important part to play.

No way was I going to miss the famous two's latest adventure. A final trip together into our past. The last few pieces in the complex jigsaw puzzle of our backgrounds. And the final straw for my eight-month pregnant wife and Esther's long-suffering husband Duncan. They were both down with a heavy dose of tracing fatigue.

'You and your bloody families – you've got one here, you know?' said Tina.

I understood how they both felt, but I'm not sure they could ever really see it from where we were. Pretty soon, where we were was on a plane bound for Shannon Airport.

We drove from the airport to her cousin Martin's home in a small town forty miles from Limerick. I felt the churning thrill of anticipation all over again. As we drove into the town Martin guided us in via his mobile. Left at the roundabout and then take the second on the right just after the hurling field. The last mile was the longest. It brought to mind the long minutes leading up to the buzzer going, the leg-trembling walk over to open the door and the entry of a new relative. The world changes.

We drove into the close where he lives. It was like *Brookside*. I mean architecturally rather than in terms of drama. I don't remember the late-lamented Scouse soap being quite this intense or involving. A tall dark-haired man in his early thirties was standing outside a house speaking into a mobile phone.

'Oh my God,' I said. 'He looks like you.' My tummy did a triple jump.

Esther didn't reply. We parked. She got out. They met. I pretended I'd lost my phone and stayed put in the driver's seat looking in the glove compartment for something that was quite obviously in my left hand. It was her moment. Part of me didn't want to interfere and part of me didn't want to face the fear. I recognized so well that amalgam of terror, curiosity and eerie recognition. The need to stay. The desire to run far away. The compulsion. The aversion. The intensity.

'And this is my brother,' I heard her say. For a second I was the support act that had missed his cue. I got out as quickly as I could but we'd been sitting down for hours and my bones were in slow motion. He did look so like her: the eye colour, the hair colour, the shape of the face. And they're only cousins. Only cousins? They shared a set of grandparents. Their fathers were brothers. For adopted people 'only cousins' is like the phrase 'only a hundred thousand pounds'. Esther and Martin had professional interests in common too. They both work in management consultancy so they'd already found areas in their phone calls beyond 'isn't this amazing' and 'who would have thought'. We met his girlfriend Caroline who had an elfin quality and reminded me of Sinead O'Connor. Christ knows. Maybe she was her cousin.

We arrived on Thursday evening and the next day was spent driving the thirty or forty miles to meet Uncle Eddie and to see his photographs. Esther couldn't wait to see an image of her father for the first time in her life and I was fascinated by the prospect of seeing Stella's other policeman. Esther was nervous and excited about meeting her uncle. As we took a morning stroll through the town, admiring the cathedral, medieval tower and loitering youths, it was clear she needed support and reassurance.

'You want flesh and blood – this is as near as it gets. This man is your father's brother. We have reached the destination, Esther.'

The destination was planet Esther. It was like a classic episode from a sixties cult sci-fi series. Her cousin Martin – her two other cousins – everywhere we went we seemed to encounter people who looked like her. This was everything she had been looking for. There was the same dark brown hair and prominent nose, the same shape of face and depth of eyes. And Eddie: here was a man who might be termed a 'character'. He was stocky. He could have played prop in his day I'm sure, but he was from the planet all right. 'No DNA test required.' Eddie kept peering at her from behind his huge horn rims, from slightly sunken eyes framed by prominent cheekbones. I could barely understand a word he said but I understood every subtext of his every glance. I knew the wonder behind that look so well. It's the look that stares in amazement and searching curiosity, the look that can't quite comprehend or believe the reality of what's there. He was looking for his dead brother.

We all wandered up to the ruined farmhouse where Esther's father and Eddie had grown up. Eddie, a wonderfully independently minded bachelor, was determined that Esther see it. The old man tried to untangle the rope holding the wrought-iron gate on to the adjacent fence so we could all trudge in over the mud and walk right up to the home that once was. Eddie fiddled and pulled but couldn't quite untie the rope. I stood aside and watched as Esther came to his aid. Standing behind him she had a good go at it. Their profile was identical. This seventy-three-year-old, thick-set guy 'sweating Irish stew' and this tall, svelte, sophisticated Edinburgh woman with a first-class honours degree in maths and a couple of academic tomes to her name. But they had an identical look as they focused on that obstructive tangle of rope. What a snapshot of the amazing world of adoption and tracing. And then, as I saw a mystery of her life unravel, so did the rope. In we went.

Esther, an uncle, two cousins and a half brother. Just a few years before she would never have believed it.

I saw Esther's face for the first time as I'd seen my own after meeting Stella in 1991. I remembered that rush to the bathroom in the hotel and that rush to the head when I caught my reflection in the mirror. I'd seen my features in a whole new context. Their provenance and origins were at least partly explained. I'd seen Esther's face in love, anger, frustration and exasperation – often at me, but now I saw her face in others.

There was a quasi-religious feel to this searching business. Every house we'd entered on the Limerick trip had pictures of Jesus on the walls and Poundstretcher Marys on the shelves. We'd seen a kind of grotto near one relative's home. Inlaid in some artificial rock-like edifice was a gaudy Virgin Mother, looking theoretically beatific but actually a bit gormless. It was all as alien to us Edinburgh Prods as a dip in the Ganges. This was where medieval obscurantism met contemporary kitsch.

But here we were on our own pilgrimage. We were searching for truths – albeit self-centred secular ones. We were after our own Holy Grail and were essentially asking the same question as the most devout worshipper of the most gaudily painted plastic icon. Who are we?

Eddie showed us the old farmhouse. The thatched roof was gone and the white-washed walls long faded. He proudly pointed out the complete wreck of a piano in the undergrowth. It was almost inaccessible. The family used to play on it. We could almost hear the music. Both Esther and I love to play and grew up with pianos in our houses in Edinburgh. They were such familiar backdrops and soundtracks to our lives. We understood a house with a piano far more than a smallholding with cows and pigs to guarantee fresh bacon for breakfast and lashings of creamy butter on fresh-baked bread. There were trees growing inside the house now and Eddie was standing over at the byre with Esther.

'Do you want a key?' I asked her.

'What?'

'A piano key?' I went into the jungle. I was determined. As I hacked through the weeds I got wet and muddy but Brother Nicholas came back with two holy relics for Sister Esther. I got a chunk of piano from the rotting carcass of the old upright (no keys were to be found) and a long piece of piano wire. She looked delighted. I knew how she felt. Nobody else quite knew what to think.

The sun was painting the fields and hills around us a rich green as we wandered back down to the cottage that Eddie, a life-long bachelor, had just vacated for a sheltered-housing unit ten or so miles away. As we waited outside he went in for the photos. Esther was about to have a sight of her father's face. I remembered how I'd stared and stared at the photos of Joseph as a young man when I'd first got hold of them. Then weeks after that there'd been the knock at the door and an old man behind it. All Esther had were the photographs.

Out they came. There he was and there she was. The same face. The same bone structure and the same nose. The same melancholy expression. It was the one I'd immediately noticed all those years before, when she came out of the darkness of the stairwell into my flat at our first meeting in 1996.

She looked briefly as we stood outside Eddie's little cottage. You need to look again and then again a bit later. It takes four or

five goes before you begin to come to terms with what you are
actually looking at.

We wandered half a mile or so up to the little graveyard on a
hill where there was a family plot. I walked a while with Esther.

'You know that story I told you – when I was jogging in
Central Park and I heard one Puerto Rican down-and-out declaim
to another in a strong Latino accent "too much crrray-zee, too
much crazy"?'

'Yes.'

'And how you thought it would be a crap title for the book
even though I really liked it: "Too much crazy".'

'It's still a crap title for the book.'

'You still think that?'

In the light of experience she gave some ground. 'Yes, but I do
like that expression more and more.' We laughed. She went on, 'I
now understand better all the things you spoke about and wrote
about. You want to run away but still be there. You want to hide
but also immerse yourself in it. You can't assimilate all the
information.'

I was going through it all again myself, albeit at one remove:
the feelings of intensity, belonging but not belonging, being a part
of it but being separate. It's the feeling of being in that bizarre and
disorientating hall of mirrors.

'Too much crazy. Too fucking far too much fucking *crayzee*!'

We laughed again. We needed to.

We'd reached the graveyard and walked over the wet grass to
the headstones. A pall of sadness and introspection came down.
The bright sun seemed paradoxical. Eddie pointed out his own
name already carved on a fine big grey stone.

'This is where I'll be.' It was the only thing he'd said all day that I'd understood first time. It was slow and clear and thoughtful. I noticed they'd had a brother called Thomas who had died in the mid nineteen thirties at the age of seven. Esther stood alone and apart from us. I asked Eddie about him.

'How did Thomas die?'

The old man said something about a fall and a cart and constant ill health.

'It must have been devastating for the family?'

'It was sad all right. He was a little friend of mine he was. There was a year between us. A little friend was Tommy.'

It was a sadness drowned in Guinness and smothered in stoicism. The depth of the pain was unspoken.

Esther was staring at the inscription of her father's name. She was treading on the bones of the past. She stood silently. All the conversations had revolved and would revolve around Frank. Her father: a great guy, a gentle man, a clever man, a hopeless alcoholic who couldn't be rescued from himself. But Frank wasn't there. He was under her feet and in her thoughts. A sleeping policeman. The search was over and this was as far as it got. There was her father. Stella's other lover. He was physically as close as she was ever going to get. Was she sad? Was she sad because she wasn't sad? I looked at her on her own and wanted to hug her there and then but turned away, left her to her thoughts and started walking back to the car.

Later, as we sat in a small town council house we saw more family photos. There were yet more inhabitants of planet Esther. She's a dead ringer for her grandmother. Frank died a lot older than he should have by rights. He was sixty-six when his body finally surrendered. That was testament to something inside him. He needed eight pints to become himself again as Esther's cousin John remembered. Eight pints to just feel normal.

But he couldn't help himself. It was a tragic love affair with the booze. We sat in the tiny front room of the house on the estate in Limerick as they told Esther all about him. All about Uncle Frank. Brother Frank. Brother-in-law Frank. All about her father Frank. Cousin Martin's mother Catherine offered us both a whiskey. Two half-pint tumblers of the terrible stuff. We needed them just to become ourselves again. Just to feel normal.

The next day we drove up to Dublin to see Stella. It was only on reflection that this seemed a foolhardy thing to do. We were like flying squirrels with a death wish, leaping from tree to tree and crashing headlong into the branches. We raced down the motorway from one family tree to another without really thinking about the impact it would have on us. Esther was heading from her father to her mother like a teenager in a broken home. Esther offered to drive. She was thankful to be in control of something. On the way we talked about it all and had a good few tension-releasing laughs at the funnier moments of the last forty-eight hours. My attempted impression of the wonderful but impenetrably incomprehensible Eddie gave us both a fit of giggles. That felt really good. We arrived in the city.

'Well,' I said, 'Stella here we come. No DNA test required here then.'

I'll let Esther tell it in her own words.

Nicky hated the Dublin hotel the minute we arrived whereas I
didn't give a damn. He was pretty funny about it so I forgave
his moaning. We squeezed in a trip to see the place where Frank
met Stella. The police station where Frank used to work is ten
minutes' walk from the hospital where Stella had been matron.
It was an intriguing place for Nicky and me, because it represented the point in space and time when we became forever
connected. Joseph had told us that Frank and Stella were
standing casually chatting in the street one day. Frank was a
sociable fellow, and with simple gentlemanly generosity, he had
introduced Stella, his old flame, to the young fresh-faced Joseph.
Why don't you come over and have a coffee one day? she said.
Why don't you come over and make a brother for the daughter
I gave away just a few months ago? That's how it happened:
Esther and then Nicky.

'It's a bloody big hospital,' said Nicky. And it was.

'I wonder where the little gate was. You know – the gate
where Stella used to let her men friends in.'

'There are dozens of fucking gates. Could have been any
one.'

'She must have cycled down here, on that path, in the dark,
in secret.'

'I need a drink.'

It's not always easy getting Nicky to fully experience a
moment like this.

This was the impressive organization over which Stella
presided as matron; she must have been a hugely powerful figure
in those days. I tried to picture her as the highly starched figure
of authority. Not difficult. 'I am a good judge of form,' she had

said to me imperiously one day. She reckoned she could spot a wrong 'un. I expect she had a blacklist of nurses who didn't meet the standard, dressed sloppily or muddling up the daily routines.

We walked towards the police station, which was grey and square and forbidding. There was a dark, smoky pub just across the road where Frank and Joseph used to drink. The policemen would have spilled out of the station at the end of the day and crowded into the pub. Frank would have savoured the Guinness and the company. But I'll bet he missed the smell of the fresh country air blowing on his face as he used to cycle up the hill to school, with the taste of fresh bacon on his lips. I'll bet he missed the changing colours of the soft hills and the warmth of the cosy farmhouse. Frank suffered from depression – that's what the family told me. Maybe he missed the security and safety of home and couldn't tell anyone. He must have had to deal with some terrible situations as a policeman in Dublin. I felt his sadness as I stood outside this harsh stone edifice of authority, or maybe I just thought I did.

We filibustered the moments before seeing Stella, filling the space with a wholesome Irish stew and a drink or two. Out of the pub, into the street, into a taxi – it was all too quick. We got to Stella's nursing-home before we were really ready. It was still familiar from our previous visit a whole year before. The tiny Filipino matron welcomed us with a broad but guarded smile and we climbed the stone stairs up to Stella's room. This was a far cry from the luxurious privilege of her matron's rooms at the hospital. The nurse furtively told us that Stella liked to be upstairs, away from all the other inmates. I could believe it. She must have hated being amongst the mass of disaffected old folks with cardigans and grey hair. Perhaps they all hated it.

Stella's room was ridiculously hot. I sat next to Stella. Robert, her nephew, was there already and he beamed a characteristically relaxed welcome. He was taking things as they come, wiping Stella's nose and helping her sip her tea. Nicky and I like Robert. He's bright and kind and reliable – funny, too. I consciously moved up into a high-energy conversation about very little, family events, objects in the room, my kids, my dog, etc., etc. I was doing OK and felt that my adoptive mum would have been proud of me.

Then all of a sudden we edged over the boundary wall of sensible chit-chat into the dark forest of the past. Nicky went first. He mentioned that he had seen Joseph recently. He gave nothing away. 'He sends his love.' Nicky repeated this phrase a number of times as a strong counterpoint to Stella's raised eyebrows and coquettish smile. 'Oh he was very good looking, like you, Nicky. I shouldn't say that, should I?' The 85° F was affecting my blood pressure.

I followed Nicky into the forest. 'We went to see Frank's brother in Limerick this weekend. Of course, Frank is dead. You knew that, didn't you?' Stella nodded. 'Would you like to see a photo of Frank?' Stella picks him out of a row of three Guards no problem. Phew. At least that piece of the jigsaw was correct. 'What do you remember about him, Stella?'

Stella looked up blankly. 'Oh, he was reasonable I'd say.'

I don't think I have ever felt quite so crestfallen. 'Reasonable?' I asked, desperately looking for some explanation.

'Just reasonable,' she said flatly. It was as if the memory of Frank didn't deserve the common courtesy of a positive adjective. I felt a little angry with her and I realized that my disappointment with this remark was very deep, but quite unreasonable. I began to feel very uncomfortable in that hot little room.

The afternoon progressed from bad to worse. Stella introduced Nicky flamboyantly to every member of staff who entered the room. Then she started becoming confused about who I was. I cared and I didn't care all at the same time. She was ill, she was tired and she was not at all herself. I knew that. But it hurt all the same.

Once back at the hotel, Nicky went for a sleep and I decided to go for a brisk walk to clear my head. I set off purposefully at an even pace. Then, noticing a little excess energy in my legs, I began jogging. Before I knew it I was running at top speed, my legs pounding the road. I ran and ran and ran and ran down the long straight boulevard from Stillorgan to Black Rock. I could see the sea and I needed to get there. We had always lived by the sea in Edinburgh, and sometimes you just need to soak in that pewter-blue strip of immovable cold liquid. Sometimes it is really a very calming sight. I got there and breathed slowly for a while. I walked back refreshed.

One more rendezvous awaited us; a meal with the Lackey cousins and Stella's sister-in-law, now a widow. They treated us to a lovely Indian meal in the centre of Dublin. We had a good evening, mostly due to Nicky's stories about Limerick and his general good humour. I, however, was shrunken and exhausted and a little stuck for polite conversation. I was suspended in a continuous loop, which sounded a bit like, 'What the fuck's it all about? What the fuck's it all about?' and I thought it best to keep it to myself.

'You just weren't match fit,' said Nicky afterwards, drawing on his beloved football to ground the situation. We sat in the hotel lobby amidst drunken wedding guests and he talked me down. 'The human brain just isn't designed for this, Esther. You took on too much. Too many relatives in too short a space of time. Now you just need to give it time and let it all sink in. It'll all look different next week.'

He was right. And the sound of his clear, confident voice was very reassuring. This was my brother being completely brotherly at just the right moment.

We shuffled off to our rooms, past the kilted aftermath of a Scottish–Irish wedding. Nicky looked at me quizzically as if to take a final reading on how I was, and I could see he was full of empathy. He gave me a much-needed hug, and I felt so much warmth towards him and so much gratitude that I nearly cried.

I remember looking across the table to Esther during that Indian meal. She was finished. Wiped out. Too much crazy. Way too much crazy.

I'm glad I was there for her and she appreciated it too. That meant a lot. And there'd been a role reversal. Now I was the wise counsel, helping her to get it all into perspective, and she was the grumpy, uncommunicative sibling attempting to cope with a genetic onslaught. I drew on my professional resources and I drew on my feelings for Esther.

That weekend I saw Esther submerged in it. Sometimes she

coped, sometimes she didn't. Now I understood how excluded she had felt from my quest and that she at last understood how easy it is to be so totally swept away by it. The journey's over. We both know that. Where do we go from here? Any of us?

We flew back to London early the next day. As we stepped into arrivals and traipsed towards baggage reclaim she looked at me and smiled. 'Here we are then. Back in Kansas. Terra firma.'

We were home. There's no place like home, is there?

St Thomas' Hospital, London, 27 March 2004

I was holding her and I didn't want to let her go. Tina was half asleep in the hospital bed to our side and I gazed at this beautiful child in my arms. Blissfully happy moments like this help to make sense of our time on the planet. She was just three hours old. Isla. Another little girl. There's no chance of a blue-eyed son now; not unless one turns up at my door in forty years time or writes an oblique letter of introduction. I looked at Isla's mummy in her narcotic haze and wanted to reassure her that there would be no unpleasant surprises of that sort. She'd been through quite enough in the last few hours.

The eyes of both my girls were tightly shut. What was Isla thinking? What dreams were playing in her mind? I hope she reads this book one day. I hope all the girls do, and then they'll realize how lucky I was and how lucky they are.

Then Isla opened one of her tiny eyes for the first time since the cold blinding glare of the operating theatre had suddenly replaced the comforting cradle of her mother's womb. She had arrived to a cacophony of voices, a harsh flurry of commotion and the pitiless flare of the storm troops' searchlights. That was earlier. Everything was calm now. Her eyes opened and she attempted an ill-focused little squint at her daddy's proud face. She seemed quite contented. He looked deliriously happy. Tiny babies do possess this Zen-like aura. They appear wise but within days, hours even, they forget everything they've ever known and the journey starts again. Then she spoke to me. I swear to you she did.

'What is the book about, Daddy?'

'It's about a little boy who wanted to know where he came from.'

'And where was that?'

'From a kind of love I suppose. But soon after that he found a much a better kind of love.'

'Does it have a happy ending?'

'Oh yes.' I looked at her with an inexpressible love and gratitude. She was healthy. She was beautiful.

'Are there goodies and baddies?'

'No, Isla. Just people doing their best.'

I stuck my pinkie into her little hand and she gripped it for the first time. Such strength. I hope we hold hands again when I walk her down the aisle. In the twilight hour before I eventually slip away she may take my hand and grip it as tightly, for one last time. I pray she is there at the end with all her sisters. She might kiss my forehead and smell my skin one last time as I bent down to kiss Dad as he lay in the hospice bed. And here I was, Isla's daddy, holding her at the beginning; in the first few hours of her life in this bizarre new world.

'What is life, Daddy?'

'That's quite a question, Isla.'

'It's all so new and different. I'm trying to get my head round it. What's it like?'

'It's a magical painful funny fascinating wonderful confusing game of chance.'

She gave me a quizzical look, as if to say, Is that all you can come up with?

'And what about your daddy. What was he like?'

How did she know what I was thinking? At the birth of all of our children, Dad was right there in my thoughts. Right there in my heart. I answered her.

'He was the best daddy in the world. The best daddy anyone could hope for. The best daddy I could ever have had. He was always there to look after me. He was warm and welcoming to everyone. So full of love.'

'I'd like a daddy like that,' she said, almost to herself.

She went on, 'The story in the book is a bit confusing. You had two mums and two dads. I want to know who your real mummy and daddy are.'

'Well, we're *your* real mummy and daddy because we'll always be here to look after you. And we'll love you with all the love we have and so much more – so much more that we won't know where it came from. That's what real mummies and daddies do. They're the ones who are always there for you.'

'Then why did your first mummy give you away?'

'Because she couldn't look after me all by herself. She couldn't be there for me.'

'Are you going to give me away?' I felt icy inside at the thought.

I glanced at Tina as she slept fitfully and I thought about the horrors that scenario would call forth, the nightmares that would bring. If someone were to come for Isla in a few days' time Tina would die inside and I'd think about this tiny little girl every day for the rest of my life. She'd be frozen in time. I steadied myself.

'No, Isla. We're going to look after you for ever and a day and then one day after that you'll look after us,' I said hopefully.

Her other eye prized itself open at this point and she flashed those dark irises around, full of the new-found wonder of it all. If only she could see more of it. Then, in exhaustion, her eyes closed and she fell into a deep sleep. All knowledge of what went before slowly slipped away.

There she was, asleep in my arms. I leant over, grabbed the remote, flicked on the high-tech hospital telly and saw that Scotland were losing a rugby match to Ireland. It was another pretty awful performance. Instinctively I wanted to speak to Dad about it but he's gone. Gently, but with the confidence of a father of four, I laid Isla in her cot, which was already festooned with photographs of her big sisters and drawings they had lovingly created for her. She was beautiful all right. I so wanted to tell Dad about her. He would have been so proud of all his Campbell girls.